THE CENTER FOR PUBLIC INTEGRITY

ANIMAL UNDERWORLD

INSIDE AMERICA'S
BLACK MARKET
FOR RARE AND EXOTIC SPECIES

For information, address PublicAffairs, 250 West 57th Street, Suite 1321, New York, NY 10107.

Library of Congress Cataloging-in-Publication Data

Green, Alan, 1950–

  Animal underworld : inside America's black market for rare and

  exotic species / Alan Green and the Center for Public Integrity.—

  1st ed.

    p. cm.

  ISBN 1-891620-28-2 (hc)

   1. Wild animal trade—United States. 2. Black market—United

  States. 3. Rare animals—United States. 4. Endangered

  species—United States. I. Center for Public Integrity. II. Title.

  SK592.U6G74 1999

  333.95'42137'0973—dc21

                                         99-39245

                                            CIP

First Edition

10 9 8 7 6 5 4 3 2 1

In memory of my mother

CONTENTS

Among the animals on display at Six Flags Wild Safari, in Jackson, New Jersey, are addax, rare antelope whose long, thin, spiraling horns slant up and back like an ornate pair of tight, mirror-image S curves. The four-foot-tall mammals, which typically weigh nearly three hundred pounds, are much better suited to life on their native North African Sahara Desert than this theme park's grassland: In summer, their grayish coats turn heat-reflecting off-white. Their large, splayed hooves allow them to easily traverse the sand dunes. And addax can go without drinking, instead fulfilling their need for fresh water from the moisture in the shrubs and grasses that constitute their diet.

Yet the addax has been pushed to near extinction in such countries as Chad, Niger, and Mali. For starters, the antelopes have been indiscriminately overhunted, often by poachers firing automatic weapons from motorized vehicles. The addax population has also been ravaged by severe and prolonged droughts, habitat loss from livestock grazing, and the stress brought on by throngs of overzealous and aggressive tourists.

What's more, military troops have used the hapless animals for target practice. As a result, it's estimated that only two hundred to three hundred addax remain in the wild—a number that has prompted the two major wildlife-monitoring agencies outside the United States to conclude the obvious: The species is in danger of disappearing.

That leaves the fate of the addax largely in the hands of zoos, wildlife preserves, and theme parks such as Wild Safari, whose fifteen addax live in a fenced-in area dubbed the African Plains. The placid antelopes, seemingly unfazed by the daily parade of vehicles, share their territory with Barbary sheep, East African crowned cranes, and white-tailed gnus; across the cattle grids, giraffes, marabou storks, and a dozen other species amble over their designated turf, some idling long enough in the three-lane service road to bring the crush of summer traffic to a standstill.

The gates are shut the first week of November, when the three-hundred-fifty-acre drive-through park closes for the season. Because many of the thousand-plus animals at Six Flags Wild Safari—the desert-dwelling addax, among them—probably couldn't make it through New Jersey's harsh winters, they are soon relocated to heated buildings. It's a process that requires great care.

Such concern for animal welfare is characteristic of Time Warner, Inc., which managed Wild Safari from 1992 to April 1, 1998, when the entertainment company sold its interest in the Six Flags chain to Premier Parks Inc., a large theme-park operator with headquarters in Oklahoma City. Time Warner's Volunteer Project Grants, which are designed to support community-service work, have gone, for example, to an animal-rescue organization's newsletter in Burbank, California. The company's scholarship giving has supported New York University's Science and Environmental Writing Program. HBO, Time Warner's pay-television service, produced the widely acclaimed *To Love or Kill: Man Versus Animal,* a chilling documentary about society's heinous treatment of animals.

Ted Turner, Time Warner's vice chairman, has his own distinguished record regarding animals and their environments. The media and entertainment mogul, whose fortunes have been built on such properties as Cable News Network and the Atlanta Braves, is the Nature Conservancy's single-biggest individual donor of conservation easements, having set aside more than 148,000 acres of land he owns to prevent development and ensure that sufficient habitat is left for wildlife. Turner's Atlanta-based superstation, WTBS, has long been home to the popular National Geographic Explorer series. The Turner Foundation has funded such animal-friendly organizations as Earth Island Institute, whose projects include campaigns to save whale and dolphin habitats, sea-turtle nesting beaches, and San Francisco Bay's harbor seals. And the family foundation also launched the Turner Endangered Species Fund, which assists private landowners in conserving desert bighorn sheep, Mexican wolves, and other imperiled species.

It should be no surprise, then, that the animals at Wild Safari would have been cared for so well under the management of Time Warner—that they would be moved en masse from their summertime habitat and so carefully shielded from the threats of harsher weather. This is just the sort of commitment that has helped Wild Safari earn its standing as a valued resource for wildlife preservation.

But with the relocation to winter quarters comes a parallel migration—a one-way exile that unceremoniously removes dozens, sometimes hundreds, of animals from the drive-through park. In years past, most of them have been entrusted to Henry Hampton, a North Carolina broker who's hauled away Wild Safari's camels, zebras, and Ankole cattle, as well as llamas, fallow deer, and white-bearded gnus. The park has also sent herds of blackbuck antelope to Hampton, along with North American black bears and Cameroon goats, eland, aoudads, lechwes, Beisa oryx, and dama gazelles. One year, Hampton hauled away nearly two hundred of Wild Safari's animals.

Hampton, whose business is transporting and brokering animals, is licensed by the U.S. Department of Agriculture to ply his trade. His facilities are inspected annually to ensure compliance with the federal Animal Welfare Act. His clients include the Miami MetroZoo, Florida's Lion Country Safari (which has even given Hampton its newborn lions), and the White Oak Conservation Center, a respected wildlife conservation facility whose animals come by way of the Los Angeles Zoo and other well-known institutions. In short, who better than Hampton to find suitable homes for surplus animals?

As it turns out, however, this roundup has nothing to do with conservation of species. Instead, it's merely the first leg of an arcane and largely invisible process that shunts Wild Safari's animals from place to place, laundering them into obscurity until they're deposited with auctioneers, backyard hobbyists, or dealers like Steven Patrick Forest, who runs an exotic-animal hunting operation on his Texas ranch that boasts fifty species of game. The right fee brings you the chance to bag a Nubian ibex or four-horned sheep, a yak, an eland, or a Persian gazelle. For $2,250, you can pick off an addax at the Forest Ranch, maybe even one that came from Wild Safari. Henry Hampton trucked three of its young males to the Forest Ranch in 1996. But Wild Safari's population of the disappearing antelope was hardly affected, because spring always brings babies, just as autumn inevitably brings the North Carolina trucker to quietly haul them away.

INTRODUCTION

There was nothing particularly unusual about the pickup leaving Reston Animal Park on a frigid Thursday morning in November 1995. One of the Virginia petting zoo's longtime employees was at the wheel of the truck, attached to which was a twenty-foot cattle trailer. The hulking worker, who'd completed his preparations long before sunrise, sometimes hauled goats, monkeys, and other animals to schools and birthday parties in Reston and other well-to-do suburbs of Washington, D.C. The mobile menagerie was a service that the zoo's owners liked to promote, a supplemental stream of income that, they claimed, helped them provide exemplary care to their collection of animals.

But on this morning the petting zoo's truck headed north and west and kept going, crossing the Potomac River into rural Maryland on its way toward the Pennsylvania border. At first light there had finally appeared hints of the trailer's cargo, as alternating pairs of bulging eyes peered just over the rear door. These were nilgais, the largest of the Asian antelopes. Although regarded as sacred in their native India and let be by reverent villagers, the powerfully built animals are not particularly esteemed in the United States: They are exhibited at only a half-dozen major metropolitan zoos, and you can bag one at a private hunting preserve for a few hundred dollars—about the cost of shooting a Rio Grande gobbler. Some Texas entrepreneurs are farming nilgais for human consumption, although so far there has been little demand for the lean antelope meat.

No other animals were visible, but a pair of eight-month-old black bears, named Lolli and Macon, were also supposed to be on board that November day. For nearly half a year I had investigated this petting zoo's operations and on each visit had found myself drawn to these cubs: I watched them play together, followed along when they were paraded across the grounds, and listened transfixed as one, then the other, stood with its front paws high on the bars of their cage and, for minutes at a time, whimpered like a puppy. I had also tried to learn details of their past and future, but my questions to the zoo's young staff invariably brought the same vague response: The cubs had been born at a Wisconsin zoo and would return there at season's end to participate in a breeding program. Where in Wisconsin? I wanted to know. What sort of breeding program? Were visitors allowed? There were never any answers. The keepers either didn't know the truth or didn't want to share it.

In many ways, these bear cubs epitomized the allure of zoos. Animals in the wild may be threatened by hunters, poachers, disease, and starvation, but those in captivity have presumably been granted safe haven. Animals in the wild are often elusive, their presence revealed only by tracks in the earth or shadows on a distant ridge, whereas the lives of zoo animals unfold daily in plain view, sometimes from birth. As a result, we develop relationships with zoo animals and care about their individual lives. With Lolli and Macon, however, the details remained hidden.

As the months passed, however, I learned at least part of the story: The cubs had been sent to Reston Animal Park from R-Zoo, a federally licensed facility in Neshkoro, Wisconsin. Despite its name, R-Zoo is really just a breeding compound and holding facility for animals awaiting ship-

ment elsewhere. There are no exhibits at R-Zoo. The public is not welcome. Because there are no signs or markings to indicate its location, you
can drive by without even knowing you've passed it.

R-Zoo is owned by Mark Schoebel, a second-generation animal dealer
who in 1986 was accused by the federal government of illegally transporting bears and other wildlife across state lines. Evidence gathered by
the U.S. Fish and Wildlife Service revealed that Schoebel had supplied
bears to the owner of an Illinois game farm who was charged with shooting the animals, dismembering and decapitating them, packing the carcasses in dry ice, and shipping them via a New York firm to Korea, where
the gall bladders are used in traditional medicines and prized as an aphro-
disiac. At the time, a glut of bear galls had buyers across Asia concerned
about the quality of their purchases. This way, customers could actually
cut the bile-filled sac out of the limbless remains and thus be assured of its
freshness and authenticity.

Federal agents uncovered evidence that two dozen bears had also been
sent from R-Zoo to Korea via a California broker. A search warrant executed at Schoebel's facility turned up receipts showing the sale of yet more
bears to an exotic-meat dealer in a Chicago suburb. Schoebel pleaded guilty
to four counts of wildlife infractions and in return received a fine and four
years probation. But he retained his USDA license to breed and sell animals.

Schoebel continued to breed and sell animals, each spring farming out
newborn bears to the likes of Reston Animal Park and each autumn re-
claiming the animals. It is a mutually beneficial relationship: The zoo gets
the crowd-pleasing babies, which lure patrons through the gates, while
dealers like Schoebel are temporarily relieved of the responsibility of caring for the animals. But finding new homes for those eight-month-olds is
problematic. Major metropolitan zoos are already overrun with black
bears. Unruly hundred-pound juveniles are of little interest to the pet
trade. The hand-raised bears lack the skills required to live in the wild, so
they can't be released. Few animal sanctuaries have the space or facilities
to properly take care of the bears. There is, in short, no place for them,
and they are of real worth only when disassembled: The skins are made
into rugs. The claws become jewelry. The flesh is packaged for restau-

rants. The paws go to Asia, where they're regarded as delicacies. And most valuable of all are the gall bladders, which can earn smugglers a few thousand dollars apiece. Was this, I wondered, the fate that awaited Lolli and Macon?

In a chance telephone conversation, a zoo cashier volunteered that the young bears would be leaving the following day for their Wisconsin birthplace. So I packed food, water, a change of clothes, and even a makeshift urinal. I borrowed road maps, filled my wallet with cash, loaded up on film. And at five the next morning I parked a quarter-mile from the zoo, where for an hour I waited anxiously in the predawn cold.

The pickup wended its way through a deserted residential neighborhood—exposing me, I imagined—and then passed across a commercial strip heavy with rush-hour traffic. I was still on pace as we reached the first highway, but my concerns soon mounted. Was my car's gas tank too small? Would I lose sight of the truck as merging cars in a construction zone left me boxed in too many lengths back? Would the driver catch on to the tail and either abort the trip or else park his rig and wait for me to go by? Worst of all, what if the bears weren't actually in the trailer? Maybe they were being moved out in another truck. Maybe their departure had been postponed.

My chance to find out came in northwestern Maryland, seventy-five miles from the zoo. When the driver and his helper stopped for breakfast, I parked in an adjacent lot and sneaked behind the truck. The darkened trailer at first revealed only the nilgai antelopes, which stood motionless as I approached. There was no sign of other animals. Finally, however, there appeared two pairs of eyes at the head of the trailer. I pointed my camera in that direction, and the flash revealed Lolli and Macon, chains around their necks, sitting side by side on a ledge overhanging the bed of the pickup. We stared momentarily at each other, then the light faded and their faces again disappeared in the blackness of the cattle trailer.

◄○►

My interest in these bears and this petting zoo was entirely accidental. I had actually hoped to explore the inner workings of the National Zoo, in Washington, D.C., where for a year and a half I had worked as an ape-house volunteer. I liked the National Zoo's keepers and appreciated their concerns for the animals' well-being. I was on hand in 1993 for the construction of the zoo's Think Tank—a novel exhibit that put orangutans before computer terminals in the hope of gauging their intelligence. I watched with rapt interest as the zoo's golden lion tamarins were taught vine climbing and other survival skills—a kind of boot camp designed to prepare the tiny monkeys for reintroduction to their native Brazilian forests. I had even applied for a position as a zookeeper—a dramatic (friends and family said absurd) career change after two decades in journalism—but was passed over for lack of seniority among the volunteers. Spending a year rotating from one exhibit to another (assuming I could wangle the necessary permission) seemed a novel way of researching a book on the much-heralded transformation of zoos from entertainment-oriented amusement parks to conservation-minded bioparks.

But keepers at the National Zoo urged me instead to first look at Reston Animal Park, where there were persistent rumors of animal mistreatment and odd goings-on. By all accounts, the twenty-year-old petting zoo was no model of humane care. An employee had been convicted of animal abuse for allegedly striking a huge Aldabra tortoise in the nose with a two-by-four. At season's end, animals are routinely trucked off to auction, with no regard for their ultimate fates. There was the story of a black angus left to die in the zoo's dump. A neighbor discovered the forty-pound calf, which a veterinarian concluded probably hadn't eaten for days. Apparently suffering from shock, the badly dehydrated calf was soon dead.

In short, Reston Animal Park was as the National Zoo's keepers had described it. But thousands of documents I discovered in a court archive told a more complicated—and compelling—tale: Reston Animal Park had links to some of the nation's premier zoological parks.

Although major metropolitan zoos publicly claim to have no dealings with roadside attractions like Reston Animal Park, these documents showed otherwise. Before the operation had even been granted a business license, in fact, Chicago's Lincoln Park Zoo—a self-proclaimed standard-bearer of zoological ethics—sent Mack S. " Jack" Crippen, Jr., the park's would-be proprietor, a pair of lion cubs. And once Crippen, an eccentric animal collector and wealthy landfill operator, obtained the license, other supposedly reputable zoos followed suit, sending him everything from a leopard cat to a blackbuck antelope. Even the National Zoo sold Pet-a-Pet, as Reston Animal Park was then called, rare muntjac deer—a 1977 transaction that the National Zoo's then-director, Theodore Reed, claimed never happened. "I don't recall that and had nothing to do with that," Reed insisted. "I'd slaughter the animals before I'd do that."

But he had indeed sold Crippen the tiny "barking" deer, as receipts confirmed and Reed finally acknowledged. And two years later the petting zoo's animals would suffer for the indiscretions of Reed, Lincoln Park, and all the others: With his marriage failing, Crippen feared that the petting zoo—situated on choice suburban-Washington farmland owned by his parents—might go to his wife as part of a divorce settlement. So he quietly engineered a scheme to dispose of the animals and close down Pet-a-Pet, thereby putting these assets out of his wife's reach. In effect, Crippen held the equivalent of a months-long fire sale, unloading more than two hundred thirty animals on auction barns, pet owners, dreadful exhibits, and dealers such as Henry Hampton, disposal man for Six Flags Wild Safari. Spider monkeys landed at a local university's psychology department. A young chimpanzee named Mario was sold to New York University's Laboratory for Experimental Medicine and Surgery in Primates, where he spent the next two decades as the subject of human hepatitis research. And there was a sixteen-year-old elephant named Topsy, a Ringling Brothers and Barnum & Bailey castoff, whose bum leg and reputation for unruliness made her $12,000 asking price far too steep for the twenty zoos approached. So a plan was hatched to donate the elephant and claim a charitable deduction. Crippen found a willing taker in the Washington Park Zoo in Portland, Oregon, long recognized for its commitment to elephant conservation. In this instance, however, the zoo showed only its unsavory side: The general curator proposed to pay $4,000 for Topsy and in return to provide a letter for the Internal Revenue

Service putting the elephant's value at $20,000. What's more, the zoo would promise to sell to Crippen—by then a private citizen without even his roadside menagerie—Topsy's first-born calf, no questions asked. The deal ultimately fell through, however, and the petting zoo's court-appointed receiver—engaged to dispose of the remaining assets—sold the elephant to an unsavory animal dealer, who pawned her off on a low-rent traveling circus. Topsy was later put to death after she injured her trainer.

Why would the caretakers of the nation's elite zoological parks send animals to Crippen's private menagerie? After all, Pet-a-Pet was exactly the sort of second-rate operation scorned by the zoo establishment. Members of the American Association of Zoological Parks and Aquariums (renamed the American Zoo and Aquarium Association—the AZA—in 1994) held out their accreditation as proof of their high professional standards, and they drew haughty distinctions between themselves and those unable to measure up. Circuses were not admitted to the AZA. Neither were traveling petting zoos nor the infamous roadside attractions that interred animals in concrete-and-steel hoosegows. The AZA was a club that would not welcome Pet-a-Pet—at least through the front door.

And yet, these same high-minded zoo directors freely transacted business with Crippen. On one hand they shunned operations such as his but on the other were nonetheless willing, sometimes even eager, to partner up in deals, no matter how questionable. Burdened with unwanted surplus, the National Zoo and its well-regarded counterparts willingly overlooked the animal-care standards to which they supposedly subscribed. When they had animals to dispose of, a recipient's lack of credentials or affiliations was meaningless. The goal was to clear out inventory. And if that meant off-loading animals on a private collector with no standing in the so-called legitimate zoo community, so be it.

But it became increasingly clear that zoo directors were treating Pet-a-Pet, which reopened as Reston Animal Park under the ownership of a Crippen employee, as they would anyone else with a cage and a checkbook. The paper trails that pointed from Reston to high-profile municipal zoos in turn led to a hodgepodge of pet owners, wretched menageries, opportunistic breeders, disreputable dealers, charlatans posing as conservationists, and middlemen adept at making animals vanish. For all the us-versus-them chest thumping of zoos accredited by the AZA, the trading-partner manifests often made the two camps seem almost indistinguishable. And of particular surprise, even the high-minded National Zoo indiscriminately off-loaded its animals to this same group of supposed zoo-community pariahs.

When the National Zoo, a unit of the venerable Smithsonian Institution, needed to dispose of unwanted monkeys, for instance, a keeper drove them to an unaccredited zoo near Camp David, Maryland, whose repeated failure to pass animal-welfare inspections resulted in a temporary suspension of its exhibitor's license. Exotic Père David's deer once part of captive-breeding programs were dumped on a Midwestern animal dealer, thus fueling a trade that added an exotic new trophy at the nation's private hunting preserves. When the National Zoo retired its herd of East Asian sika deer, the animals were all sent to a Virginia roadside zoo known for frequent escapes, endless complaints of animal mistreatment, and carcasses disposed of in public trash cans. A brown bear was even sent to Studio Animal Rentals, a Florida firm whose proprietor, William Vergis, trained animals for use in movies, commercials, and wrestling-bear acts—at least until he was run out of the state for carrying on his exploitative trade without a permit. Not long afterward, the U.S. Department of Agriculture stripped Vergis of his animal exhibitor's license. The charges leveled against him included mistreatment of bears.

Even animals sent to presumably legitimate organizations sometimes endured sorry fates, as they were laundered through the system to the usual suspects. A couple of oryx from the National Zoo's Conservation and Research Center were sent to International Animal Exchange, a commercial dealer deemed upstanding by much of the zoo community, which in turn shipped them to Henry Hampton. Two more of the African antelope went to the Bamberger Ranch—a Texas facility that ran an oryx-breeding program for the AZA—and were then passed on to the Forest Ranch, the Hill Country hunting preserve where Wild Safari's "surplus" addax were sent to die.

◄○►

The truck passed through Maryland, then West Virginia, and headed north for the Pennsylvania line. It was a clear, sunny day, with intermittent patches of high clouds and a half-inch of fresh snow in the upper elevations. Along some stretches the interstate highways were almost deserted—just an old Honda following a late-model pickup and its trailer, the two accelerating in tandem on long, flat stretches and crawling through hilly passes as if tethered by a hundred-fifty-foot tow bar.

Despite my earlier worries, tailing the truck proved to be relatively easy. I stayed far enough back to be unobtrusive but close enough to keep the pickup in easy view. When the driver stopped for gas I used a service station up the road, then followed him back onto the highway. Only once did I nearly falter: When the truck pulled into a rest stop, I pressed on to the next exit and waited atop the on-ramp. For a moment I glanced at a map, hoping to get a fix on our course, and as I did the truck sped by on the road below. I glanced up just as the trailer was leaving my field of view, disappearing behind a line of trees.

After two hundred miles our destination was still impossible to determine. We were within easy reach of Ohio, Michigan, and western Pennsylvania—states, I had learned, that are overrun with exotic-animal dealers and the sort of unregulated hunting operations where bear and nilgai antelope are served up as target practice from twenty paces. A westerly turn could send us to Indiana, whose almost-anything-goes laws have made the state a dumping ground for exotic animals. We could press on to Illinois, home to at least two packing houses where bears are brought in live and slaughtered for the meat trade. Or we could keep going to Missouri, which, by virtue of having the nation's largest exotic-animal auction, is the premier crossroads for exotic-animal trading and brokering.

Or maybe we really were bound for the R-Zoo game farm—a nine-hundred-mile trip that would take us through Chicago, Madison, and up near the Wisconsin Dells to a rural outpost of fewer than four hundred people. The idea that I could follow the truck that far without being noticed—particularly on dark back roads—began to seem ever more ludicrous, and staying incognito once we arrived would obviously be impossible. Would I sit outside Mark Schoebel's compound and wait for another truck to follow? What if that took a week? And how would I know if the bears were on board? My impromptu stab at detective work suddenly felt pointless. As the odometer kept turning, the chase took on an embarrassing, almost sickening, air of futility.

◄○►

For as long as anyone can remember, the Irvine Park Zoo in Chippewa Falls, Wisconsin, has had a curious relationship with Mark Schoebel: Cougars, deer, bison, and other babies are born at the small municipal zoo, and Schoebel soon arrives to take them away. No money appears to change hands. No one but Schoebel seems to know where the animals go after he takes them away. For years, city officials would not say what—if anything—the zoo got in return. But residents were finally let in on the arrangement: Schoebel loans animals to the Irvine Park Zoo, and their babies are his to take.

City officials have been reluctant to discuss the matter publicly. Members of the local zoological society once requested documents that might have exposed the exact nature of the arrangement, but the parks and recreation department at first stonewalled and then imposed search and copying fees so high they put the documents out of reach. What's more, zookeepers were ordered to not discuss Schoebel's activities with anyone.

Among the animals that Schoebel trucks away from the Irvine Park Zoo are black bears—on average, three or four of them each spring. Schoebel has other sources, as well, including mom-and-pop breeders, who keep pairs of adult bears and, as if blessed with a warm-blooded annuity, each spring sell him the babies. Sometimes, however, the source of Schoebel's cubs is a mystery: U.S. Fish and Wildlife agents found records to indicate that, over a two-year period, his R-Zoo operation bought seventy-four bears but sold one hundred thirty-two. They could only speculate about the source of the additional fifty-eight.

Schoebel deals in more than bears. His fur-farm license permits him to sell live raccoons, skunks, and otters or their pelts. His commercial deer-farm license lets him ship out whitetails by the dozen, in some instances to a private hunting ranch whose clients can shoot game that have been put in a five-acre pen. His game-bird and animal-farm license allows him to add waterfowl, quail, weasels, badgers, moose, and other species to his product line. His federal dealer's license lets him buy and sell everything from monkeys to cougars to nilgai antelope, which he does with great regularity. He consigns ostriches and lions to exotic-animal auctions. He peddles giraffes and ponies, macaws, coyotes, tortoises, and zeedonks—genetic anomalies fashioned from the crossbreeding of zebras and donkeys. In a single five-week period, Schoebel took delivery of more than fourteen hundred prairie dogs, which he in turn sends to pet stores and medical research laboratories in the United States and abroad. At one point, he proudly claimed eight thousand baby animals for sale.

But with the ever-growing demand for exotic animals, Schoebel, like his cronies, is always in search of more inventory. And there's plenty out there, compliments of an elaborate network of breeders, dealers, and middlemen, many with ties to roadside zoos, university research facilities, and even state wildlife agencies. Remarkably, Schoebel has also been able to turn to the Racine Zoo, in his home state, and Duluth's Lake Superior Zoo, which are both members of the AZA, the trade association for the nation's best-run, and presumably most ethical, zoological parks. Wisconsin zoos actually protect Schoebel, a state wildlife official says, because they depend on him to clear out the aging, unwanted surplus they're no longer interested in caring for. Another wildlife officer puts it more graphically: Schoebel and dealers like him, he says, clean the runny noses of the nation's zoos.

◄o►

New Richland is a tiny Amish farming community seventy miles northwest of Columbus. The homes are modest, but the barns are impressive. There is a one-lane wooden bridge just off the main route, but the likelihood of ever having to yield to an oncoming car is slim. There's no fast food in New Richland, but the town has a gas station and mini mart, and this is where the truck carrying Lolli and Macon stopped, and for ten, fifteen, twenty minutes, stayed put.

We had arrived there after an unexpected change in course two hundred fifty miles into the trip: The northerly route was abandoned for an interstate going westbound, and we were soon crossing the Ohio border on a path toward Columbus. It was now clear that Schoebel's Wisconsin game farm was not on the itinerary after all. The bears and nilgai antelope were going somewhere else.

By now we were nearly five hundred miles from Reston Animal Park. Although I had managed to maintain the tail, any hope of remaining undetected had evaporated just outside Columbus: We picked up a two-lane road whose traffic thinned out more with each passing mile, leaving me with less and less cover. As we headed down the half-mile feeder road to New Richland, we were a two-vehicle caravan.

At a T intersection, the truck turned left into the mini mart and I went right to a lot, where I parked with a clear view of the road. I assumed that this would be a quick refueling stop and again studied the maps for clues of our destination. But as more time passed I worried that the driver had slipped out a driveway invisible from my vantage point, that he had taken a back road through the surrounding farmland and at last eluded me after a ten-hour pursuit. So I finally headed for the gas station, and when I arrived the driver was waiting for me: He maneuvered his rig around the mini mart and headed toward my car. I made a quick U turn, fled the station, and backtracked up the feeder road to a hilltop perch.

When the truck finally moved a few minutes later, I took off after it. But I was about three-quarters of a mile back, and my view was obscured as the road dipped in some spots, angled behind trees in others. I thought I saw the trailer head east on an out-of-the-way back road and raced to follow. But that road soon forked, and there was no sign of the truck in either direction—no trailer visible beside the homes to the right, no distant clouds of dust kicked up on the gravelly roadway to the left.

I sat at the deserted fork and debated: Right or left? Left or right?

◄o►

Thomas Solin has a flow chart in his office that's the size of a small blackboard. It is a confusing jumble of lines, arrows, boxes, and words that track the movement of diseased elk to and from a Montana game farm. The elaborately drawn diagram, which in each quadrant requires minutes of close study, shows the herds from which the contaminated elk might have originated and the states to which exposed elk may have in turn been sent. It is a puzzle that must have taken weeks, maybe months, to complete, an elaborate, multistate road map that graphically demonstrates the painstaking work sometimes required to follow an animal's trail. Solin points to the chart as a telling illustration of the work required of wildlife and public-health investigators. But there is, he admits, a problem with this otherwise impressive effort: "It's based on records," he says, "and you know the validity of records."

Fraudulent records, as Solin knows, are a hallmark of the wild-animal trade. He knows that animals change sex from one record to another, that animals listed as dead never really died, that animals supposedly transported to one state were actually moved elsewhere, that animals listed as one species are in fact another. Solin knows that documents are whited-out and photocopied, then filled in with false information. He knows that animals imported illegally from outside the United States are shipped out of state, then shipped back home with what appears to be proper documentation. He knows that records don't jibe from one jurisdiction to another, that the consignor claims to have sent a dozen animals and the consignee insists he received only nine. He knows that ear tags used to identify animals mysteriously fall off, that tattoos are removed, that names are changed, that dates of birth are fictitious, and that animals certified as healthy have never been seen by a veterinarian. Solin also knows that animals sometimes listed in game-farm records as captive-born were really wild-caught, in violation of the law. And he knows that individuals in his state have been willing to exploit a gory legal loophole: It's illegal to take bears from the wild, the exception being those that are orphaned. So the bear merchants simply shoot the mothers and remove the babies.

As chief of the Special Investigations Section of the Wisconsin Department of Natural Resources, Solin studies and analyzes records and occasionally seeks court orders to subpoena them. (He also supervises undercover operations when the paperwork—or lack thereof—raises enough red flags.) He goes after those who illegally take the state's protected flora and fauna, and the records sometimes expose the wrongdoing. Among those whose records Solin has scrutinized is Mark Schoebel. Solin has pored over them for years, and he seems resigned to the idea that he'll continue to do so at least until one of them retires from his chosen profession.

If anyone could help find Lolli and Macon, then, it was probably Tom Solin. And I certainly needed help: My left-right debate at the New Richland junction had been paralyzing, and after half-hearted advances in both directions, I grudgingly reversed course and began the five-hundred-mile trip home. I arrived home after 2 A.M. and at sunrise drove back to the petting zoo. The truck and trailer were behind the locked fence, so Schoebel's Wisconsin game farm—another day's drive from New Richland—obviously hadn't been the final destination. Later that morning I began a weeks-long search in hopes of learning what had been the destination.

Solin speculated that the bears had been transferred in Ohio to another truck and then returned to Wisconsin, though he could find no evidence of that. But the third or fourth Ohio wildlife officer I contacted told me that he knew where the bears ended up: Had I looked forty-five degrees right at that last intersection, he said, I would have seen in the distance a ranch-style house owned by an Amish animal dealer—a horse and fallow-deer trader who also keeps a black bear in a stall of his barn. The Amish man had recently built new cages in his yard, arousing the attention of wildlife investigators, who had busted him for obtaining his bear illegally. It seemed a good bet that Lolli and Macon had been dropped off there, though a later search by state officials turned up nothing.

Documents that surfaced over the following weeks showed why Solin so mistrusts the printed word, and why nothing is as it seems in the rare-animal trade: The Virginia Department of Agriculture said that it had never issued the permit required to import Lolli and Macon, and the state's fish and game agency said that, according to its computers, Reston Animal Park had one bear, not two, on exhibit that year. The circumstances of the cubs' departure were equally muddled: The petting zoo's veterinarian filed papers claiming that the cubs had been trucked to Schoebel's compound, which of course wasn't true. On the same day, the vet filed another document stating that Lolli and Macon had been shipped to the Woods & Waters exotic-animal auction, in Delphos, Ohio, not far from New Richland. But Ohio officials said that the petting zoo lacked a permit to sell black bears at the auction—or anywhere else in the state, for that matter.

Coincidentally, on the very day that Lolli and Macon were in transit, Schoebel filed paperwork to show that he was sending thirteen bears to a wild animal dealer whose family operates the Woods & Waters auction. Ohio officials said that he, too, had no permit to sell black bears.

Everyone seemed to have theories about the bears' fate, some simple, some convoluted: They were still in Ohio. They had been moved to Wisconsin. They had been sold at auction and carved up for their parts. They had been smuggled into Mexico and would eventually end up at a Chinese bear farm—an operation where bile is each day milked from animals with shunts implanted in their gall bladders. Another theory had it that the cubs had been transferred on paper to Schoebel, then on paper again to the Ohio wildlife dealer, who in turn transferred them back to Schoebel—a creative ruse involving no interstate movement on legs two and three of the deal, and therefore generating no revealing documents.

There was also a theory from a veterinarian with the Illinois Department of Agriculture: He said the state police had called him after stopping Schoebel's son, who was driving a truck filled with bears. The trooper wanted to know if any Illinois law was being violated; the vet told him that the shipment was perfectly legal, that the younger Schoebel could continue on his way. The vet said that the truck had been stopped not far from an exotic-meat dealer upstate—the same dealer, it turns out, who a decade earlier had received the bears that earned Schoebel the fourth count of his federal plea agreement. That's where Schoebel's son was headed, the vet said. He was certain of it. But of course he had no evidence, no records, no documents. Like all the other theories, it was just more speculation.

─◄○►─

Two and a half years after following the truck to Ohio, I returned to Reston Animal Park. It was exactly as I remembered it: The bison were still in the upper field, the ratites down below, the gibbons on their island, the ducks by the pond. Only Lolli and Macon were missing, and of course some nilgai antelope.

In the end, the search for the bear cubs proved futile. Virginia authorities couldn't help: Once the animals left their borders, they became another state's responsibility. The authorities in Wisconsin and Ohio couldn't say whether the bears had actually been shipped there; besides, bears carry no diseases that affect agricultural herds, so their importation is of little, if any, interest. The U.S. Department of Agriculture, which licenses both Reston Animal Park and Mark Schoebel's game farm, looks only for violations of the federal Animal Welfare Act, and in this instance there was no apparent evidence of any. The U.S. Fish and Wildlife Service is concerned primarily with enforcement of the Endangered Species Act and illicit international trafficking, not with the movement of two domestic black bears across state lines.

It usually ends this way, because captive-bred wildlife is by and large no one's responsibility, no one's jurisdiction, and really no one's concern. As a result, the animals are part of an elaborate and sinister shell game, quietly shunted from place to place by those more interested in profits than protection of the species. But search through enough records and follow enough trails, piece together enough evidence from a cross-country dragnet, and much of the deception is ultimately revealed: You can uncover the laundering schemes, pinpoint the animals' destinations, and document how the self-appointed guardians of exotic species are quietly in league with the most disreputable traffickers. At the same time, you can understand how the federal, state, and local laws designed to protect wildlife are flawed, riddled with enough loopholes to permit those bent on exploiting the system to do so with virtual impunity. And you can gauge the consequences of society's inattention to the scandals small and large, consequences that include the spread of diseases with potentially serious human repercussions.

Of course, you can track some animals for weeks, months, even years, and they nonetheless just vanish. Others appear, out of nowhere, in their place. There was a pair of bear cubs, for example, that had taken Lolli and Macon's place. The young keeper said their names were Ben and Jerry. She said they weren't born at Reston Animal Park, but she believed they had come from a breeding farm. She didn't know where exactly the breeding farm was located, but she did know that the young black bears would return there when the animal park closed its doors later that fall.

ANIMAL UNDERWORLD

HERE TODAY . . .

Aaron was born on a scorching Sunday afternoon in July 1997. He weighed one hundred twenty-seven pounds and stood five feet—a half-foot shorter than the average newborn Masai giraffe. Onlookers were stunned by the delivery, which was actually routine. Aaron's mother, Grif, went through labor standing up and in the end sent her new calf into a six-foot free fall. Not long after smacking the hard earth, the spindly legged infant stood and took his first steps—a herky-jerky walk that looked as if he were staggering on four rubbery stilts. The following day, veterinarians at the National Zoo in Washington, D.C., pronounced both mother and son healthy.

Giraffes have been a popular part of the National Zoo's collection since 1926, when Hi-boy and Dot, who had been captured during a Smithsonian-sponsored expedition, were released from quarantine and put in the Bird House, where the inhospitable surroundings soon left them dead. A decade later, four young giraffes, who had endured a blistering and stormy six-week voyage to the United States, were ushered from their crates into a corner of the zoo's new Pachyderm House—a great stone building distinguished by indoor-outdoor environments and huge, lifelike murals of African landscapes. The newcomers were so enthralled by the panorama, which a Works Project Administration artist had peppered with grazing herds of zebras and other hoofed stock, that they actually tried to eat leaves off the painted walls. The crowds of visitors, who that same day got their first look at the impressive Elephant House, were thoroughly entranced by the spectacle.

The National Zoo's quartet of giraffes thrived in their new home, as would their successors: The first baby was born beside that trompe l'oeil landscape in the spring of 1945, and a half-century later Aaron was number forty-three. But the birth of a zoo giraffe is never routine, no matter how many have preceded it, and this one was no different: The calf was the subject of doting newspaper and TV coverage, and great throngs of zoo visitors immediately came out to see the newborn and his mother. It was an enthusiastic crowd largely made up of stroller-pushing parents, counselors with their campers in tow, and the typical crush of tourists who flock to the nation's high-profile federally funded zoo. Aaron remained the park's number-one attraction for weeks, as camera-toting animal lovers, sometimes lined up three deep at the rail, called to the young giraffe in hopes of summoning him their way. Oblivious to the attention, or perhaps just uninterested in it, he lazed in the shade or followed his mother around on increasingly long and sturdy legs.

It was a scene reminiscent of Amber's birth, twenty-five months earlier, although her arrival had an added significance because newborn zoo giraffes have been disproportionately male. John Lenhardt, then the zoo's assistant curator of mammals (he left in 1997 for Disney's Animal Kingdom), was gleeful that on her fourth go-around, thirteen-year-old Grif finally delivered a female. By helping to redress the male-female imbalance, this birth, he proclaimed, would be important to the future of North American zoo giraffes.

But Aaron's arrival changed the sensitive dynamics of the National Zoo's lone giraffe family and in the process appeared to make Amber's status there uncertain. One longtime keeper told a reporter that because the two-year-old would menace, and possibly injure, her newborn brother, another home for her was now being sought. Around the Elephant House, employees informed visitors that Amber's departure was also being prompted by the sexual advances of her father, eighteen-year-old Lionel. Inbreeding, they explained, could have detrimental consequences for a carefully managed captive gene pool, and steps must therefore be taken to separate the two.

And then one day Amber was gone, although visitors near the giraffe yard scarcely noticed. In truth, the young female had been all but forgotten when Aaron was born: The throngs that had so fervently turned out to see her two years earlier now seemed to be interested only in her younger sibling. Few zoo visitors inquired about where she had been sent.

The zoo, in fact, had put Amber up for sale immediately after her birth, just as it had immediately begun shopping other giraffes born there. Statements about daddy's friskiness and threats to her younger brother had an element of truth, but they were also a convenient public-relations smoke screen: The zoo, once so excited about this female's arrival, wanted her gone to free up space for another new arrival. Amber's ultimate destination was really of little consequence.

The same fate apparently awaited Aaron. Two days after he was born, as great waves of zoo visitors were descending on the Elephant House, a veteran keeper let on that it might one day be difficult to find a home for the fully weaned calf because the giraffe market was saturated. "Giraffes just happen," she said. "It's like a baby factory."

—◦—

Actually, giraffes don't always just happen. Some zoos use contraceptive implants or injections to keep the giraffe population in check. Others resort to castration. There is also a less dramatic approach: keeping males and females apart. But even an overabundance of North American giraffes hasn't influenced officials of the National Zoo, whose policies have ensured a never-ending inventory of two-year-olds valued only as an income stream, no matter how meager it might be.

The National Zoo has a prescribed procedure for removing an animal: The department chief makes an initial recommendation, and the proposal works its way through the chain of command to the zoo's director. When authorized to dispose of another giraffe, as it is about every two years, the staff surveys market conditions, sets an asking price, and begins the search for a buyer. The hope is that the animal will land at another facility accredited by the American Zoo and Aquarium Association, which counts virtually all of the nation's high-profile zoos among its one hundred eighty-three members. By trading only within this community, a zoo can publicly claim that its unwanted animals have gone to reputable institutions.

So colleagues are phoned, e-mails are sent, a listing is prepared for the AZA's members-only monthly newsletter, *Animal Exchange,* advertising the now-celebrated, soon-to-be-unwanted giraffe. Unfortunately, this approach is often futile because many of these same AZA zoos are inevitably trying to unload their own surplus animals. As a result, the National Zoo's curators are sometimes forced to take dramatic action. The asking price for Amber, for example, was initially set at $25,000, then slashed to $10,000 when no takers surfaced. The animal touted as being so critical to the future of North American giraffes was, in fact, of interest to no one—least of all the National Zoo.

When even a bargain-basement price doesn't bring a buyer from the roster of AZA zoos—as would be the case with Amber—staff members are free to look elsewhere. They're bound, however, by at least some restrictions: Disposing of animals at auctions is prohibited; so is selling them directly to hunting preserves. But breeders and dealers are acceptable business partners, provided that they're "accredited" by the AZA or have earned the blessings of the National Zoo's administration.

Before doing business with a dealer, though, a department chief must try to determine an animal's final destination and the competence of the ultimate buyer. A nonaccredited zoo must either undergo inspection by a National Zoo staff member or produce references from an AZA affiliate attesting to its high animal-care standards. In short, the National Zoo's policy appears to guarantee that its unwanted animals will end up in good hands.

—◄о►—

Among the dealers who have met the National Zoo's seemingly rigorous standards is Edward Novack of Cairo, New York, who sells exotic animals to the suppliers of auctions and commercial hunting operations. Their ranks include a Montana game farmer who has transported bighorn sheep—a species supplied to him by Novack—to other game farms, where they were killed by paying "hunters." In 1991, the San Diego Zoo sold Novack a European boar, which he in turn sent to Mark Smith, a dealer/exhibitor in Reddick, Florida. (Smith was formerly the director of Reston Animal Park; he, in fact, was the one who left the half-dead black angus calf in the petting zoo's dump.) When Smith went through a bankruptcy/foreclosure proceeding, the zoo's boar ended up at a canned hunt—a privately operated shooting ground where "trophy" animals are sometimes killed in enclosures no bigger than their cage. The San Diego Zoo's public relations director told the magazine *Animal People* that it had immediately stopped dealing with Novack and others involved in the transaction. He also said that the AZA had been notified of the incident so that it could warn its members not to do business with them.

Yet the Miami MetroZoo sent Smith more animals, and the directors of AZA zoos in more than two dozen other cities, including Chicago, Cleveland, Milwaukee, and Washington, D.C., continued to supply Novack. In fact, just a few months after the San Diego Zoo's revelation, the National Zoo handed Novack an eleven-month-old giraffe named Michael. Two years earlier, it had given Novack a giraffe of the same age.

Novack transported Michael to Burton Sipp, a professional horse trainer, pet-store and petting-zoo owner, and self-described animal-rights activist who was once characterized by a superior-court judge as "a man whose own lack of integrity is unimpeachable." That opinion was rendered in 1982, after Sipp agreed to help New Jersey authorities catch crooked jockeys in exchange for not being prosecuted on criminal charges stemming from a racetrack forgery scam. Two years later, Sipp was indicted on charges of inflating, for insurance purposes, the values of nine thoroughbred horses that died while under his care. He later pleaded guilty to witness tampering and was banned worldwide from racing. In 1990, Sipp was indicted by a New Jersey grand jury in another insurance scam—this time, for falsely reporting the theft of rare birds from his pet store and, the indictment alleged, for filing fraudulent insurance claims. Sipp says that two teenage employees actually stole the birds and hid them with a Virginia man. In the end, he was acquitted.

If administrators at the National Zoo had bothered to check with the U.S. Fish and Wildlife Service, they would have learned that five years earlier, Sipp had been stripped of his federal permit to buy and sell captive-bred endangered species. Had zoo curators asked New Jersey veterinary officials about Sipp, they would have heard something like this: "He's a shining example of defiance and disobeying the rules." Copies of Sipp's animal-inventory records, readily available from the New Jersey Division of Fish, Game, and Wildlife, show that numerous animals out of Sipp's backyard have ended up at auctions or with pet owners, while others land with dealers like Wild Safari's favorite, Henry Hampton.

The National Zoo's administrators must have overlooked these sources of information about Novack and Sipp, because they signed off on the removal of Michael the giraffe—a transfer, the public was told, necessitated by worries that adults like Lionel become increasingly intolerant of younger males, even their own offspring. The relocation efforts hardly saved the young animal from harm's way: He lived sixteen months at Sipp's Animal Kingdom Zoo before his neck was broken by an adult male giraffe on loan from another roadside menagerie. This sort of incident was not unprecedented at Sipp's. That same month, a baby roan antelope froze to death at Animal Kingdom Zoo, as did a nilgai antelope and an axis deer. A young female monkey was beaten to death by others in her cage. Two impalas apparently died from eating hay contaminated with nightshade—a poisonous plant that causes fever, hallucinations, and convulsions. A female gemsbok and a roan antelope—the mother of the frozen baby—may have died of natural causes that December, though no one could say for certain.

Despite Sipp's sorry background and animal-care record, his operation has also become a dumping ground for AZA-accredited zoos in such cities as Buffalo, New York; Columbus, Ohio; and Scottsbluff, Nebraska. Chicago's Lincoln Park Zoo, a supposed leader in wildlife conservation, sent Sipp its unwanted sable antelopes. Birds have come his way via FaunaLink, a reputed wildlife conservation organization headed by Donald Bruning, the chairman and curator of the ornithology department at the Bronx Zoo. And when researchers at Bucknell University no longer had any use for their ring-tailed lemurs (a species classified as endangered) and their Japanese snow macaques (which can carry a disease fatal to humans), they have sent the primates to Sipp's petting zoo.

But Sipp's place in the chain isn't just to display these castoffs at his roadside menagerie. He's a prolific dealer, a launderer of animals for zoos and others in need of a seemingly legitimate outlet to send their surplus. (If nothing else, the fact that Sipp calls his operation a zoo affords those who do business with him the cloak of respectability, even though Animal Kingdom Zoo in fact adjoins Sipp's pet store.) When the Buffalo Zoo gets no takers after advertising its mandrills in the *AZA Animal Exchange*—a kind of Blue Book for pre-owned exotics—it simply ships them to Sipp; he in turn deals them off to Catskill Game Farm, a petting zoo that's been the subject of whispers by members of the AZA because of co-owner Jurgen Schulz's sales to hunting ranches and his dealings with exotic-animal auctions. When the University of Memphis sent Sipp rare bushbabies once used in research but then deemed too expensive to care for, he consigned some of the small, arboreal primates to an Ohio auction and sold others to individuals, some via magazine ads with headlines like *Reduction Sale!*

In short, the curators at the National Zoo surely have good reason to shy away from Novack and Sipp. But when you're trying to dispose of a giraffe, something very disquieting soon becomes apparent: If there are no legitimate takers, you may have nowhere else to turn.

—◄o►—

Giraffes are the planet's tallest mammals, with some males reaching a height of seventeen feet. There are eight subspecies, all of which belong to the species *Giraffa camelopardalis*. (*Giraffa* is possibly derived from an Arabic word whose meanings include "creature of grace" and "one who walks swiftly.") Each of these eight subspecies has different markings. The reticulated giraffe, for example, has the most distinctive pattern—large polygonal spots separated by narrow white lines, or reticulations—whereas the Masai, the largest giraffe, has a leafy pattern of spots on a yellowish background. Interbreeding among species on the African savannas sometimes produces a jumble of patterns, and giraffes ranging in color from near black to a creamy all white have even been seen.

Giraffes can run at speeds of up to thirty-five miles per hour. Like humans, their necks are composed of seven vertebrae. Their horns are solid bone, covered with skin. They have extreme long-range visual acuity, enabling them to track predators and keep in visual contact with other giraffes over several miles. Contrary to popular belief, giraffes are not silent: They grunt and snort, although quietly. Despite their sloping appearance, their forelegs are actually only slightly longer than their hind legs.

Giraffes can go for weeks without water. To drink, a giraffe must either straddle a pool of water or bend its legs—a position that makes it vulnerable to predators. Adults are not regularly preyed upon, but more than fifty percent of first-year calves are killed by lions, hyenas, and wild dogs. A mother giraffe will defend her young by standing over it and kicking at the encroaching predators.

Giraffes form scattered herds over a large range. Males use their heads to batter one another in a struggle for dominance (a ritual called necking), the ultimate victor fathering most of the group's offspring. Males are sexually mature at forty-two months but, relegated to their place in the dominance hierarchy, usually don't get a breeding opportunity until they are at least eight years old. Females first conceive after five years. Both have a life expectancy of a quarter-century.

The giraffe's natural habitat once encompassed the arid and dry savanna zones south of the African Sahara Desert. But the lanky ruminants were eliminated from most of the West African and southern Kalahari range, their numbers reduced to zero by hunters after hides, trophies, and meat (gamy in flavor, sometimes likened to veal, with the eighteen-inch tongue and huge marrow bone much-prized delicacies). The killing continued in other parts of Africa as well; in fact, giraffe populations declined so dramatically during the early part of the twentieth century that the species appeared headed for extinction in the wild. Only worldwide condemnation of the slaughter gave the giraffe a reprieve.

In zoos, giraffes would seem to need no advocates. They're among the animals collectively referred to as "charismatic megafauna"—the lovable, attention-getting species that bring crowds through the gates. Gorillas, pandas, and Bengal tigers belong to this elite fellowship, which the zoo community prefers to call "flagship species"; at the aquarium, whales and sharks are their waterborne counterparts. Charismatic megafauna may or may not be classified as endangered. They may be as big as elephants or as small as koalas, but they're never skittish and secretive like the tiny muntjac deer, nor do they have the unsightly snout or tight skin of a pygmy hippopotamus or Brazilian tapir. What these animals share is universal appeal. They're the ones whose names come by way of contests, and they—not the tree shrews or New Guinea singing dogs—receive letters of condolence from schoolchildren when a cage-mate dies. The public singles them out and pays them inordinate attention, while zoos and their not-for-profit support organizations feature them on calendars, annual-report covers, and, most important, direct-mail solicitations.

The giraffe's appeal is obvious: Even if the public doesn't get to see the animal in full gallop—its head and neck swinging in a breathtaking rotation like nothing else in nature—its elongated features, distinctive markings, and swaggering gait are enough of a draw. As a result, giraffes are a favored staple of American zoo collections, with some displaying as many as ten.

But the baby factory described by the keeper at the National Zoo leaves it and many of its counterparts stuck with unwanted animals: In 1995 and 1996, for example, more than forty AZA zoos were trying to sell giraffes, most of them just a year old. (The lone adult was the Detroit Zoo's male hybrid of two giraffe subspecies—"trash," in the parlance of the zoo community, because its mixed lineage renders it unfit for breeding.) When the networking efforts generate no interest from AZA members, which more often than not is the case, curators simply hand over their giraffes to the dealers who haul off their other surplus animals.

Among these dealers is Larry Johnson, a middleman who in 1996 hauled away a giraffe from San Diego Wild Animal Park. That same summer, Johnson filed paperwork with the Texas Health Commission testifying that he was consigning a giraffe to Global Wildlife Center, in Lafayette, Louisiana. Texas and Louisiana authorities rubber-stamped the documents, since Johnson's veterinarian certified that the animal appeared healthy. But the address to which the giraffe was supposedly sent—a post office box in Lafayette—hadn't been used by the Global Wildlife Center for five years. What's more, the safari park is actually in Folsom, Louisiana, one hundred forty miles from Lafayette, and officials there say they received no giraffe from Johnson or anyone else that summer. With the aid of a bogus document, the giraffe had disappeared.

Another of the dealers is Novack, who hauls away animals from zoos across the United States. In the spring of 1994, for example, the Buffalo Zoo handed its New York neighbor—and frequent trading partner—a nine-month-old giraffe. Novack transported the young giraffe to a dealer in Maine, and five months later it landed in the sales ring at Lolli Brothers, the big Missouri exotic-animal auction whose patrons include the proprietors of sideshow-like roadside attractions, hunting-ranch operators, and their ilk. In the summer of 1996, officials of the Phoenix Zoo withdrew a long-running listing in *Animal Exchange* and pawned off on Novack a year-old reticulated giraffe. The following spring, Novack was advertising it in *Animal Finders' Guide*—the chief trade publication for exotic-animal dealers.

Yet another recipient of zoo giraffes is Bob Brackett, the owner of Little Ponderosa Livestock Company, in Winchester, Illinois, home to an animal auction and a private menagerie that provides Brackett with merchandise for sale barns in other states. Jurgen Schulz, the exotic-animal dealer and auctioneer who was exposed in 1991 for supplying animals to shooting preserves, nonetheless still gets surplus giraffes from members of the association. Charles "Buddy" Jordan, a Texas dealer who supplies auctions and has supplied at least one hunting ranch, gets surplus giraffes and other animals by way of AZA zoos in Montgomery, Jacksonville, and Seattle. The largest number of surplus giraffes go to International Animal Exchange, a purely commercial operation that ships many of them to Japan, Thailand, and other foreign countries. Nothing seems to get in the way of business. After Kansas animal dealer Jim Fouts was exposed by *60 Minutes* in 1990 for reconsigning zoo animals to auctions attended by canned-hunt operators, he was declared persona non grata by AZA members. Since then, however, Fouts not only has supplied animals directly to at least one canned hunt but has also received numerous surplus zoo animals, including at least a half-dozen giraffes, from AZA members in Abilene, Texas; Denver; Pittsburgh; and Wichita, Kansas. Earl Tatum, the other dealer featured in the *60 Minutes* exposé, was forgiven for his misdeeds by some zoos, although even AZA officials, who are loath to publicly criticize any of their constituents' trading partners, make an exception for Tatum. "Some of us sit around here and say, 'Why would anyone still use the guy?'" says Jane Ballentine, the AZA's director of public affairs.

The San Diego Zoo Wild Animal Park is among the half dozen AZA members that have continued to supply giraffes to Tatum; he in turn has dumped the animals on other Missouri dealers, including one who unloads zoo stock at auctions in Iowa, Louisiana, and his home state, and another who both operates an auction and sells any interested parties the animals out of his drive-through park. So much for the post-*60 Minutes* pledge of the San Diego Zoo's executive director, Douglas G. Myers: "We are devoted to doing the best for each animal as we work toward preserving the entire species."

Some of the surplus giraffes disposed of through these animal dealers end up at roadside menageries. Others end up at substandard overseas zoos or with eccentric collectors like pop star Michael Jackson. Still others are sold and resold, shunted through the exotic-animal netherworld until their fates are impossible to determine. Maybe they land at a game farm or a hunting ranch—in other words, on death row. Maybe they're turned into animal feed, as some zookeepers privately suspect. Or maybe they're the source of the giraffe loins and boneless cuts advertised by such exotic-meat purveyors as Butcher Boy Food Products in Warren, Michigan, whose catalog is available on the Internet. Butcher Boy's owner says that giraffe, camel, and lion are often hard to come by, although substitutes are available, including bear and nilgai antelope.

Happily for many zoo directors, tracking this sordid commerce via public records is often difficult, if not impossible. These zoo professionals are, after all, at the front end of an elaborate shell game, and they play the same aggrieved hand when details of how the game is played are occasionally exposed: *This dealer is licensed by the USDA, and we therefore had no reason to suspect any wrongdoing. This animal supplier is an accredited affiliate of the American Zoo and Aquarium Association and came highly recommended by our peers. Our charter prohibits the resale of animals in such a manner, and if our internal investigation turns up evidence of wrongdoing, legal actions will be forthcoming.* "We should have known," said Jeff Jouett, then-spokesman for the San Diego Zoo, when in 1991 documents were made public showing that two dealers entrusted with the zoo's animals had ties to trophy-hunting ranches. "We don't condone hunting ranches and we don't deal with people who do. I'm shocked. I'm disappointed. And I'm glad it was pointed out to us."

-◄o►-

Every year, the Massachusetts Zoological Corporation must submit to the Commonwealth's government a detailed fiscal report covering the activities of the Franklin Park Zoo and the Walter D. Stone Memorial Zoo, which since 1992 have operated under its control. Because the two zoos are legally part of the Boston parks system and a substantial portion of their operations are subsidized by the state, auditors in the state government understandably need to keep tabs on revenues, expenditures, quality of animal care, and so on.

In addition to these annual reports, the Massachusetts Zoological Corporation's eleven-member board was directed by the state legislature to submit a "state-of-the-zoos" report by the first day of 1996. The zoos had long been considered among the nation's worst, with exhibits little better than those of many roadside operations. With their facilities in such disrepair and their scant collections so poorly managed, the public stayed away. The occasional proposals to revive the ailing institutions usually gave way to talk of shutting them down (the Stone Zoo, in fact, was padlocked for a time). The semi-private Massachusetts Zoological Corporation was charged with taking control of the zoos from the Boston-area parks commission and resuscitating them—emulating their counterparts at Zoo Atlanta, for example, who turned an equally pathetic facility into a highly regarded institution.

By law, the state-of-the-zoos report was to have been delivered to the clerks of the Massachusetts Senate and House of Representatives, as well as to the overseeing committees in both chambers. But walk the great marble-floored corridors of the Massachusetts State House, go from Senate to House committees in search of the report, and the hours-long exercise ultimately proves futile. The report was never delivered, say committee staff members. Or perhaps it was delivered, say others, but no one can remember ever seeing a copy.

Try the Massachusetts Bureau of Animal Health, in a nearby Government Center office tower, and records of the zoos' animal-trading activities are also impossible to locate. Although sending animals from one state to another typically requires the filing of paperwork, there are no documents to be found for these zoos or, for that manner, any of the state's other zoos.

This is not unusual. Although great efforts are made to track the movement of animals into the United States, to flush out illegal shipments and ensure that appropriate quarantine procedures are followed, captive-born exotics—whether monitor lizards or mammals extinct in the wild—are of little concern to anyone. State veterinarians are interested in cattle and other livestock, not in the thousands of lions and tigers in private hands. State game commissions focus their meager resources on the protection of native animals. The U.S. Fish and Wildlife Service monitors the importation of endangered species but assigns a low priority to captive-bred animals. The USDA, which enforces the federal Animal Welfare Act, has nearly seventeen pages of regulations pertaining to the handling and transportation of dogs and cats, but the care of snow leopards and other wild animals is dismissed in just seven pages. And the exotic species are guaranteed much less protection: Domestic kittens, for example, can't be sold in commerce until they're two months old and fully weaned, but a day-old lion may be carted to an auction and sold to the highest bidder. What's more, government prosecutors, as a rule, have virtually no interest in protecting these animals. Given a choice between pursuing a drug-trafficking case or an animal-permit violation, prosecutors rarely opt for the latter.

As a result, the fate of exotics is left largely to their self-appointed guardians, most notably AZA zoos. To hear them tell it, their stewardship has produced extraordinary accomplishments: cooperative efforts with state and federal agencies to foster the reintroduction of the red wolf and black-footed ferret; the Species Survival Plans, which ensure genetic diversity; field research into habitat loss; fauna interest groups; scientific advisory groups; and the Conservation Endowment Fund, which provides finances for such projects as the reintroduction of Bali mynahs to Bali Barat National Park, in Indonesia, the bird's sole remaining habitat.

Dare to ask AZA members why they so freely dump their communities' animals into private hands, however, and the replies echo the organization's stock disclaimer: Endangered-species conservation is not something they can accomplish on their own; partners are needed. "What is most important is that the animals are in the hands of those properly qualified to care for them," the AZA says. "Each AZA institution has their own methods of determining if an animal recipient is qualified."

Actually, a trailer or cage is often all that zoos require. There is no real due diligence. A recipient's qualifications are immaterial. So are his breeding or resale plans. Time and again, zoo animals are sent to either those unqualified to provide them care or those uninterested in doing so. The discarded animals are nothing but the foundation for dishonorable commerce, with zoos and dealers linked as silent business partners.

It's a long-standing nod-and-a-wink arrangement meant to provide the zoos deniability: They hand over their unwanted animals and hope that the dealers' misdeeds aren't traced to the source. It's a sorry game of don't-ask, don't-tell, and it's conducted in a way designed to bury the truth. If these publicly funded institutions have nothing to hide, why won't they provide a full accounting of where all the unwanted animals went?

—<o>—

Lionel disappeared in the spring of 1998, although the nineteen-year-old giraffe's absence wasn't readily apparent. From the public walkway that encircles the National Zoo's Elephant House everything looked perfectly normal. Anyone who counted two giraffes instead of three likely had the same thought: Lionel must be indoors.

Sadly, Lionel had died. The Masai giraffe, which for years had been treated with ibuprofen for arthritis, had developed a troubling hoof problem, and, after consulting with Lionel's keepers, the National Zoo's veterinarian decided that treatment was necessary. A giraffe's unique anatomy and physiology make anesthesia risky, but the seriousness of Lionel's condition dictated that the longtime zoo resident be knocked down for treatment.

Unfortunately, there were complications: Lionel's neck convulsed not long after he was anesthetized, and the zoo's veterinarian, who had never before administered such strong sedatives to a giraffe, immediately injected an antidote to counteract them. It didn't work, and Lionel never recovered. His death may have been propitious, though: A necropsy revealed that the aging giraffe had serious joint problems—bone scraping on bone—that had undoubtedly caused him great pain. In the wild, giraffes and other animals will not reveal physical abnormalities—a means of concealing from predators that they're potentially easy pickings. Lionel never showed any signs of discomfort, though he did have a somewhat unusual gait. Maybe he was hiding his pain, motivated purely by instinct. Or maybe his unusual walk was a means of compensating for his discomfort.

During Lionel's life at the zoo, he sired nine calves, including Amber. She was born on June 5, 1995, and by August of that year was already being offered for sale in the AZA's members-only *Animal Exchange* newsletter. There was talk of sending her to an Asian zoo, but higher-ups at the National Zoo yielded to staff protests that she might get substandard care overseas.

Like all other transfers from the National Zoo, the details were not available to the public. Although the federally funded zoo enumerates breeding loans in its annual reports to the Smithsonian Institution, information about sales, trades, and donations is conveniently omitted. And although most zoos file the paperwork required by state veterinarians when their animals are moved across state lines, the National Zoo has never even done that. This record-keeping system was developed to give agriculture and health officials the means of tracking diseases to their source. It's a convenient—albeit rarely used—way for the public to track the movement of animals to and from zoos, a continually evolving paper trail that offers insight into at least some zoo commerce. But officials of the National Zoo claimed ignorance of state laws. Only in the face of pointed questioning did Robert Hoage, the zoo's director of public affairs, relay word in a letter that the zoo would finally start complying with the law.

Because the zoo did not file these documents, only keepers and other zoo employees would have known about Amber's move to a drive-through safari park in Port Clinton, Ohio. That facility is owned by International Animal Exchange of Ferndale, Michigan, which is so controversial that some AZA zoos refuse to do business with it. "I know a lot of people in the AZA who won't deal with them," the lead keeper at one zoo says. "Someone mentions IAE and we give the evil vampire cross and say no, no, no." Despite such sentiment, International Animal

Exchange manages to acquire large numbers of surplus giraffes from AZA zoos and then ships them to Mexico, Thailand, Turkey, and a host of other overseas destinations. The foreign buyers have included Aritake Chojuten, a Japanese firm known for having been involved in the smuggling of two infant gorillas—in violation of international treaty—to Spain, where records were concocted to make it appear as if the animals were captive-born. Aritake Chojuten then sold the infant gorillas, whose parents were believed to have been slaughtered, to a Japanese zoo. Another Japanese dealer that has bought giraffes from International Animal Exchange is Keihin Choju Trading Company, an animal supplier once involved in transporting three gorillas from Africa with bogus permits. Two of the great apes died in transit. Ironically, keepers at the National Zoo, out of concern for Amber's well-being, had demanded that the young giraffe be sent to Ohio, rather than overseas.

As for Aaron, he too was put up for sale shortly after birth. With the giraffe market glutted, however, no one wanted the year-old giraffe.

But now Lionel's death had made threats from an adult male immaterial. Worries about inbreeding were not immediately germane, as male giraffes don't become sexually mature until approximately their forty-second month. And Grif was not pregnant when Lionel died, so for the foreseeable future there would be no births—no fears that Aaron might pester a newborn. If zoo officials wanted to keep Aaron with his mother, to let the public that had celebrated his arrival watch him grow to adolescence, they seemed to have the perfect opportunity.

But the National Zoo didn't want Aaron. Following Lionel's death, debates began about the future of the giraffe collection: Bring in a new male, bring in another female, let Grif go solo for awhile. Aaron's fate wasn't a debatable issue. Everyone knew that the young male would be leaving, although no one could say when or where he would be going.

A docent stationed at the giraffe yard said there would be discussions with other zoos, that coordinators of the Species Survival Plan—the cooperative breeding program of the American Zoo and Aquarium Association—would render a decision about Aaron's fate. He said that zoo populations would be surveyed to see where Aaron's bloodlines were most needed—the same process that had determined Amber's move to an Ohio "zoo." It all sounded like the perfect model of conservation, except for one detail: There is no Species Survival Plan for giraffes, no interzoo blueprint for how best to ensure that giraffes in captivity thrive. As a keeper at this same zoo had once admitted, giraffes just happen.

BLIND FAITH

The Discovery Channel Destination Store, in downtown Washington, D.C., is a 30,000-square-foot shopping adventure that's in perfect sync with the cable programmer's image and mission: The store's four museum-like floors, whose displays include a bomber cockpit and a cast of a *Tyrannosaurus rex* skeleton, are filled with globes and telescopes, trail guides and hiking gear. There are science kits and gardening tools, along with fossils, kites, and, of course, all things animal—everything from bird feeders and leopard sculptures to books about reptiles, T-shirts imprinted with mammals, and videotapes that follow creatures of the sea.

In September 1998, the store was spotlighting tiger merchandise. Items included a computer mouse pad emblazoned with a tiger's face, a Siberian tiger "sponsorship kit" (a means of aiding conservation efforts), and a Siberian tiger stuffed animal—a $28 toy, with a share of the profits earmarked for the World Wildlife Fund's activities celebrating the year of the tiger in the Chinese lunar calendar.

There were other special events as well that month, most notably a Saturday bash to introduce Discovery Channel Publishing's new book, *Wild Discovery*. Judging by sales, many in the large crowd had come in search of the glossy volume, whose title comes from the popular show of the same name. But others were there only because newspaper ads had touted an appearance by a small troupe of animals. And they weren't disappointed: On the store's ground floor, onlookers were treated to close-up views of an owl, a python, and a pair of baby alligators. But the real attraction that Saturday—the one that the kids particularly appreciated—was a large feline billed as a Florida panther.

The endangered big cat is under siege in its Everglades home, as its habitat disappears and it falls victim to such environmental contaminants as mercury. Who better to educate the public about the great predator's unhappy fate than the Discovery Channel, which (along with its sister station, Animal Planet) is by far the preeminent source of quality TV programming about the world's wildlife?

But the animal impresario on hand that day, Bert Allen Wahl, Jr., was hardly the sort of wildlife specialist worthy of the cable operation's image. In fact, five weeks before his Discovery Channel store appearance, Wahl's USDA exhibitor's license had been canceled after he failed to renew it. What's more, shortly after the event in the nation's capital, Wahl's Florida license to exhibit cougars was not renewed (he appealed the decision and, as of this writing, the matter is in litigation).

Wahl is among the legions of self-proclaimed wildlife experts who have cashed in on the public's seemingly insatiable desire to see and learn about animals. Despite their lack of formal training or credentials, these so-called authorities—many of whom operate not-for-profit organizations—have managed to pawn themselves off as trusted sources of information, hoodwinking schools, community groups, and such respected media outlets as the Discovery Channel. Armed with well-honed spiels about saving endangered species or preserving habitat, these imposters come off as legitimate guardians of wildlife. What the public never sees are their citations for animal-welfare violations, their receipts for the transfer of exotic species to unqualified collectors, and, in some cases, their rap sheets, earned for their mistreatment of the very animals they claim to be saving.

Wahl, who operates the Tampa-based Wildlife Rescue, Inc., obtained a state permit in 1984 to keep wildlife for rehabilitation and exhibition purposes. Four years later, the Florida Game and Fresh Water Fish Commission sent him a letter that said, in part: "The Division of Law Enforcement has received complaints concerning the exhibition of your cougar. We have subsequently obtained documentary evidence that you have abused your cougar in public by striking the animal with various objects during your shows. Commission officers have recently filed charges against you with the Palm Beach County State Attorney for cruelty to animals."

In fact, that year the commission slapped Wahl with four charges of abusing his cougar—a cat that Wahl claims is an endangered Florida panther, but one that state wildlife officials insist is actually a mixed breed. (He was acquitted on two of the charges and the other two were dropped by prosecutors.) In 1992 and 1993, the state wildlife agency cited Wahl four more times for animal cruelty and abandonment and for maintaining wildlife in substandard cages. Neighbors repeatedly complained about Wahl's wildlife "facility"—a junk-filled, fenced-off space beside his house in a residential neighborhood.

After the Game and Fresh Water Fish Commission began proceedings to revoke Wahl's wildlife rehabilitation permit, an official of the commission wrote to the chief of the law enforcement division, Colonel Robert Edwards:

Mr. Wahl has demonstrated a continued pattern of refusal to comply with the most basic requirements for the keeping of wildlife. Not only does he make pets out of injured wildlife, rather than releasing it as required, but he also treats his wildlife in an inhumane way, keeping it under substandard conditions. Even after repeated citations, he continues to violate the same regulations. He also refuses lawful inspections of his facility and orders his workers to do the same. He refuses to follow the direction of inspectors to provide humane care or to release wildlife. We are constantly receiving complaints about his operations from his neighbors and must drop other important duties to respond to these complaints. These are the most blatant violations of law we have ever experienced by a wildlife rehabilitator.

So well known was Wahl that in the summer of 1994 U.S. Representative Peter Deutsch of Florida urged then-Secretary of Agriculture Mike Espy to undertake an investigation of his operation. A year later, Debbie Wasserman Schultz, a member of the Florida House of Representatives, wrote to the director of the Game and Fresh Water Fish Commission: "According to recent convictions, his wild cats, including the Florida Panther, are subjected to abuse and a restrictive and unsuitable living environment. It would be terribly wrong to allow this abuse of defenseless wildlife to continue. Please do not reinstate his license."

Federal authorities also were concerned about Wahl's treatment of animals, including his so-called Florida panthers. In March 1995, USDA's Animal and Plant Health Inspection Service filed a formal complaint against Wahl, alleging that he failed to maintain proper acquisition records, that he kept his animals in substandard housing, that the refrigerator/freezer containing the animals' food was littered with blood and insects, that he denied inspectors access to his facilities, and that he kept deer in a backyard cluttered with rusty wire fencing and lumber with protruding nails. (On this last charge, Wahl maintained that because deer were accustomed to living amid briar patches and other obstacles, the rusty wires really didn't present a danger.) In May 1997, an administrative law judge found Wahl guilty of various Animal Welfare Act violations and fined him $1,000. That same year, a Florida court declared Wahl's big cats a public nuisance and, much to the relief of neighbors, ordered him to remove two of the animals from his Tampa home.

Between the fall of 1996 and the spring of 1997, Wahl deposited six cougars at a Florida "sanctuary" that had recently been fined $5,000 by the federal government for its substandard facilities, and which was again under investigation for its animal-welfare practices (the USDA canceled its exhibitor's license a year later). Five of Wahl's cougars soon died, apparently from feline leukemia. What's more, two of the big cats were pregnant when they arrived at the sanctuary—a fact that had escaped Wahl—and their cubs were stillborn.

In short, Bert Wahl's background does not exactly jibe with his public image as a dedicated conservationist. And his record hardly seems to make him the sort of wildlife expert with whom the Discovery Channel might want to be aligned. But examine the résumés of the self-proclaimed exotic-animal authorities, and it's clear that this sort of unholy alliance is hardly unusual. In fact, the heroes and villains are such regular—and apparently comfortable—bedfellows that it's sometimes hard to tell the players without a program.

◄o►

The star of the *Newton's Apple* segment on tigers was a white Bengal named Taari, a rambunctious five-month-old with inch-long canines and oversized paws. The three-minute segment, first broadcast on public television in 1997, was in keeping with the informational, yet fun, approach that has made this science show for kids such a long-standing and highly acclaimed success.

On hand with cohost Brian Hackney was Cynthia Gamble, the president of the Center for Endangered Cats, in Forest Lake, Minnesota. Gamble had brought Taari to the TV studio to talk about such things as the tiger's behavior and genetics—how it learned at a young age the physical skills that would later be required for hunting, how the exotic feline's coloring should not be confused with albinism. Prompted by questions from Hackney, who joined Taari and its handler in a hay-filled pen fortified with chicken wire, Gamble also explained how the endangered cat's population is declining as its habitat is increasingly lost to humans. Hackney concluded the obvious: "So the best bet we have of seeing a tiger like this is in captivity."

Gamble is one of those who make it possible for the public to see these captive tigers up close. The Center for Endangered Cats is among an increasing number of not-for-profit organizations founded to enlighten the public about the plight of disappearing species, and like other such groups it does so through media appearances and presentations at schools, outdoor shows, conventions, and small zoos.

Some wildlife educators refuse to use live animals in their presentations. They insist that placing the animals in unfamiliar environments not only causes them undue stress but also tells audiences nothing about their normal behaviors. Others use only indigenous animals in their live presentations, relying instead on slides or video to teach about nonnative exotics. Gamble, however, uses "feline ambassadors" as part of her "cats in crisis" presentation, augmenting her lecture by showing off the likes of a snow leopard or a Siberian lynx. Audiences generally enjoy the close contact with these rare animals, which they might not otherwise get to see in person.

Although Gamble often appears on behalf of the Center for Endangered Cats, its founder and driving force is executive director Craig Wagner. Like many whose careers involve exotic animals, Wagner's interest began with pet ownership: He drove by a "cougars for sale" sign, impulsively bought a pair of cubs, and brought them home to his stunned wife. Before long Wagner was breeding big cats.

Wagner's activities caused some displeasure in his small western Minnesota community, where neighbors concerned about living in such close proximity to wild and dangerous animals mounted an effort to banish the sanctuary. But others took Wagner's side. Dozens of volunteers helped build and maintain facilities for the center's two dozen big cats. Support was offered in the form of membership donations. Local schools called on Wagner to help highlight efforts to protect the environment. "It's too easy for almost anyone to buy cougars and other wild animals," Wagner once said in an interview. "You don't need any special qualifications."

Indeed, Wagner himself doesn't have any formal qualifications. The self-taught wildlife specialist, who professes ignorance about any skill other than working with cats, was at one time a restaurateur and a professional racquetball player. But despite his lack of credentials or formal training, it's certainly been easy for Wagner to acquire snow leopards,

Amur leopards, and other rare animals. They come from Oakhill Center for Rare & Endangered Species, an AZA "Related Organization" in Luther, Oklahoma, and Ashby Acres Wildlife Park, in New Smyrna, Florida, an animal-dealing enterprise that has counted on a steady stream of AZA surplus.

What may be most notable about Wagner's sanctuary, however, is that he runs it from Minnesota because there is a warrant for his arrest in neighboring Wisconsin, where he was busted on horrendous animal-cruelty charges. What's more, the objects of his sometimes-fatal neglect and abuse were endangered cats, a fact he's managed to keep hidden from his benefactors.

Wagner's troubles started in June 1990, when a Wisconsin game warden learned from a veterinarian that Wagner had brought in two young snow leopards for examination. Because he lacked both state and federal permits to possess the endangered cubs, as well as other large cats that were later found at his home, he was cited for four violations of state law.

Although the cats officially became the property of the state, Wisconsin, like other states, lacks the facilities to house confiscated animals, and so Wagner was permitted to keep his pets while he secured the necessary permits. But in July, the game warden monitoring the animals' care found, on three consecutive days, that they had received neither food nor water. In addition, a tiger and a lynx were chained in a filthy yard. Wagner, meanwhile, was nowhere to be found.

When he at last appeared, Wagner admitted that he hadn't been taking good care of the cats, that he had run out of food, and that his meat freezer wasn't working anyway. The animals were finally fed, but the care was short-lived. In fact, at one point the game warden concluded that the cats may not have been fed for five days. Wagner had apparently left town, entrusting to friends the care of his animals.

In August, Wagner told the game warden that he planned to construct a building for his cats, whose ranks now included seven Siberian lynx, a Siberian tiger, a snow leopard, two cougars, and a black leopard. A month later, however, the construction had not yet started. The freezer was still broken. The leopard and tiger were chained outside in the yard, once again without food or water. Wagner was issued a fifth citation for violating regulations of the Wisconsin Department of Natural Resources.

But still nothing changed, at least until late October. That's when the starving tiger killed the black leopard and ate it. In return, Wagner allegedly beat the cat with a two-by-four. Follow-up visits by the game warden over the next month revealed the same continuing pattern of hungry animals without water.

Wagner was charged in state circuit court with crimes against animals, which in Wisconsin are misdemeanor offenses. He was found guilty in March 1993 and received a nine-month jail sentence, which was stayed by the judge. He was also placed on probation for two years and ordered to pay more than $45,000 in restitution for the care of his animals, which were seized by the county but later returned to him. (Not all of them were returned, however: Two of Wagner's seven Siberian lynx died in the custody of the individual entrusted with the animals' care.) As part of the sentencing conditions, Wagner was prohibited from selling, transferring, or loaning his cats without the court's approval.

The probation order was extended another two years, but Wagner left the state with his animals, set up a not-for-profit organization, and began wooing his Minnesota neighbors. Because Wagner failed to comply with the restitution order, a warrant for his arrest was issued in early 1997—about the time that *Newton's Apple* was preparing to highlight the fine work of the Center for Endangered Cats. Probation officers in Polk County, Wisconsin, occasionally see Wagner on Minneapolis newscasts talking about the need to better protect animals, but of course the fugitive is legally out of reach. And nearly a decade after Wagner's cats were seized, county and state agencies in Wisconsin are still squabbling over who should get stuck with the bill for the animals' care.

Wagner, who calls all the charges against him trumped up, can't concern himself with the remaining $35,000 of his restitution. He wants to expand his operation and build an educational complex to better facilitate public awareness. He even hopes to acquire land in other countries (there's already a parcel in Ecuador, he claims). Until then, however, he'll have to make do with the Minnesota state fair, the Colorado and Georgia Renaissance Festivals, a Connecticut photo shoot with actress Glenn Close and Peter Matthiesen—acclaimed author of *The Snow Leopard*—on behalf of the International Snow Leopard Trust, and special events in any state but Wisconsin, where the Department of Corrections Apprehension Request still remains in force.

◄o►

In the summer of 1997, the U.S. Department of Agriculture's Animal and Plant Health Inspection Service set out to formulate guidelines for the training and handling of exotic and wild animals. The timing wasn't coincidental: There had been a recent spate of high-profile incidents involving the mistreatment of exotic animals, including the death of an elephant owned by the King Royal Circus of Von Ormy, Texas, and the alleged abuse of big cats—striking them with PVC pipe and ax handles—by David McMillan, whose Tiger's Eye Productions, in Oviedo, Florida, teaches animal training and sells newborn tiger cubs as pets. McMillan adamantly denied the accusations, likening his techniques to the spanking of an unruly child—an attention-getting device that may briefly sting but doesn't injure or otherwise harm the cats. Animal-rights activists not only wanted McMillan to be punished (APHIS would ultimately decide that sanctions were unwarranted) but they also sought assurances that the government would impose sanctions on anyone whose training and handling techniques jeopardized the well-being of exotics.

On the latter demand, at least, APHIS could offer no such guarantees, as its rules about acceptable handling and training methods were overly vague. By setting in motion this inquiry, the government hoped to determine what constituted recognized industry standards as well as humane practices.

Any new regulations could have far-reaching impact, as APHIS licenses some twenty-one hundred exhibitors, including zoos, circuses, and marine-mammal parks. As a result, USDA's Animal and Plant Health Inspection Service was besieged with industry comments, many of which insisted that it would be difficult, if not impossible, for the government to impose across-the-board standards. Each species, it was argued, has unique characteristics, and therefore universal edicts would be misguided. What's more, others insisted, each individual animal has a different disposition, and therefore even general guidelines for a given species would be pointless.

Among the well-known animal-handling specialists offering advice to APHIS on how to protect exotic animals was Bobby Berosini, a Las Vegas entertainer who, in 1989, was secretly caught on videotape taunting and apparently beating his orangutans backstage at the Stardust Hotel. Berosini was later stripped of his U.S. Fish and Wildlife Service permit, which had allowed him to buy and sell captive-born endangered species, but he nonetheless still maintains a troupe of nine great apes that pose with customers for photographs ($15 a pop) and perform a vulgar circus-style act that includes giving onlookers the finger.

The comments from Hawthorn Corporation, an exotic-animal breeder and exhibitor in Grayslake, Illinois, which were submitted by the Washington law firm of Shea and Gardner, focused in part on the proper way to care for elephants. Missing was any reference to the charges of elephant mistreatment heaped on John Cuneo, the owner of Hawthorn, by the very agency to which these comments were submitted. The government charged Cuneo with shipping tuberculosis-infected elephants across the United States, posing a potential health threat to humans. Cuneo denied the charges, but temporarily surrendered his exhibitor's license; a few months after filing his comments with APHIS, he agreed to pay a $60,000 fine and give up his license for another three weeks. It was an African elephant owned by Cuneo that, in 1994, trampled her trainer and went on a rampage through the streets of Honolulu, threatening bystanders before police shot and killed her.

Not everyone offering recommendations to APHIS was as well known. There was, for example, Joan Byron-Marasek, the director of Tigers Only Preservation Society, in Clarksburg, New Jersey. Byron-Marasek is a former circus employee, and TOPS, as it's known, bills itself as a sanctuary that for more than two decades has been "totally and passionately dedicated" to the protection and conservation of endangered and threatened species, in particular all tiger species. Such promises are apparently good enough for Ringling Brothers and Barnum & Bailey Circus, which in 1992 donated six retired tigers to Byron-Marasek's so-called conservation center. (While Ringling enthusiastically promotes its top-flight retirement home for elephants, it will not admit to sending Byron-Marasek tigers, nor will it say where else it has sent its unwanted big cats.) Today, TOPS is home to about twenty large carnivores.

Byron-Marasek was the subject of news reports in early 1999 when a tiger allegedly escaped from her twelve-acre compound and, after wandering freely for seven hours, was shot and killed by police. But she actually got in the refuge business in 1976, when she bought two Bengal tiger cubs from David McMillan, who was then the big-cat trainer at Great Adventure, the New Jersey theme park later renamed Six Flags Wild Safari. (McMillan, who told a New Jersey state zoologist that, in his opinion, the ownership of captive-bred animals should not be regulated, also sold tigers to a resident of a mobile-home park in northern Virginia who was busted for displaying his animals without the required USDA exhibitor's permit.) Because she had no place to keep her tigers, Byron-Marasek stashed them in a barn beside an apartment she and her husband rented. The landlords were themselves exotic-animal exhibitors who impressed Byron-Marasek as being conscientious and responsible. But months later, Byron-Marasek accused this couple of trying to poison her tigers by spraying insecticide at them. She claimed that they had exposed her tigers to toxic ammonia fumes, from urine and feces, by nailing shut the barn's windows. She said that they cut the hoses so her tigers couldn't get water. She insisted that a live, twelve-gauge shotgun shell was thrown into her tigers' cage, making possible a scenario in which an animal biting the ammo would have its head blown off. She complained that, against her instructions, the landlords bought a powder-type fire extinguisher for the barn, which could also poison her tigers. A state zoologist who investigated the allegations found none of them to have merit.

In 1987, Byron-Marasek applied to the Interior Department for a captive-bred wildlife registration permit, which authorizes one to buy and sell endangered or threatened animals not native to the United States.

Her application was denied, in part because her facilities were found to be inadequate, her cats' diet unacceptable, and the educational material she intended to distribute outdated. What's more, her knowledge of the field was called into question, because three of the tiger subspecies she sought to have covered by her permit were extinct.

Byron-Marasek finally managed to get a captive-bred wildlife registration permit in 1988, the same year she sued a New Jersey meat dealer for allegedly selling her poisoned horse meat that, she claimed, killed one of her tigers and left four others brain-damaged. The case was dismissed four years later after Byron-Marasek, who is known to her neighbors as the "Tiger Lady," failed to show up for a scheduled deposition. An appeals court ruled that her noncompliance was deliberate.

In 1997, Byron-Marasek enlisted the assistance of Rainforest Relief, a conservation organization, in an attempt to forestall construction on land abutting her property. The problem, she insisted, was that storm-water runoff from the neighboring development might poison her tigers. Rainforest Relief's fruitless petition to Governor Christine Todd Whitman of New Jersey asked that TOPS and its tigers be declared a state treasure and that a buffer zone be created around the sanctuary to protect it in perpetuity. There was, the petition noted, a thirty-acre forested preserve in which the tigers could roam freely, and their numbers included the world's largest tiger, a rare Siberian named Jaipur. In truth, the tigers are caged in a small portion of the compound because state law prohibits them from running freely, and the nine-hundred-pound Jaipur had died a decade earlier. According to Byron-Marasek, it had been poisoned.

Also writing APHIS with their ideas about standards for training and handling exotic animals were Kirsten and Troy Hyde, the proprietors of Animals of Montana, Inc., in Bozeman. The USDA-licensed exhibitors, who arranged photo shoots of their pet animals in wild-like settings, had a unique idea: mandate a two-to-three-year apprenticeship for all new owners of exotic animals.

In their comments to APHIS, the Hydes bemoaned the changes they'd seen in their thirteen years of raising exotics. "We see and get calls from all kinds of people throughout the United States looking for an exotic as a 'tame pet,'" they wrote. "Those are words to make a person shudder thinking about it. We do not think of any exotic animal as a 'pet' nor 'tame.' When you are dealing with these animals our word is 'trained.'" Of particular concern to them was the ownership of animals for reasons of "status" or to make a quick profit.

The Hydes (who are no longer marital or business partners) were particularly well versed in profiting from exotic animals. Month after month, their ads in *Animal Finders' Guide,* the pet-trade periodical, offered for sale both their unwanted surplus and even their not-yet born. This advertisement, from a spring 1997 issue, is typical: "Montana Babies Abounding: coyotes due April 1, red fox due April 15, wolves due May 1, cougars due May 25. Call for information." In the same issue: "For sale: 1 male 2 years old river otter; 2 males 5 years pure-bred timber wolves; 1 male 8 months cougar; 1 pair of breeder coyotes; 1 pair breeder red fox. All hand-raised and used in still photography and motion picture sets." The Hydes also advertised black bears.

In 1996, when planning a summertime visit to relatives, Troy Hyde petitioned the Wisconsin Department of Natural Resources for permission to bring along Mocoqua, a pet black bear the couple jokingly referred to as their nanny, and which they photographed pushing their young son in his stroller. Wisconsin authorities at first refused the request but ultimately relented after Troy pledged in writing that the three-and-a-half-year-old female would not be displayed or exhibited during his two-week stay.

Despite the promises, Hyde brought the chained animal to a local tavern, had it climb onto the bar, and allowed patrons to take pokes at it. Hyde's proclivities were very much in evidence that day: He carried a full-size wooden baseball bat in a holster, which was at the ready should there be trouble. Wisconsin authorities learned of the breach of promise only after Hyde and his pet bear had left the state.

—<o>—

On the afternoon of March 5, 1998, the toughest seat to get on Capitol Hill may have been in the Gold Room of the Rayburn House Office

Building. The National Wildlife Federation had reserved the space for a legislative briefing on endangered species and human population issues, followed by a screening of *Tiger!*, a TV special that it had coproduced with WTBS. As the 1:30 P.M. start time approached, the Gold Room's hundreds of seats were already filled. In fact, representatives of the NWF, the nation's largest member-supported conservation group, had spent the morning telephoning some of those to whom invitations had been sent with an odd, and slightly embarrassing, request: Please wait until the briefing has finished before trying to enter the room. An overflow crowd was anticipated, and the organization wanted to make certain that essential legislative personnel were not denied entry.

Ordinarily, an event of this sort draws a sparse audience. But as a way to generate interest, NWF had faxed and e-mailed a notice that there would be a special "guest appearance" by a white tiger cub from the Columbus Zoo. It was an effective gimmick: When the five-and-a-half-month-old Bengal tiger, named Rama, was ushered into the room, throngs of young congressional aides eagerly pressed in to snap pictures. Scenes of the event played that evening on local TV. A page-one picture of the tiger—and two thoroughly smitten members of Congress, who had been on hand to offer remarks—appeared in the following week's issue of the Capitol Hill newspaper *Roll Call*. The year of the tiger had spawned many events promoting big-cat conservation, but none likely played to a more high-powered—and perhaps enthusiastic—crowd.

Unbeknownst to District of Columbia officials, however, the National Wildlife Federation—a great advocate of wildlife laws—had brought the sixty-pound tiger into the nation's capital without first securing the proper permits, according to the city's chief of animal disease control. And the Columbus Zoo had not filed the appropriate health certificate, as D.C. law mandates. This same city official says that such behavior is typical of the NWF, which, she says, seems to believe that it's above the law.

What's more, the organization's choice of animals was particularly baffling. Although white tigers appear occasionally in nature, Rama was nothing but a genetic aberration, the inbred offspring of a line of tigers traceable to the Cincinnati Zoo. Because of inbreeding—the endless mating of brothers and sisters, fathers and daughters—white tigers are a physical mess: They are often stricken with cataracts, club feet, near-crippling hip dysplasia, and other physical problems. Edward Maruska, the director of the Cincinnati Zoo, rejects the view that white tigers are genetic freaks, but he has little support from his colleagues. The coordinator of an AZA-sponsored captive-breeding program for Siberian tigers, has condemned breeding white tigers because they are of mixed ancestry and serve no conservation purpose. The prevailing wisdom is that they are merely artificially manufactured showpieces favored by roadside menageries and other profit-seeking hucksters, not by bona fide conservationists.

The National Wildlife Federation said that it had chosen the Columbus Zoo for its tiger because it would deal only with an AZA-accredited zoo. In truth, however, the Columbus Zoo didn't own the white tigers but had them on loan from the Nashville Zoo, which is not accredited. Nashville's other white tigers have landed with D.C.'s Country Junction, a nightclub/roadside zoo in Lowell, Indiana. It loaned clouded leopards to Bert Wahl. Its Bengal tigers have gone to dealer Jim Fouts, who in turn has sent his stock to Roxy Luce and her husband, one-time exhibitors based in Trenton, Florida. Until the couple retired and passed the "portable zoo" business to their son, they bred big cats and dragged them to photo shoots at Wal-Mart stores and elsewhere—species preservation work, Luce says, that paid for further breeding. Additional funds to continue the family's mission were generated by the sale of white tiger cubs, which were featured in *Animal Finders' Guide* ads.

The Columbus Zoo's loaner white tiger and other cubs made many public appearances beyond Capitol Hill, as they were designated props for Jack Hanna's TV and personal appearances (Rama's résumé included the daytime talk show hosted by Maury Povich). Three weeks before the congressional event, for example, Hanna, the director emeritus of the Columbus Zoo, was featured at a groundbreaking ceremony for the Dallas Zoo's one-acre, $4.5 million Exxon Endangered Tiger Exhibit. The ceremony coincided with the largest-ever international meeting of tiger experts, government officials, and others working to stave off threats to the species.

Assisting Hanna that day was Heidi Riggs, of the Bridgeport Nature Center, eighty miles from Dallas. Although the organization bills itself as a big-cat conservation center, it's really just another front organization that lives off of animal dealing and $10 photo opportunities. (Six months after the groundbreaking, the USDA announced that it was suspending Heidi Riggs's exhibitor's license for one month for a variety of Animal Welfare Act violations, including her mistreatment of tigers.)

The center's staff "rescues" tigers from exotic-animal auctions and elsewhere and breeds them like rabbits: Just before the Dallas meeting, Bridgeport Nature Center was advertising for sale eight white Bengal tigers born between November 1996 and October 1997, and ten heterozygous Bengal tigers ("all animals are hand raised and very tame"). Its buyer list includes I.B. "Trey" Chapman, the onetime proprietor of Alamo Tiger Ranch, in Alamosa, Colorado. Chapman's so-called sanctuary was billed as a safe haven for abused or neglected animals, but in fact the not-for-profit ranch rented big cats for TV commercials and, like all the others, charged people to pose with the cats for photos. Ten days after the groundbreaking ceremony in Dallas, the U.S. Department of Agriculture announced that Chapman and his wife had been forever barred from exhibiting animals.

Exxon Corporation, of course, uses the tiger as its corporate symbol and has donated millions of dollars to various tiger conservation efforts. Among those Exxon has hired to display its regional tiger mascots is James Stephens, of Water Wheel Exotics, in Avella, Pennsylvania, who was tabbed to travel a five-state area with a Bengal named Cody. A former horse farmer and truck driver who for years operated a mobile petting zoo and animal-leasing service, Stephens breeds big cats and other animals on his farm, endowed with loaners from "sanctuaries," such as one in Ohio that supplied boxer Mike Tyson with tigers. Stephens proudly claims—"in the tradition of P. T. Barnum"—to own the world's largest cat, a twelve-hundred-pound, freakish-looking crossbreed of a lion and Siberian tiger (a "liger"), a genetic mutant that's the antithesis of the goals of the Save the Tiger Fund, which Exxon enthusiastically supports. To make matters worse, Stephens was cited for repeated Animal Welfare Act violations over a three-year period; in September 1997, he agreed to a $30,000 fine and had his federal exhibitor's license suspended for a month. Stephens was also nailed by Ohio authorities for failing to keep a young tiger "under the direct control and supervision of a knowledgeable and experienced animal handler during a public exhibition." And he says that his animal-exhibiting career suffered yet another setback in 1998, when he was fined another $32,000 by the USDA and stripped of his license.

An animal handler who has claimed to also own an Exxon tiger is Bhagavan Kevin Antle, who was an assistant to Jack Hanna during his appearances on *Good Morning America* and *Late Night With David Letterman*. Known alternatively as Kevin Bhagavan, Kevin Antle, Mahamayavi Bhagavan Antle, Ghagavan Antle, and Dr. Kevin Antle (he supposedly earned a doctor of natural sciences degree from the Chinese Science Foundation), Antle also claimed to own the MGM lion, even though Metro-Goldwyn-Mayer Inc. sent him a cease-and-desist letter, and he implied in his literature an affiliation with Greenpeace, until he was told to cease and desist. Antle is a self-described big-cat conservationist who presides over The Institute of Greatly Endangered and Rare Species (TIGERS), which operates a mobile petting zoo, leases tigers for TV commercials, and charges people at shopping malls and festivals to have their pictures taken with an animal. Antle hauls around a crossbred lion and tiger to such places as casinos in Biloxi, Mississippi. He is also known for owning a lion that, in 1991, had to be pulled off a terrified model during a photo shoot in Manchester, New Hampshire. That same year, the federal government charged Antle with repeated violations of the Animal Welfare Act, including substandard housing for big cats, and to settle the charges he agreed to pay a $3,500 fine. He was also cited in Massachusetts that year for illegally displaying his cats, and he was threatened with arrest and confiscation of the animals if he didn't immediately leave the state. What's more, Antle was the target of an unsuccessful 1991 Tennessee lawsuit regarding his alleged beating of a Bengal tiger with a wooden shaft. The following year, the big-cat expert accompanied Hanna on his TV appearances, handling a variety of animals for the famed zoo director.

Other Year of the Tiger events produced by conservation-minded organizations have lent an air of legitimacy to an equally suspect cast of characters. For example, *National Geographic* devoted thirty-four pages to a cover story that chronicled threats to the big cat's survival as well as efforts to protect the species. Amid descriptions of antipoaching initiatives and the valuable field work of Hornocker Wildlife Institute, a well-respected conservation organization in Moscow, Idaho, is a photograph of a woman in her home playing tug-of-war with a young tiger. On the facing page is a picture of another cub lying placidly in a beat-up playpen, light streaming through the frosted glass panes of a door. "Betty Young plays with Butterball, one of 52 tigers at her ten-acre compound in northwest Arkansas," the caption reads. "Young takes in tigers given up by owners unprepared for a 400-pound pet, breeds them—even trains them to use a jumbo-size litter box. After she nursed Major Bill (right) from an illness, he took to sleeping in her bed. 'He snores,' says Young, 'but I'm used to it.'"

Actually, Young doesn't breed the genetically indeterminate castoffs occasionally deposited with her. But the positive spin about her Riverglen Tiger Shelter, in West Fork, Arkansas, is certainly standard fare. "The nonprofit feline conservatory takes in tigers from zoos, circuses, and individual owners who are no longer willing or able to take care of the cats. Currently, 50 tigers live there," the *Arkansas Democrat-Gazette* explained in a 1998 story. "We provide accurate information and create public awareness concerning tigers, both captive and wild," Young's Web site once proclaimed. "Riverglen provides comfortable shelter, proper diets and other specialized services (medical, etc.) for neglected, abused, and abandoned tigers."

Riverglen also provides entertainers and pet owners with a generous supply of babies, because the so-called sanctuary has operated like a tiger-cub mill. In 1995, for example, seventeen tigers were born at Riverglen; the following year, the count was twenty-six. During that same period, Young "rescued" a single tiger: The sheriff's department in Benton County, Arkansas, brought her an eighteen-month-old tiger that was seized from someone not permitted to own it.

Young has no trouble getting rid of her tigers, which she advertises month after month in *Animal Finders' Guide:* "White tiger cubs. Perfect

blue eyed babies due in spring. Serious inquiries only, please. Permits."
By exploiting a loophole in the Endangered Species Act, she can "donate" or "loan" her tigers to virtually anyone. Myron Jones, for example, who keeps wild animals in pens and a barn on his small family farm
in Creve Coeur, Illinois, received a "breeder loan" from Young. Local officials first learned of Jones's private menagerie—shielded from neighbors by a high fence and acquired, in part, from exotic-animal
auctions—after he showed up at a Peoria movie theater's presentation of
The Lion King with a lion cub in tow. Ron and Joy Holiday (as they
were known professionally), who performed illusions such as trans-
forming a woman into a tiger, got as a "gift" from Young a pair of three-
month-old Bengal tigers—one white and one orange—for "educating
and entertainment." In October 1998, the white tiger killed the Holi-
days' business partner, Charles Lizza III, with a bite to the neck. Six
weeks later, the same tiger killed Doris Guay, a.k.a. Joy Holiday, after
which sheriff's sharpshooters killed the tiger. Another of Young's tigers
went as a "gift" to Randy Miller, whose company in Big Bear City, California, Predators in Action, trains exotic felines and other animals to do
specialty stunts—staged attacks on humans, for example—for motion
pictures. The *Los Angeles Times* once described Miller, the founder of a
successful seltzer company, as a "kooky trendsetter" who kept a cougar
and bobcat as pets in his Hollywood condominium. (He later built a
home in the Hollywood hills to accommodate his animals—a structure
complete with a three-story glass cage that, he says, featured ponds and
waterfalls.) The trainer described for the newspaper the magic-show act
he fantasized most about performing: "First, the tiger mauls me and kills
me. Then they drag me out of the prop and levitate my body until it van-
ishes. Finally, I turn up in the middle of the audience which, by now, is
going absolutely wild."

Young also "loaned" a white tiger to entertainer Kirby Van Burch.
Every day but Monday, at 2 P.M. and again at 8, Van Burch wows
crowds with his magic act at a theater in Branson, Missouri, a country-
music mecca. He previously performed a similar routine in Las Vegas,
where, in 1988, a leopard being transported to a casino for his show was
killed by a trainer using excessive force. Young also made a "breeder

loan" to Joe Taft, who runs Exotic Feline Rescue Center in Center Point, Indiana. Taft says that his sanctuary gives animals a home for life, a claim that obviously puts Young's paperwork in question. In fact, he adds, Young was in financial trouble, and gave him the tigers.

Young made another "breeder loan" to Anna and Lamont Cox, of Chatsworth, California. Shortly thereafter, the couple's animal-exhibiting business was charged with violations of the Animal Welfare Act; a consent decree hammered out with the USDA brought them a $5,000 civil penalty. Young engaged in a "breeder exchange" with a Texas couple doing business as Tiger Tales Productions and dedicated, in their words, to "maintaining a breeding program that will ensure that when there is a repopulation effort, unaltered cubs and adults will be available to live in their native lands." But the private Texas zoo with which Tiger Tales Productions was affiliated says the relationship ended, and before long the operation was reborn with a new mission, touted via classified ads: a high-priced zookeeper school.

Not all of Young's animals go out on loan, however. For example, in the summer of 1995 she "donated" a three-month-old tiger to Predators Plus of Sorrento, Florida, yet another take-your-photo-with-the-tiger business. (Predators Plus claims in a filing with the government that it bought the tiger.) Predators Plus, whose animals also came from Oakhill Center for Rare & Endangered Species, the AZA-affiliated organization that supplied Craig Wagner, went out of business a year and a half later after one of the partners disappeared with five of the big cats. She later resurfaced and announced that she and her husband were forming their own exotic-animal compound.

In February 1996, a female tiger at Betty Young's compound escaped through an open gate; at Young's request, the Arkansas Game and Fish Commission personnel who were tracking the animal shot it to death. Two years later, there was tragedy of another sort: A three-hundred-pound tiger attacked a volunteer at Young's compound and bit into his neck. Young pulled the tiger off the worker and held his carotid artery, which was gushing blood, then called an ambulance. The victim of the attack survived, and health officials placed the offending tiger under quarantine. Major Bill, featured so prominently in *National Geographic*'s year-of-the-tiger special as Young's snoring, nighttime companion, undoubtedly missed that familiar mattress during his days of isolation.

◄o►

Jim Fowler had come to the pavilion outside the *Today* show studios to introduce the stars of the annual live nativity scene at Radio City Music Hall: a dromedary camel, a reindeer, some sheep, deer, and Sicilian donkeys. It was a week before Christmas 1997, and Katie Couric, the cohost of the *Today* show, toured the makeshift pen with Fowler, who in his typically good-natured way offered a few particulars about these animals—how reindeer shed their antlers, how the one-humped male dromedaries have canine teeth not unlike a lion's.

And who better than the folksy Fowler to educate TV audiences about these animals? He had, after all, been at it since the early '60s, first with *Mutual of Omaha's Wild Kingdom,* then as a regular on *The Tonight Show,* where Johnny Carson's exaggerated tales of Fowler's exploits—of him out-wrestling wild tigers and stalking bull elephants—made the Georgia-born naturalist a late-night celebrity. For the past decade, however, Fowler has instead been featured on NBC's morning news show, where his popular wildlife reports from around the globe have been aired twice monthly. More recently, he has been an on-air pitchman and program host for Animal Planet, the sister offering of the Discovery Channel, and is often seen on other TV outlets as well.

On this December morning, Fowler and Couric engaged in their familiar banter, she feigning giggly concern about being gored by a ram or spit at by a camel. But Fowler, who has decried the news media's portrayal of animals as nothing but dangers to humans, used a question about the donkeys to inject at least one serious theme: "Of course, these have been beasts of burden for years—around for human beings," he told Couric. "We humans have really been pretty good at utilizing and exploiting animals." Fortunately, he added, the animals he'd brought along were cared for by Dawn Animal Agency, whose farm in New Jersey was home to nearly six hundred orphaned animals that had been rescued from unhappy fates.

In truth, Dawn Animal Agency once owned a farm in New Jersey but had long since moved to New York state. And rescue is not entirely accurate either: In recent years, it had amassed a long list of alleged violations of the Animal Welfare Act. Among the charges: failing to protect the animals' food and bedding against contamination and vermin infestation, failing to keep the premises free of garbage, and failing to maintain accurate records of animal acquisition and disposition. In 1993, to settle these charges, the animal-rental operation agreed to a civil penalty of $2,000—a sanction imposed on only a small number of those licensed as exhibitors or dealers.

Things were no better in New Jersey, when, for a time, the operation was called Sanctuary for Animals and boasted an advisory board that included such celebrities as Ed Asner and Joanne Woodward. The decrepit farm was overrun with hundreds of dogs, horses, goats, and sheep, as well as a collection of exotics that included elephants, macaws, and primates. Revenues for feed were generated from donations and animal rentals, but the sheer number of boarders often left the sanctuary in arrears and the animals, as a result, subjected to substandard housing.

In direct-mail solicitations, Leonard Brook, a trustee of the sanctuary, wrote of one day expanding the facility, although not until finances improved; until then, he promised, it would accept only a minimum number of needy animals. Instead, Brook overwhelmed the sanctuary with black bears and other exotics he'd bought from some of the nation's most prolific animal dealers. His trading partners included Frank Weed, a breeder who flooded the pet trade with some two hundred cougars. Weed called his operation the Florida Endangered Species Research Association, but the title apparently didn't impress federal inspectors: After two years of citing Weed for egregious violations, including the withholding of veterinary care, they finally shut him down for good.

Like the Discovery Channel, Jack Hanna, and other trusted sources of information about wildlife, it appears that Fowler inadvertently aligned himself with an animal supplier whose business practices are sometimes at odds with the conservation messages that the TV star espouses. "While it is not possible to do extensive background checks on every employee of every organization we work with, we adhere to strict standards," Fowler maintains, "and require the same of those who work with us." But Dawn Animal Agency isn't the only animal supplier that Fowler may not have wanted to rely on. Unaccredited petting zoos such as Reston Animal Park have provided him with animals for his educational spiels. When Fowler appeared on *Today* to educate the public about the plight of the grizzly bear, his supplier was Jeffrey Watson of Bedford, Indiana, who buys castoffs from a dreadful Washington state drive-through park and trains them for use in TV commercials and movies. (Watson's specialty is full-contact "maul" scenes.) For his talk about lion cubs, Fowler turned to Furry Friends Zoo, in New Hampshire, whose owners sell lions, some as young as four weeks, to private collectors. When Fowler needed a tiger, Betty Young sent one from Arkansas to Predators Plus, the defunct Florida photo-shoot operation. When the subject was ringtail cats, Fowler turned to Wildlife Educators of America, which was run by Karl Anderson. "This is an educational program; they go to schools," Fowler told *Today* show cohost Matt Lauer in January 1997. Three years earlier, Anderson had plea-bargained his way out of misdemeanor counts for illegally selling protected species; in return, he agreed to a fine, probation, and short jail stay for illegal possesion of wildlife. After he relocated to California, history repeated itself: Anderson pleaded no contest to charges of keeping protected animals without the proper permits and relegating some to substandard cages. A local newspaper, the *Ventura County Star,* dug into Anderson's background and dredged up even more from Oregon records: "Charges that Anderson had sold animals were not pursued by prosecutors, although state police investigators' notes include copies of a receipt signed by Anderson recording the sale of a protected western pond turtle to a Florida pet store," staff writer T. J. Sullivan reported. "Police files also contain a copy of a published advertisement offering the sale of a protected ringtail cat, which investigators traced to Anderson."

Another of Fowler's TV sidekicks has been Harold Kafka, the owner of the now-defunct Scotch Plains Zoo. Kafka made a number of *Today* show appearances with Fowler, including one on May 10, 1997. Four months earlier, a trio of New Jersey state officials toured the private facility to decide whether the animal-care violations that had been amassed over the years had been rectified sufficiently, or whether Scotch Plains Zoo should be shut down. Among the highlights of the walk-through was the birdhouse inspection: "Because of the strong paint and ammonia smell in the building, division personnel had to exit the building repeatedly in order to obtain fresh air." There was also the tour of the giraffe barn: "The stench of ammonia at the second story level was so strong the inspectors could only stay a few minutes." And in another enclosure: "Because of the icy conditions outside, the four flamingos were locked in the shed. Upon inspection, conditions were found to be grossly inadequate. Although heated, no light was provided. A small dirty window allowed no light to enter. The floor of the cage was two inches deep in damp wet bedding and excrement. The smell was unbearable and worse than all other buildings encountered." Twelve days later, on January 28, the New Jersey Division of Fish, Game, and Wildlife informed Kafka that it would not renew the permits covering most of his animals. On May 13, three days after his appearance on the *Today* show with Fowler, Kafka withdrew his appeal of the decision and was ordered to divest himself of his animals.

Following the 1993 publication of his book *Wildest Places on Earth,* Fowler hit the talk-show circuit, bringing along, naturally, some mammalian props. Among those who joined him on *Larry King Live* was Bert Wahl, who parked a golden-brown feline on the talk-show host's desk. "Larry, this is a Florida panther," Fowler said. "Now, the thing that's amazing is that we're about to lose these from the face of the earth. There are only thirty of these left in the Everglades, which I consider one of the wild places in America." Of course, this "Florida panther" was Wahl's apparent knockoff, whose lineage had been traced by the Florida Game and Fresh Water Fish Commission to big-cat breeder Robert Baudy (whose accomplishments include the cross-breeding of leopards and jaguars), and from there to Everglades Wonder Garden, a roadside attraction near Fort Myers. "Although Mr. Wahl's cougars may have some genetic material from a Florida panther, they are not purebred and our biologists do not consider them panthers," Jerry Thompson, of the state wildlife agency, noted in a memo.

Fowler has had plenty of other wildlife specialists to help out, and his retinue has wowed audiences with everything from vultures to bearcats to kinkajous, sometimes even endangered species. On one October day in 1995, for example, Fowler was in New York to receive an environmental award, and he made the rounds with a snow leopard, going from *Good Day New York* to *Late Night With Conan O'Brien.*

Fowler's tag-along, Craig Wagner, was in his element: He was described on O'Brien's show as a savior of endangered species, and he told the *Good Day* audience about his training methods, which were designed to permit animals and humans to bond. Perhaps he wasn't given enough time, but the executive director of the Center for Endangered Cats omitted the part about controlling a tiger with a two-by-four.

3

DISAPPEARING ACTS

In the spring of 1998, the American Zoo and Aquarium Association inadvertently let the world in on one of its most closely guarded secrets: *AZA Animal Exchange,* an eighteen-page, *TV Guide*-size monthly newsletter that's all fine print. Each issue consists, from beginning to end, of listings submitted by AZA members of mammals, birds, and reptiles that—for one reason or another—are no longer needed or wanted. For decades, the AZA had mailed this Blue Book for pre-owned zoo animals to its member institutions and to a select group of affiliates, with the stipulation (almost universally ignored) that copies not go to unaccredited dealers, auctioneers, and other undesirables. Then, in late 1996, the AZA launched an electronic version of the monthly newsletter on its Web site—a password-protected edition that permitted members to continuously update their offerings, search three years' worth of listings, and even track daily price fluctuations of tigers and bears, much the way commodity traders monitor the market gyrations of grain or cocoa futures. It was an appropriate addition for member zoos eager to rid themselves of a crushing surplus, but the headquarters of the AZA, in Bethesda, Maryland (it has since moved to nearby Silver Spring), made a slight software error: Anyone logging on to www.aza.org could use the site's internal search engine to find "exchange," then proceed to the menus for the confidential newsletter.

The AZA quickly grasped the dimensions of its blunder and fixed the glitch, preventing outsiders from learning which animals at which institutions had been quietly tagged for disposal. At the Denver Zoological Gardens, for example, the expendables included a Bactrian camel, four waterbuck antelopes, three dama gazelles, two Diana monkeys, three capuchin monkeys, one bison, five lesser kudu, and a pair of endangered Amur leopards. Omaha's Henry Doorly Zoo advertised eighteen black tufted-ear marmoset monkeys that actually belonged to the University of Nebraska's Psychology Department. One day's listing for the National Zoo and its Conservation and Research Center consisted of the following: five Asian small-clawed otters, five Australian snake-necked turtles, ten bearded dragons (Australian reptiles), one black-naped oriole, a pair of blesbok antelopes, a half-dozen Burmese brow-antlered deer, four cusimanses (weasel-like mongooses), four dwarf caimans, one golden-breasted starling, a quartet of green iguanas, two large tree shrews, three Low's squirrels, two magnificent ground pigeons, one Masai giraffe (year-old Aaron), four Reeves' muntjac deer, eight rhinoceros iguanas, one roadrunner, three rock cavies, six Savanna monitors, three tegu lizards, the zoo's lone spangled cotinga (a rare South American bird with a $1,500 asking price) and an American bison (purchased three years earlier from Reston Animal Park and, along with the blesbok antelopes, sold four months later to Little Ponderosa Livestock Company, in Illinois, home to an unaccredited private collection, an exotic-animal auction, and an animal-dealing enterprise that consigns wildlife to out-of-state auctions).

On a single day, AZA zoos were looking to rid themselves of six hundred mammals, nearly four hundred reptiles, thousands of fish, hundreds of birds, and a variety of invertebrates. But the listings in *Animal Exchange* reveal more than just sheer totals. They show, in stark detail, the large number of zoos trying to simultaneously unload the same species, making zoo-to-zoo transactions unlikely and, therefore, disposal outside the AZA community all but inevitable. The listings reveal that African lions, black leopards, and every kind of monkey are often free for the asking, whereas birds and reptiles now sought after by pet owners—and easily disposed of by zoos—command sky-high prices. They show dramatically higher prices for females compared with the bargain-basement costs for the less desirable males ($3,000 for a female red kangaroo, for instance, versus $500 for a male). And in numerous instances *Animal Exchange* demonstrates the sorry eagerness of zoos to get rid of their aged and decrepit animals, some of which had entertained the public and earned gate receipts for a quarter century or more. They are the same animals that zoo directors relied on to bring their institutions media coverage, community support, and the new taxpayer-funded habitats. They are the animals that the zoo establishment proclaimed to be "ambassadors of their species" when debating critics about the need for, and value of, zoological parks. And they are the animals that adoring patrons followed from birth to adolescence to parenthood, as the cycle continued behind the cage bars and Plexiglas walls. Yet despite these years, even decades, of affiliation with a community and meritorious service to it, the nation's zoos simply earmark the aged animals for disposal through the pages of *AZA Animal Exchange* as if they were so many pieces of unwanted groundskeeping machinery or concession equipment.

The newsletter also exposes not-so-admirable truths about the AZA's Species Survival Plan, a much-touted breeding-management and conservation arrangement that sometimes results in animals being moved between institutions. This voluntary system, a kind of computer dating service for threatened and endangered species, was conceived as a hedge against extinction—a series of captive-breeding master plans designed to ensure genetically diverse and demographically stable populations and, where possible, to foster the reintroduction of endangered and threatened species to their natural habitats. The AZA coordinates nearly ninety SSPs covering one hundred sixteen individual species, and its members enthusiastically point to the program as proof of their commitment to the maintenance of healthy and self-sustaining captive populations. But when the coordinators of Species Survival Plans decree that animals should no longer be allowed to breed, they are often administering what amounts to exile or even death. These SSP has-beens are routinely listed in the *Animal Exchange,* making them available to the same disreputable middlemen who launder other zoo animals. Snow leopards, chimpanzees, and Siberian tigers, all once valued for their contributions to gene-pool diversity, are simply disposed of with no regard for their fates.

Finally, the newsletter punctures the proclamations of the zoo community that financial considerations play no part in the relocation of animals, that movement among zoos is done according to some master plan whose only consideration is species conservation or an individual animal's well-being. In fact, many zoos treat their animals as little more than last season's merchandise, slashing prices on unpopular or unwanted specimens much the way department stores mark down clothing. In August, for example, the Palm Beach Zoo at Dreher Park in South Florida, advertised a male llama for $750. By November, the year-old animal was priced at $500. The following April the price dropped to $350. In June, the llama was advertised for $300. A month later: $100. The Cincinnati Zoo's pair of bongos: $25,000 in April, $20,000 in May, $18,000 in July, and $15,000 in August. No zoo, however, can match Oklahoma City's price-cutting zeal, as one animal after another becomes fodder for the red-tag sale: A striped hyena goes from $500 to $200 to $100. A tiger is $500, then $400, then $250, then $150, and finally $100. The male hog deer go from $500 to $400 to $300, while the females drop in price from $2,000 to $1,500 to $1,200.

Despite all this, zoo directors publicly cling to the big lie. "We began to wean ourselves from animal dealers about ten years ago," Palmer Krantz III, the executive director of Riverbanks Zoological Park and Botanical Garden in Columbia, South Carolina, and an immediate past president of the AZA, told a reporter for the *Dallas Times Herald* in 1990. "Zoos themselves are far more sophisticated. There is just very little reason to use an animal dealer for anything other than transportation. . . . Coupled with that is the philosophy that animals should not be bought and sold, that they should be common property." To his credit, Krantz shuns dealers in favor of sending surplus animals only to other AZA-affiliated members. But his zoo's listings in recent *Animal Exchange* newsletters reveal that the common-property philosophy never, apparently, took hold: Brazilian agoutis ($100 each), a Central American spider monkey ($300), white-faced sakis ($500 each), DeBrazza's monkeys ($300 each), a Baird's tapir ($1,000), black howler monkeys ($300 each, then free for the asking), black-footed penguins (first $500 each, then $250).

When a bargain-basement price fails to attract buyers, some zoos offer to pay shipping, throw in the animal's cage, or just cut their losses entirely. For example, the Baltimore Zoo advertises a male Thomson's gazelle at $400 and then at $150; when the gazelle remains unsold six months later, the zoo gives up and announces that it's free to an approved institution. Still there are no takers, so the curators of the Baltimore Zoo dump the animal on Red McCombs Wildlife, one of about two dozen dues-paying "Related Organizations" that are part of the AZA—a designation it offers to wildlife organizations, nature centers, private zoos, and in the case of McCombs's facility, a breeding farm whose animals have been consigned to auctions, but rarely returned to accredited zoos.

This is the beginning of the laundering process. After the relocation efforts—bona fide, half-hearted, or perfunctory—prove futile, as they so often do, many of the animals are shunted off on AZA Related Organizations or Commercial Members, or those with some formal connection, however tenuous, to the zoo establishment. These affiliations with the AZA are supposedly proof that they're reputable trading partners, thereby insulating zoos from criticism. So animals are freely sent to the likes of Safari West, in Santa Rosa, California. Eland, oryx, addax, and other hoofed stock come to this two-hundred-fifty-acre preserve by way of AZA zoos in San Diego and Fresno, California. Safari West then sends dozens of these same species to NBJ Ranch, in Bulverde, Texas, which is not accredited by the AZA. Charles "Buddy" Jordan, the owner of NBJ Ranch, in turn sells these same species to private collectors and consigns them to exotic-animal auctions—practices that the AZA has condemned and zoos' charters sometimes prohibit. But the zoos are of course absolved of responsibility, because their animals only went to Safari West—an institution endowed by their trade association with an imprimatur of respectability.

Besides, who could say whether it was in fact a particular zoo's animal that landed at a canned hunt or in an auction ring? When animals are repeatedly sold, swapped, and shipped from one place to another, when they're moved through a system fraught with incomplete, even bogus, record-keeping and laundered like drug money, their origins soon become impossible to pinpoint or verify. This gives all parties to the deal adequate cover. Should a zoo be forced by public outcry to explain the fate of an animal, it will invariably launch an investigation and then declare that the animal is grazing happily on the dealer's north forty, that the animal trucked to the auction ring was either born right on the ranch or belonged to someone else. Or the zoo director will announce that he's received unqualified guarantees that no hunting has ever taken place on the dealer's property and indignantly suggest that it was reckless for such allegations to be leveled without any proof. It is a practiced two-step that silences the critics, gives zoo officials the moral high ground, and ensures middlemen uninterrupted access to the animals they covet. The illusion that castoff animals are being well cared for, that their guardians are performing their roles as charged, remains intact.

For example, Red McCombs, who ended up with the Baltimore Zoo's gazelle (as well as a rhinoceros never even advertised to other zoos), is a controversial figure in the exotic-animal business. Best known for his ownership of professional sports franchises, including, since 1998, the Minnesota Vikings football team, McCombs has a five-thousand-acre Texas spread that's used, in part, as a holding and breeding facility for animals in the AZA's Species Survival Programs. But there have been reports in the news media that McCombs's ranch has also been home to exotic-animal hunting—accusations that both he and the AZA zoos supplying him have denied.

In 1995, for example, an animal-rights group picketed the Denver Zoological Gardens after learning that it had sent animals to McCombs. Members of the Rocky Mountain Animal Defense ridiculed the zoo for doing business with McCombs, citing a twelve-year-old brochure advertising trophy hunts on his property. But Angela Baier, the zoo's director of marketing and public relations, had a ready explanation: "They never did have a hunt," she told the *Denver Post*. "They made a brochure but scrapped those plans and decided to focus more on conservation. If they could turn back the clock and change one thing, it would be the stupid brochure."

Interestingly, a relevant piece of evidence about McCombs's background was somehow overlooked: an article from the February 2, 1981, issue of *Forbes* about Texas hunting ranches. In "The Least Dangerous Game," which described how old-time ranchers were turning to more-lucrative exotic game, B. J. "Red" McCombs was quoted as saying: "With exotic game, I can cover my costs—and then some." A photograph accompanying the two-page article showed a pair of hunting guides on McCombs's Indian Creek Ranch kneeling beside a dead trophy animal. The caption: "For $650, a Russian boar's head to impress the neighbors." McCombs today describes that seventeen-hundred-acre property, which he sold in 1982, as a "pay-for-what-you-kill-type ranch."

Although many AZA zoos consign animals to McCombs, sometimes the animals don't actually arrive at his compound. The Tulsa Zoo, for example, once filed paperwork claiming that it had sent McCombs a zebra; in truth, McCombs delivered the animal to a drive-through park eighty miles away. And despite the large number of animals flowing into McCombs's ranch, including those he holds for the AZA's Species Survival Programs, it's virtually impossible to find documents showing that he in turn is sending animals back to accredited zoos, supplying them with the sort of fresh genetics that would justify his participation in these conservation programs. What's more, when the surplus zoo giraffe disappeared in Louisiana, delivered to the bogus post-office box, McCombs's ranch foreman, Don Housman, was listed on the original paperwork as the transporter.

Denver Zoo officials also maintained to reporters that they send animals only to AZA-accredited institutions. Not so. They routinely send animals, in fact, to individuals with no AZA affiliation, including Larry Johnson, the California dealer who arranged to transport the giraffe to the phony Louisiana address. Another is Jim Fouts, one of the dealers exposed by *60 Minutes*. Among the animals that the Denver Zoo sold Fouts—after *Animal Exchange* listings proved ineffective—were Dall's sheep and dama gazelles, species often available at American trophy-hunting operations. No public records exist to show what Fouts did with the animals, however, so officials of the zoo can publicly maintain that they're alive and well. Who, after all, could prove that they're not?

◄◦►

Sometimes zoos double as stockyards. For example, during a single week in early 1997, ten fallow deer died at Space Farms Zoo and Museum in Sussex, New Jersey. Tuberculosis, brucellosis, and a variety of other diseases sometimes ravage deer herds, but these ten deaths might instead be explained by a sideline run from the zoo: butchering its animals for human consumption. By year end, in fact, the list of animals slaughtered under state-issued permit also included eight white-tailed deer, a trio of sika deer, and one of its thirteen bison. These animals shouldn't be confused with the road-killed deer that are advertised in *Animal Finders' Guide: Ground meat! We process venison received from cut and wrap shops, ground and packed and frozen in approximately 50 pound poly bags, ideal diet for big cats and canines. $7.50 per bag fob our farm.*

Slaughter is just one way that zoo animals die, trucked off to butchers after the public has fattened them up sufficiently with feed from the quarter-a-handful vending machines. Some, for example, die of freakish acts of violence. At the zoo in Greenville, South Carolina, six vandals, ages eight to fourteen, scaled a fence, pelted wallabies with bricks and stones, killed one by smashing its head against a wall, and returned the following evening, perhaps to finish off the others. A trespasser at a zoo in Florida shot an ostrich through the head. A baboon at a Maryland zoo died when a visitor threw it a banana apparently laced with strychnine. A deer was beaten to death by an intruder at a Massachusetts zoo. Two deer were killed by an archer at another Massachusetts zoo. At a third zoo in that state, a former curator recalled his own director's after-hours entertainment: shooting the park's peacocks off a fence with a bow and arrow.

Sometimes animals are bludgeoned to death by intruders or tortured and left to die. Two monkeys were stolen from the Dreher Park Zoo, in Palm Beach County, Florida, by a teenager awaiting trial on grave-robbing charges—an initiation ritual for a satanic cult. "Knowing that he robbed graves to take a skull, you got to figure he had something in mind with the monkeys," a West Palm Beach police sergeant told a reporter. The monkeys were rescued, unharmed, from a small bird cage in the home of the suspect's mother.

Sometimes young eland antelopes and other relatively harmless petting-zoo animals are shot by neighbors or passersby after they wander off the grounds. Sometimes tigers, Amur leopards, and other big cats are shot and killed after escaping from their cages. Even marauding packs of neighborhood dogs have been known to invade zoos and kill off entire exhibits or leave brutalized, half-dead animals in their wake. Sometimes animals are killed by their siblings, just as in the wild, other times by unrelated exhibit-mates. A guillotine door that closes at the wrong moment will sometimes break an animal's neck. Animals introduced into strange, new enclosures sometimes panic and run headlong into a wall, breaking their necks. Animals occasionally die during castration or other medical procedures. Over the past three decades, orangutans in domestic and foreign zoos have died from paint poisoning, billiard-chalk ingestion, and, in one gruesome incident, wounds inflicted by a lion after a great ape escaped from its quarters. At least three orangutans, including one at Salt Lake City's Hogle Zoo, accidentally hanged themselves when they got caught in exhibit ropes. Like other zoo animals, orangutans have died of complications from polio and various diseases passed to them from humans. Sometimes animals are shipped upside-down in their crates and die before ever reaching their new homes. In 1989, three sea lions owned by the Cleveland Metroparks Zoo died after being transported in improperly ventilated vehicles, with no veterinarian along to monitor their care.

Sometimes carcasses are incinerated; other times no attention is paid to the disposal technique. At a Virginia roadside menagerie—the one chosen by the National Zoo as the home for its retired herd of sika deer—an entry on a federal inspection report reads: "Seven visible bovine carcasses were located in the junk pile at the north side of the facility near the dogs on chains. . . . The bovine carcasses were partially dismembered, some burned, in various stages of decomposition. One carcass was heavily infested with maggots."

Sometimes animals die for no obvious reason, leaving even veterinary pathologists to venture their best guesses. During one recent year, for example, three endangered Rothschild's mynah birds (a.k.a. Bali mynahs or Bali starlings) died at the National Zoo. One was found dead in its exhibit, but a necropsy revealed nothing that would permit a definitive diagnosis. The second one, also found with no signs of trauma, apparently died from an obstruction in its gizzard—a material that may have been silicone caulk. The third died of trauma after a snake evidently tried to catch and eat it. Shed snakeskin was found in the overhead wire of an adjacent cage, so there was speculation that the late-September death resulted from the resident attic population moving in for the winter. But no one could say for certain how the bird had really died.

The public usually pays attention to the death of such "charismatic megafauna" as pandas, but the demise of other zoo residents usually goes unnoticed. In the spring of 1998, however, as Disney's Animal Kingdom was preparing to open, there was an uproar over revelations that about two dozen animals—half of them small mammals—had died there in the previous year and a half. The dead included four cheetah cubs (drank poison), a Sable antelope (became entangled in an electric fence), and two crowned cranes (flattened by tour vehicles).

Executives of the Walt Disney Company insisted that the body count was not so unusual, and they were right: Compared with other drive-through parks, the tally was relatively modest. At Lion Country Safari in Loxahatchee, Florida, six chimpanzees died in one recent year, including four that never lived past one month. The following year two chimpanzees drowned and a third was euthanized after it attacked workers and killed one of its exhibit-mates. In 1990, when the *Dallas Times Herald* investigated International Wildlife Park, the now-defunct drive-through safari owned by International Animal Exchange, the AZA-accredited animal disposal service, its reporters found records to show that, in the early 1980s, five hundred sixty-four animals had died over a ten-month period, including more than one hundred from infection or inflammation and a dozen from hypothermia.

At Six Flags Wild Safari, in Jackson, New Jersey, the death count in a single three-month period at the drive-through park was twenty-six: giraffe (skull fracture), baboon (head trauma), scimitar oryx (fractured neck), eland (fractured neck), blackbuck antelope (fractured neck), rhea (gore wound), peacock (predator), black swan (hypothermia), fallow deer (drowned), elk (peritonitis), rhea (peritonitis), white-bearded gnu (infection), emu (shock from blood loss), baboon (congestive heart failure), elk (pneumonia), black swan (pneumonia), llama (blood disease), blackbuck (gastrointestinal disorder), wallaroo (lumpy jaw), bontebok (birth complications), zebra (tetanus), ostrich (slipped tendon, euthanized), blackbuck (compound fracture, euthanized), rhea (compound fracture, euthanized), ankoli cattle (compound fracture, euthanized), white-bearded gnu (severe fracture, euthanized).

--◄○►--

Some zoos euthanize animals, though they dare not admit it publicly. The subject is so controversial and uncomfortable, a former zoo director says, that he never even heard his colleagues talk about it at professional meetings. Zoo officials believe that patrons, by and large, are unable to handle the revelation that animals are intentionally put down. They also fear that animal-rights activists will charge the zoo with wanton slaughter.

It's unlikely, however, that reasonable people would argue with the ongoing decisions to euthanize animals in the National Zoo's collections, including a Przewalski horse that was lame because of multiple leg fractures; an aging Burmese brow-antlered deer unable to get up and down because of arthritis; a Darwin's rhea whose hocks were so swollen that it would walk only when pushed; a Goeldi's monkey with a terminal kidney condition; a twenty-five-year-old Persian onager—an Asian wild ass—with chronic arthritis, worn-away teeth, dermatitis, and other incurable conditions; and a clouded leopard with malignant tumors, difficulty breathing, blood in its trachea, and an inability to eat or drink.

Sometimes, however, the purposeful killing is guided by less-humane institutional policy. A two-decades-old memo, written by the National Zoo's assistant director for research to the director and other key zoo officials, reveals how euthanasia may be used as a population-management tool when other options have been exhausted:

> For at least a year, I have been trying to place surplus crab-eating foxes in zoos. They have been listed on the [AZA] animal exchange for over one year. I have sent one pair each to Los Angeles, San Diego, and Salisbury [Maryland], but have been unable to find adequate homes for the remainder of our surplus. I have personally telephoned at least 30 zoos in the U.S. trying to twist arms. I think we have no choice but to euthanize a selected number of individuals and either vasectomize males or tie the tubes of some females to prevent further uncontrolled reproduction. I request permission to euthanize about 6 animals to bring our population of 14 down to 8. This would free up space at [the zoo's Conservation and Research Center] which will be needed for maned wolves and bushdogs.

Actually, the Conservation and Research Center has 3,200 acres of forest and meadow in Virginia's Blue Ridge Mountains, and so space was not the real issue for this scientist, whose major areas of interest include the reintroduction of captive mammals to the wild. Housing an extra half-dozen crab-eating foxes requires only some wooden fencing on a patch of grass, and so money wasn't the real issue, either. But keeping the entire population of crab-eating foxes would have required a long-term commitment to their care. When animals are no longer useful—whether for research, breeding, or exhibition—they're to be banished, shunted off on any facility willing to take them, in rare cases even euth-anized. As for the crab-eating fox, it has vanished entirely from zoos in North America, thus leaving the South American mammal only a minor pet-trade oddity.

The same curious institutional mentality that deemed the lowly crab-eating fox expendable was evident a decade later, when curators at the National Zoo initiated a review of their primate collection plan. One thorny issue they faced—the same issue facing their colleagues every-where—was the fate of the zoo's surplus males, a situation compounded by an unusually high ratio of males to females at birth. The decision came to this:

> We must choose among halting reproduction, housing surplus males in suboptimal conditions, euthanizing surplus males, sending surplus males to biomedical research, or allowing the groups to reach social equilibrium through aggression. NZP [National Zoological Park] must actively decide which among these alternatives it will support and implement.

How is it possible that no other options were available to officials of the nation's best-known zoo? This, after all, is the federally funded "BioPark" whose mission is to emphasize the unity and diversity of the living world, to reveal communities of plants and animals living in har-mony with their environments. Housing nonhuman primates in sub-standard conditions, relegating them to medical research, or even letting the weakest get sacrificed while the dominance hierarchy is played out hardly seems to jibe with this notion of examining nature in all its glory. And if killing surplus males is the National Zoo's idea of a viable option for primate management, then it's no wonder that zoo directors cower when the word euthanasia is uttered in public.

◄○►

Euthanasia is not the ordinary means by which animals are removed from zoos. Many die of disease or old age. Some are sent to other zoos that are building new exhibits, expanding collections, or in need of fresh genetics. Others are sent to research institutions concerned with nutrition, propagation, or medical threats to a species' well-being. And many others, with nowhere else to go, are entrusted to roadside menageries, individuals ill-equipped to provide them care, and dealers interested only in exploiting the animals for profit.

Throughout the 1990s, for example, researchers at the National Zoo's Conservation and Research Center found themselves with an overabundance of captive-bred Père David's deer, a species that disappeared from its native China at the turn of the twentieth century. The large-antlered deer—named for Père Armand David, a French missionary and explorer—was saved from extinction by the 11th Duke of Bedford, who in the early 1900s rounded up the eighteen specimens in European zoos and established a breeding herd at Woburn Abbey, an hour's drive from London. All the world's Père David's deer, including those reintroduced to China beginning in the mid-1950s, are descended from these eighteen "founders." It is a prime example—perhaps the first—of human efforts to successfully rescue a species teetering on extinction.

The National Zoo's Conservation and Research Center has been part of that rescue mission since 1974, when the facility opened on a former cavalry post in Front Royal, Virginia. The undertaking is emblematic of AZA zoos' efforts to recast themselves as modern-day arks—species-preservation strongholds that are determined to enrich the world's biodiversity through captive breeding. Starting with nineteen Père David's deer, the CRC let breeding run amok until its herd numbered more than one hundred. Unfortunately, the animal has never been of interest to AZA zoos (only a dozen display them), and none of these hundred-plus animals were destined for repatriation on Chinese game reserves. And so scientists at this arm of the Smithsonian Institution decided to pare their inventory.

From October 1990 to November 1991, the CRC sold twelve of its surplus Père David's deer to Auerhahn Ranch, in Pipe Creek, Texas. Shortly thereafter, the *Houston Chronicle* reported that the owners of the ranch, Robert and Betty Kelso (the latter a member of the San Antonio Zoo's board of directors), opened their one-hundred-sixty-five-acre spread to paying hunters and sold some of their surplus to other breeders and ranchers. Michael Robinson, the director of the National Zoo, proclaimed that the Kelsos had misled his institution, and he hurried to Texas to demand the animals' return. Robert Hoage, the National Zoo's director of public affairs, told a reporter for *Washington City Paper* that the institution does not supply facilities that allow the hunting of animals born in zoos. "At the time, we thought we had checked it out pretty well," Hoage told the paper. Fortunately for Hoage and Robinson, reporters never asked about the pair of two-year-old sable antelopes—another popular trophy animal—that the National Zoo also sold to Auerhahn Ranch. With the public assured that the matter was being resolved, the controversy quietly faded away.

But the animals never were returned to the zoo, and subsequent transactions involving the Père David's deer also raised questions. Throughout the 1990s, the CRC placed only nine of the rare deer at AZA-accredited zoos. During the same time, it sent more than a hundred of them elsewhere: In addition to the dozen sent to Auerhahn Ranch, eighteen (along with nineteen muntjac deer) were sold to a game farmer in Greenfield, Indiana, who breeds hoofed stock for alternative-livestock speculators, not for accredited zoos. Twenty were sold to Amagita Grande Ranch, in Houston, whose owner amasses large numbers of zoo castoffs, breeds more, and then ships them by the dozen to Mexico. In 1997, when the CRC apparently decided to shut down its Père David's deer breeding operation, it sent nine to Fauna Research, Inc., in Red Hook, New York, a commercial member of the AZA. Fauna Research bills itself as a designer and provider of trapping and transport systems for deer, antelopes, giraffes, and other animals. But the firm, which is owned by Mark and Martha MacNamara, has other business interests as well. It is a commercial breeder of alpacas. It moves exotic hoofed stock to the property of wealthy suburbanites who wish to see wildlife when they look out their windows. It also operates a for-profit capture and relocation service for communities in search of a humane solution to the proliferation of native white-tail deer. Another of its enterprises is Highland Premium Venison, which the MacNamaras run from a farm eleven miles away in Germantown, New York; the listing for Fauna Research in the AZA membership directory, however, makes no mention of their state-licensed slaughterhouse. Finally, the CRC sold fifty Père David's deer, for $500 apiece, and donated another ten to Little Ponderosa Livestock Company, in Winchester, Illinois, which is not affiliated with the AZA. Owners Robert and Donna Brackett operate an auction and sometimes consign animals from their private menagerie to similar sales across the country. Their business is one of the few in Illinois outfitted with special restraining equipment to humanely facilitate disease testing, and the operation's involvement with a group of Père David's deer presumably might have given pause to the National Zoo's administrators: Sixteen months before Bob Brackett began hauling away the CRC's animals, fifteen of these rare deer passed through the Little Ponderosa's "squeeze chutes" on their way to W.R. Fewox, in Frostproof, Florida. Fewox is the proprietor of Dixie Wildlife Safaris, a private hunting operation whose two dozen offerings include sika deer, water buffaloes, and nilgai antelopes. Père David's deer aren't on the trophy price list, but the great-antlered animals are available on special request. The price to kill one: $6,000.

By the end of 1998, the CRC was left with a single male Père David's deer—a clear admission that its breeding program was being shut down, that the rare Chinese deer would take its place beside the crab-eating fox on the CRC's list of abandoned conservation efforts. The taxpayer-financed drive to save this animal had accomplished only one thing: It had given the nation's dealers and canned-hunt operators a lucrative new showpiece.

The National Zoo is in good company. In 1995, for example, the Buffalo Zoo advertised a female DeBrazza's monkey in the *Animal Exchange* newsletter, and when no takers emerged, the animal—along with a spider monkey—was sent to a roadside zoo in Scotch Plains, New Jersey. That same year, Florida's Dreher Park Zoo shipped endangered cotton-top tamarins to the same unaccredited facility. For years, the roadside zoo had also been home to an orangutan that came via Seattle's Woodland Park Zoo—a hybrid castoff of no interest to the Species Survival Plan, and therefore an animal whose placement required no real consideration. Another orangutan sent there by Woodland Park had died.

Scotch Plains Zoo, which the New Jersey Department of Environmental Protection shut down in 1997, was a classic "roadside zoo"—a privately owned, seasonal operation characterized by facilities made primarily of wood, concrete, and chain link, rather than by re-creations of natural habitats; a collection that's a hodgepodge of species rather than selected groups of animals that may contribute to interzoo conservation goals; and exhibits that emphasize entertainment rather than education. A New Jersey fish and game official says of the former owner: "This guy would let animals starve to death if he felt like it." The park's animals were sold as pets through classified ads. Following children's parties at the zoo, the Himalayan black bear was fed leftover pizza and birthday cake. Permits were not renewed, as required by law. Reports were not filed. Animals were acquired illegally. Animals escaped. Summonses were issued for failure to protect the animals from the elements and to protect the public from the animals. The barn that housed the giraffe and camel so reeked of ammonia from urine that state officials couldn't complete their routine inspections. The birdhouse reeked of paint fumes, the only ventilation in the cement-block building provided by two holes in the wall. The primate enclosure stank of feces. The food provided the animals was contaminated. A young jaguar was killed, and its handler hospitalized, when an adult jaguar managed to break down a cage wall and attacked as the pair walked by. The orangutan was housed in what a state biologist who inspected the facility describes as an isolation tank: adjacent cinder-block rooms with no water, a concrete bench for the great ape to sit on, a Plexiglas window so scratched that the public could barely see in, and a small black-and-white TV that the orangutan could watch through a three-inch-by-two-foot window. Temperatures dropped below freezing in the spring of 1997, but the gas company had cut off service for nonpayment of bills, so the orangutan, DeBrazza's monkeys, and other animals were left without heat. They were finally saved by the park's hot-dog man, who paid for ten gallons of fuel. Only then was the state able to wrest the orangutan from the animal park and send it to a sanctuary. And only then, as the wretched conditions earned the zoo unwelcome media attention and brought about its demise, did the general curator of the Buffalo Zoo ask that its DeBrazza's monkey be returned. Had he checked on the zoo's history, he would have learned that it was an unsuitable facility and, presumably, the animals never would have been sent there. But perhaps not, because this is the same zoo official who also loaned at least nine mandrill baboons to New Jersey's Animal Kingdom Zoo, the operation distinguished by the owner's long history of sales to the pet trade and at exotic-animal auctions.

Such a laissez-faire approach to the disposition of animals seems to directly violate the AZA's code of professional ethics, whose mandatory standards require that members make every effort to ensure that animals under their care "do not find their way into the hands of those not qualified to care for them properly." The public puts its trust in AZA-accredited zoos precisely because of such obligations and professional standards; one by-product of the accreditation process is that zoo officials are bound by ethical directives that would preclude animals being sent to facilities that are unable, or unwilling, to provide them good care. Certainly, an animal can inadvertently fall into the wrong hands: Referrals may not be entirely credible; inferior animal-care standards and practices may not be apparent, even after a thorough inspection. But there is no mistaking the fact that roadside menageries such as Scotch Plains Zoo and Animal Kingdom Zoo are inappropriate outlets for unwanted animals. Sending animals to either is an admission by AZA members that the organization's code of professional conduct is not always adhered to strictly.

Ironically, the AZA's commendable process of membership references and accreditation is designed to guard against animals going to precisely such places. But the zoos ignore their own edicts and, despite their claims to the contrary, permit animals to leak almost uncontrollably from their ranks. And there are always eager dealers standing by because the exotic-animal business is not only lucrative but also largely risk-free. "You can make more on illegal wildlife trade than you can on dope," a Florida fish and game officer says. "If you're caught smuggling animals, it's a misdemeanor. If you're moving illegal drugs, on the other hand, you're out of here."

And so the dealers get in line to cash in. In the booming exotic-pet business, for example, infant capuchin monkeys sell for $2,000 to $3,000, spider monkeys for twice that, a celebes ape for perhaps $10,000, and a young chimpanzee for as much as $40,000 or $50,000. And although zoo officials are adamant that primates are not appropriate pets and convene meetings to explore ways of discouraging, even barring, private ownership, the problem is largely one of their own making.

There's ample proof of that in a landmark study coauthored by Stephanie Ostrowski, a veterinary epidemiologist with the Division of Quarantine at the Centers for Disease Control and Prevention. Using the official studbooks maintained by keepers and curators at AZA zoos, Dr. Ostrowski and research assistant Dr. Natalie Keeler (at the time a veterinary student intern) examined more than thirty-two thousand individual animal records covering a twenty-one-year period. Their findings, which tracked the fates of primates listed in sixty different studbooks, reveal that American zoos have shown wholesale negligence in the placement of their unwanted animals, thereby fueling the trade they presumably so abhor. The bottom line: From 1975 to 1995, more than twenty-five hundred primates were transferred by zoos to unaccredited institutions such as roadside menageries, animal dealers, and bogus sanctuaries, where their fates then became anyone's guess.

Although curators argue that dealers are often needed to broker animals moving between zoos, Ostrowski's study showed that claim to be fiction. Animals retained in zoo populations, she found, move almost exclusively from one accredited zoo to another rather than through middlemen. The dealers are needed only when an AZA zoo can't find another member institution to take an unwanted animal. And in such cases, the animals are nearly always "lost to follow-up": No one in the zoo community can say if an animal died, was infected with a disease, gave birth to babies that were sold into the pet trade or biomedical research, or whether the animal was sold at auction, caged at a fraternity house and fed amphetamines, or perhaps even sacrificed in a religious ceremony.

AZA zoos have treated virtually every kind of primate as expendable; several species, in fact, had more animals lost to follow-up than were retained in zoos. For example, several species of lemurs—inbred and overbred until they were as common as mice and of even less genetic value—have been indiscriminately off-loaded, with approximately seven hundred fifty of the endangered primates sent to unaccredited facilities. Once the exclusive property of zoos and primate research centers, lemurs are fast becoming a staple of the private pet trade.

Being lost to follow-up in a studbook, zoo officials argue, doesn't necessarily mean a tragic fate for the animals; after all, there are private breeders whose good work has helped ensure gene-pool diversity. In some instances, they say, private breeders have succeeded where others have failed.

But time after time, that defense crumbles under the evidence. For example, the San Diego Zoo sent a pair of lemurs to an unaccredited zoo in Indiana. The zoo in turn sent the animals to the publisher of *Animal Finders' Guide,* the nation's leading voice for the dealing and private ownership of exotic animals—precisely what the AZA zoos claim to oppose. San Diego Wild Animal Park sent a lemur to its favorite dealer, Earl Tatum, who in turn sent it to Buddy Jordan's NBJ Ranch, in Bulverde, Texas. Jordan got more ring-tailed and ruffed lemurs directly from at least four AZA members: Busch Gardens, in Tampa, Florida; Gladys Porter Zoo, in Brownsville, Texas; Jacksonville Zoological Gardens; and the Memphis Zoo. Jordan subsequently sent breeding pairs of lemurs to Bookcliff Animal Park, in Fruita, Colorado. Bookcliff was so wretched that it was soon shut down by the feds, its owners barred from ever again dealing animals. He sold breeding pairs of ring-tailed lemurs and ruffed lemurs to Karen and Frank Glass, the owners of Sunrise Exotic Ranch, in Dripping Springs, Texas. A few years later, the Glasses—operating as Sunrise Exotic Sanctuary—placed a full-page advertisement in *Animal Finders' Guide* offering two dozen exotic species, including ring-tailed and ruffed lemurs. Jordan also sold lemurs to Noah's Land, a drive-through park/animal-dealing operation in Harwood, Texas, whose owner advertised these endangered species in

Animal Finders' Guide. Noah's Land also sent lemurs to a man named Tom, whose affiliation is not listed in an annual report to the U.S. Fish and Wildlife Service. Tom, it turns out, runs a Pennsylvania petting zoo whose primates—and other animals—sometimes land at auctions in Missouri and Ohio. And this is one of Tom's *Animal Finders' Guide* ads: "Zoo Production Sale: baby wallaby, baby camels, baby female zebra, ring-tailed lemurs, llamas, miniature horses, miniature donkeys, miniature cattle, shar-pei pigs, emu, watusi and deer! Reasonable prices." As for the other animals at Noah's Land, all were later sold to employees or auctioned off when the safari park closed its doors. In other words, they were lost to follow-up.

Northland Wildlife, of Grand Rapids, Minnesota, was at one time an AZA-affiliated animal supplier, and as such was inundated with primates from zoos in Birmingham, Alabama; Duluth, Minnesota; Little Rock, Arkansas; San Francisco; Seattle; and other cities. It also received endangered brown lemurs from the Duke University Primate Center, one of the nation's most respected primate research facilities. The flow slowed in 1992, however, when Northland's owner, Robert Troumbly, was indicted on a variety of federal primate-trafficking charges, including the sale of monkeys that had been brought into the United States with bogus invoices, permits, and other paperwork. But even after he pleaded guilty to one count in the spring of 1993, AZA zoos in a number of cities, including Montgomery, Alabama, and Omaha, Nebraska, continued to supply him with animals. Like most of the monkeys sent to Northland, these were lost to follow-up, so their contributions to the viability of the zoos' gene pools is unclear.

Troumbly's indictment was part of a high-profile animal-trafficking case—a federal government rarity—that targeted seven dealers across the United States. Among those indicted with Northland's owner was his long-time associate in the animal business, Antonio Alentado, a Miami-area dealer. Alentado, who pleaded guilty to trafficking in mouse lemurs and was fined $2,000 and placed on two years' probation, was able to count the San Diego Zoo among those willing to supply him with this endangered species. In addition to lemurs, the Miami MetroZoo endowed its local animal dealer with endangered gibbons. And another of

Alentado's suppliers was Monkey Jungle, a popular Miami attraction that has long billed itself as a stronghold for primate education and conservation. The twenty-acre park, which lost its AZA accreditation after questions were raised about public contact with the monkeys, has transferred to Alentado the likes of hamadryas baboons and colobus monkeys.

Thomas Nichols, a Georgia dealer, was sentenced in this same court action to a year in jail. Like his colleagues, Nichols counted on AZA zoos, including the Cincinnati Zoo, The ZOO, in Gulf Breeze, Florida, and the Greater Baton Rouge Zoo in Louisiana, for some of his inventory. Nichols's other suppliers included the Duke University Primate Center, Wisconsin-based bear dealer Mark Schoebel, and (as so often) the San Diego Zoo.

Micheal Lamkin, a Texas-based dealer of trophy-hunting stock and other animals, gets some of his primates from AZA zoos in such cities as Fresno, California; Lake Monroe, Florida; and Syracuse, New York. International Animal Exchange, which resells boatloads of zoo surplus in South Korea, Malaysia, Mexico, Sri Lanka, and elsewhere, continues to be overrun with primates from AZA zoos across the country. Edward Novack, the New York dealer who was ridiculed by the San Diego Zoo for facilitating the sale of its European wild boar to a Canadian canned hunt, nonetheless continues to be flooded with primates from AZA zoos. Novack's most generous benefactor has been the Buffalo Zoo, whose recent annual report boasts of a management plan that permits primates to grow up in natural family groups. Apparently, many of the zoo's owl monkeys, spider monkeys, colobus monkeys, mandrills, and Japanese macaques aren't part of its plan.

Larry Johnson, the California animal dealer who makes giraffes disappear by consigning them to nonexistent addresses, has been entrusted with primates from the San Diego Zoo and Wild Animal Park, including endangered lemurs and siamangs. Zoological Animal Exchange, in Natural Bridge, Virginia, one of only three commercial animal suppliers that are formally affiliated with the AZA, has primates heaped on it by zoos in Akron, Ohio; Madison, Wisconsin; Tampa, Florida; and elsewhere. The owners of Zoological Animal Exchange, Eric and Janet Mogensen, then advertise their monkey inventory in *Animal Finders' Guide*. The Mogensens also sell them directly to the likes of an Oregon pet store and one of the nation's largest pet-monkey wholesalers—a husband-and-wife team who, in March 1999, were charged with a long list of alleged violations of the Animal Welfare Act, including the failure to faithfully record the sources and destinations of their animals. After that, they're invariably lost to follow-up.

4

PAPER TRAILS

Mammoth Cave is at the end of a mile-long dirt road in southern Idaho's sage-covered high desert. A weather-beaten highway sign points motorists to the so-called ice cave, the smaller and decidedly less popular of two such tourist attractions on the scenic road that runs from Sun Valley to the Snake River Canyon. For three and a half dollars, visitors can rent a kerosene lantern and explore the perpetually frigid geologic anomaly, formed thousands of years ago by the cooling of a huge volcanic lava tube. Aboveground, in a two-room museum and gift shop cluttered with such curiosities as odd-shaped rocks and taxidermy mounts, there is a collection of bones and other artifacts said to have been found in the cave by Mammoth's proprietor, Richard Olsen.

Olsen is a taxidermist, and some of the trophies that line these walls are his handiwork. Olsen also breeds animals in and around this dusty compound, which is littered with wagon wheels, antiquated farm implements, and rusted cars that have been stripped for parts. Wild turkeys roam the grounds. Hidden behind an eight-foot-high fence, in a garbage-strewn yard with only a decrepit hut for shelter, is a pair of white fallow deer—spotted Eurasian hoofed stock whose broad, flat antlers make them a favored target of those who patronize private hunting operations. Olsen's wife of a few years, who sells tickets for the underground excursion, says that they've been trying to create an entirely new color of fallow deer. An unnamed Idaho animal breeder has supplied the couple with an ongoing inventory of genetic fodder, but their tinkering has not yet produced the sought-after breakthrough.

There are also dozens of pigs corralled in muddy wooden pens beside the parking lot. These swine are bred for Olsen's other business, the European Wild Boar Hunt. Twice a year, over a month's time, Olsen opens his ranch to the first seventy-five hunters willing to pay him $350. Archers have traditionally been the most successful patrons, although pistol, rifle, and black-powder enthusiasts have also left the grounds with carcasses weighing one hundred fifty to three hundred pounds. Olsen guarantees his customers a kill, or their money is refunded. He won't provide them with ropes for hanging and skinning, however, nor will he lend anyone his camera.

Although they're nowhere to be seen, there's also a quartet of bison somewhere on the grounds. Olsen's wife complains that they've been unable to unload their latest investment, so a local bow hunter will slay at least one of the buffalo sometime in the fall. In the past, she says, the same hunter has disposed of the couple's turkeys, deer, and other animals. She hopes he will take out the biggest of the group, but she won't explain why.

One animal that visitors can't kill at Mammoth Cave is the coyote— at least not one of those chained in front of the Olsens' modest wooden A-frame. Olsen's wife says that the coyote group's matriarch has been a family pet for three years, and although the wolf-like animal is a little excitable, it usually tolerates being touched by humans. The pups, she adds, act much like family dogs, but some of their mannerisms make them even more fun to own: At night, for instance, the young coyotes howl like their mother, but their falsetto-pitch cries make them recognizable through the darkness of the empty Idaho desert.

Among this year's offspring is Stubby, the runt of the litter (so named for his abbreviated tail). Stubby lies motionless on this torrid August afternoon, before him a rusted coffee can half-filled with brown-tinged water. When the sun is in the southern sky, the little coyote has the shade of a tree to protect him. At other times, there is no shelter from the blaze that bakes the dusty earth.

Olsen's wife volunteers that the coyotes are for sale, that a pup can be had for a hundred dollars. When I show no interest, she says that if I press her husband, he'll probably let Stubby go for seventy-five—a pretty good buy, considering the animal's disposition. I express doubts about the legality of keeping a coyote in Washington, D.C., where I'll soon be returning. She has some advice: Just put the coyote into the car and drive it on out of here.

Actually, keeping a pet coyote in the nation's capital—and many other parts of the country—is against the law. The shy and clever omnivores, which run wild in forty-nine states, are a potential menace of increasing worry to public-health officials—particularly as these wily symbols of the untamed West are displaced by development and relocate to the suburbs and even inner cities. A Massachusetts wildlife official says that were it not for Route 128, the highly traveled highway that rings Boston, troops of coyotes would probably be encroaching on the Fen and Harvard Yard.

Coyotes usually avoid people but prey on cats and small dogs. Trappers say that coyotes can't distinguish between the cries of babies and small animals and therefore attack unattended children. Ranchers, plagued by coyotes picking off their lambs and calves, shoot them on sight. In South Dakota, where the coyote is officially designated the state animal, the law authorizes the game, fish, and parks department to pay a five-dollar bounty for each dead adult or pup.

Coyotes carry tularemia, also known as rabbit fever. Like foxes, wolves, and other rodent-eaters, coyotes are part of a host-parasite cycle that can result in *Echinococcus multilocularis* tapeworm eggs passed via their feces to domestic pets and, potentially, to humans as an aberrant "dead-end" host. In humans, the migrating, immature stages aggregate as infectious, fluid-filled cysts in the liver and lungs, sometimes also spreading to the brain. The colonies of slow-growing tapeworm larvae eventually cause abdominal pain, weight loss, and symptoms that may mimic those of liver cancer or cirrhosis. Successful treatment requires delicate surgery.

In South Texas, a variant of coyote-borne rabies has plagued the population for more than a decade. The disease, which has killed both dogs and humans, spread to Alabama and Florida when coyotes that were later found to be rabid were shipped to foxpens—fenced-in enclosures where raccoons, fox, and other furbearing varmints try to outrun dogs sicced on them by hunters. Alabama public-health officials had never heard of foxpens until confronted with a rabid dog; a survey showed that more than fifty of these hunting grounds, overrun with animals trucked in primarily from the Dakotas, were operating statewide. The number of animals flooding the state startled them: Over two years, records showed, some seventeen hundred red fox had been imported from North Dakota alone. And those, they knew, were only the legal shipments.

Like their counterparts in other southeastern states, where scores of foxpens had also sprung up on backwoods tracts, Alabama authorities worried about a repeat of the rabies epidemic that over the past decade had overwhelmed mid-Atlantic and northeastern states. That costly outbreak has been traced to the relocation, in the late 1970s, of a few thousand wild-caught raccoons, some of them rabid, from Georgia to the Virginia–West Virginia border—another case of hunters wanting a fresh challenge for their coon hounds and tree hounds. With threats of rabies and *Echinococcosis multilocularis* looming, Alabama banned the importation of coyotes and red fox. Other states followed suit.

Therefore, moving a coyote across states lines typically requires paperwork testifying that the transfer doesn't violate any laws. With Stumpy, however, the rules apparently can be waived: If I've got the cash, I can put that young Idaho coyote in my rear seat and drive back East. After all, I'm told, who's going to know?

—◦—

When it's done legally, moving an animal across states lines is a simple and straightforward process: A veterinarian accredited by the USDA inspects the animal and affirms that it can withstand the trip, that any disease testing required by the state of destination has been satisfactorily performed. The names and addresses of the shipper and receiver are detailed on a standard certificate of veterinary inspection, along with the animal's breed, age, and sex.

One copy of the signed certificate remains with the animal's owner. A second copy accompanies the shipment, while copies three and four are mailed to the state veterinarian's office. One of those two documents is filed, and the other is forwarded to the receiving state's department of agriculture for review: Did the elk test negative for brucellosis, as the import law requires? Was the tiger cub's body temperature within the normal range? Were the animals moved within the allotted thirty days of the medical tests being performed? In nearly every instance the certificates are approved, date-stamped, filed, and never looked at again. After two or three years, they're either archived or discarded.

These so-called health certificates are meant to be a hedge against the spread of disease. If deer are diagnosed with tuberculosis, for instance, properly completed forms will show both an infected animal's place of origin and the whereabouts of those relocated deer that had contact with the TB-positive herd. That gives agriculture, natural-resources, and public-health officials the means to search out would-be carriers for testing and, if circumstances warrant, quarantine or slaughter.

It's an antiquated, paper-intensive system designed to protect agricultural herds and, to a lesser extent, native wildlife. Nonfarm animals have always been an afterthought in the process, in part because many are free of diseases that might put the cattle and swine at risk. So lions, tigers, and wallaroos, for example, move freely across the country, with only pro forma attention paid to the documents that accompany them: If the disease-test results meet the proper standards, no one gives the page a second look. Nor could they, in fact, since states are typically inundated with hundreds of certificates a day and have only a single caretaker to process, examine, and file them. As a result, documents with questionable information move through the entire process undetected.

Consider the case of Jake, a ten-month-old cougar kept illegally by a Virginia resident. The courts ordered that the mountain lion be confiscated and, following a hearing, awarded it to the Virginia Department of Game & Inland Fisheries. Like other state wildlife agencies, Virginia's has no facilities to keep such animals, and conservation officers scrambled to find Jake a home. Arrangements were made with the Peninsula SPCA, in Newport News, whose animal shelter adjoins a petting zoo with a collection of big cats. There are lynx housed in wire corn cribs and displays seemingly patched together on a whim or a bet: a lion and tiger are kept in one cage; in another are a black panther, two leopards, and a jaguar. The zoo's troupe of cougars menaced Jake, and after a few months Virginia wildlife officials were forced to find the displaced pet yet another home.

The job fell to state wildlife biologist Glen Askins, who spent days on a cross-country telephone odyssey, putting out the word to zoos and sanctuaries that he was trying to arrange accommodations for the young male cougar. Askins was soon contacted by a Connecticut man, who said he was building a new zoo and would be willing to take the cougar. Another state biologist drove Jake from the SPCA's quarters to an arranged meeting place in a Philadelphia parking lot, where he was transferred to the Connecticut zoo owner. It was done by the book, including the filing of the health certificate. A veterinarian had inspected Jake and testified that the cougar was fit to travel. The document noted that Jake was going to the Wildlife Center in New London, Connecticut, and the required copies were filed with the Virginia Department of Agriculture.

The transaction didn't raise the suspicions of Connecticut Agriculture Department workers reviewing the paperwork, but it should have. The New London Wildlife Center doesn't exist. Furthermore, Connecticut wildlife officers say that no one was permitted to import a cougar during the time that Jake was supposedly shipped there. That means the cougar never really went to Connecticut, as Virginia officials believed, or was brought into the state illegally.

The individual behind the hoax may have picked Connecticut as a destination—whether real or made-up—because he was familiar with its filing system: Instead of maintaining health certificates by state of origin, as is the procedure elsewhere, Connecticut workers simply dump certificates for incoming exotic species into a cardboard box, forcing anyone in search of a document to paw through five years' worth of paper. Finding anything among this scrap heap is hit-or-miss.

Connecticut wildlife officers obviously don't routinely examine the health certificates, because they knew nothing of Jake. And Virginia officials, who believed they had found the cougar a good home, have no idea of his whereabouts. "I feel bad for Jake," Askins says. "Sounds like we were fooled."

Chicago's Brookfield Zoo was also fooled. In March 1996, a health certificate completed by the zoo's veterinarian testified that one male and five female Sykes monkeys—Old World forest dwellers—were being sent to the Birmingham, Alabama, zoo. Transactions between AZA members, usually chronicled on special health certificates made available by the American Association of Zoo Veterinarians, scarcely warrant a second look, and this one certainly appeared routine.

But the following summer it was revealed that Birmingham's curator of mammals personally bought the monkeys from Brookfield and, instead of delivering them to his zoo, allegedly resold them to the owners of a private zoo in northern Alabama—a collection not open to the public. The Greater Baton Rouge Zoo, it was later revealed, was the victim of a similar con game, with three spot-nosed guenons diverted from Birmingham to the same private facility. According to an APHIS investigative report, three coatimundi donated by the Detroit Zoo to the Birmingham Zoo also ended up in northern Alabama, although the owner of this private facility says she never received the animals, so their fate is unclear. What's more, the APHIS investigation concluded that four black-handed spider monkeys donated to the Birmingham Zoo by the Staten Island Zoo were diverted in like fashion. But, once again, the owner of this private facility says there are no records to verify that any of the spider monkeys she received from Birmingham had in fact originated in Staten Island. And the director of the Staten Island Zoo seems to be equally uncertain whether the Birmingham Zoo redistributed his institution's four monkeys. As a result, the fate of those animals is also anyone's guess.

To their credit, both the Brookfield and Baton Rouge zoos undertook serious efforts to have their monkeys returned. The incidents resulted in litigation in Alabama and Louisiana. They generated investigations by the U.S. Department of Agriculture and the American Zoo and Aquarium Association's ethics board. And they spawned an audit of the zoo by the Birmingham mayor's office. The audit report was delayed for months, as it was said to contain inflammatory conclusions that warranted close scrutiny by the city attorney. Ultimately, the document disclosed that officials of the Birmingham Zoo first learned of the suspect transactions in July 1996 and began an internal investigation. But their efforts were hampered, the audit report said, by the discovery that nearly all records relating to both mammal transactions and dealings with the private zoo had been removed by the zoo official involved in the scam. He had resigned his post in April 1996, the report added, after which the records were supposedly found to be missing. As a result, the auditors wrote, they were forced instead to focus attention exclusively on the sale of ostriches, emus, and rheas to the private Alabama zoo over a three-year period. Their conclusion: A number of these ratites had been sold for below fair-market price (the owner of the private zoo contends she actually paid above-market price), while the sale of other birds could not be confirmed using the zoo's regular accounting mechanisms. Nowhere was there mention of the zoo's policies regarding its primates.

Interestingly, the Birmingham auditors had health certificates and other documents at their disposal to chronicle primate transactions but looked the other way. In early 1996, for example, the Birmingham Zoo sent a common langur, an Old World monkey, to the same private zoo in Alabama—a transaction detailed in a primate contraception report compiled by an AZA advisory group. What's more, official AZA studbooks show that Birmingham sent this unaccredited zoo a variety of primates, including more than a half-dozen black-handed spider monkeys.

The city auditors would have been wise to focus on this species in particular, rather than on the ostriches and emus. The reason: From mid-1986 to 1990, at least thirty-one black-handed spider monkeys born at the Birmingham Zoo supposedly all died there. Although black-handed spider monkeys typically live fifteen to twenty years in captivity, nearly all of Birmingham's animals lasted only two or three years before the official species studbook keeper was notified that they had died. Coincidentally, fourteen of those monkeys were reported to have died on the very same day in September 1989. (The following year, three more were reported as having died at birth and a fourth as having lived just one day.) Large numbers of deaths in a single day are usually attributable to a catastrophe, such as the pre-Christmas 1995 fire at the Philadelphia Zoo that killed twenty-three gorillas, orangutans, gibbons, and lemurs, or the 1996 barn fire at the Montgomery Zoo, in Alabama, that killed a boa constrictor, a screech owl, and a dozen other animals. But there was no fire at Birmingham, nor was there at the time any known disease so dramatically affecting captive populations of these long-limbed, New World primates (years later, a deadly virus did in fact ravage the Birmingham Zoo's spider monkey collection). Zoo officials had an explanation, however, for the 1989 deaths: It was merely a "statistical adjustment," necessitated after staff members dropped in on the monkeys' habitat, a concrete island at the zoo, to conduct physical examinations. Apparently, no one had noticed any dead, dying, or missing monkeys since the previous June, when the studbook keeper had been informed of another fatality. Although AZA zoos routinely perform necropsies, Patty Pendleton, the Birmingham Zoo's public relations director, offered no explanation for the thirteen deaths, not to mention the deaths of the four newborn spider monkeys the following year.

─◂◦▸─

The veterinarian with the North Carolina Department of Agriculture is unyielding. An hours-long search of his department's file cabinets has turned up dozens of documents I want photocopied, but he refuses my requests. Never mind that state law is clearly on my side. He wants a ruling from the department's general counsel before he'll authorize use of the office's Xerox machine. He wants to know whether other states have given similar permission and calls his counterpart in Virginia to verify that at least one, in fact, has. He wants to know why I want the information and how I intend to use it, even though the law states that no one asking to inspect and copy public records "shall be required to disclose the purpose or motive for the request." He is adamant that documents of this sort must be exempt from North Carolina's open-records law and finally proposes a compromise: I can copy information by hand from the seventy-five pages plucked from among the thousands in his department's files. I politely decline the offer, and we await the general counsel's ruling.

It's a frustrating stalemate but hardly surprising: This same document-gathering exercise, so far repeated in a half-dozen state capitals, has sometimes proved equally aggravating. The chief of the Massachusetts Bureau of Animal Health arranged a time for a search of her records and then didn't show up for the appointment; her assistant, who seemed baffled, almost indignant, by my annoyance, refused me access to the files, instructed me to return in a few hours, and ultimately produced eleven pieces of paper—the only documents on hand, she maintained, that were pertinent to my request. The New Jersey state veterinarian was off to a conference, then off on vacation, then unreachable for unspecified reasons, and for two months no one else within his entire bureaucracy could authorize a search of the files or send me the records I wanted. In Pennsylvania, perplexed employees of the state veterinarian had no explanation why the records I had requested—the documents they assumed were in their file cabinets—seemed not to exist. And now this North Carolina fiasco. It didn't bode well for an exercise to be repeated forty-eight times.

The idea was simple: State veterinary officials estimate that only 10 to 15 percent of nonfarm animals moving across state lines do so legally—that is, with the proper import permits and truthful health certificates. It's no secret that coyote pups are paid for in cash and driven to places where their ownership is prohibited. That truckloads of animals are delivered to backwoods foxpens under the cover of darkness. That venomous reptiles are sent via parcel carriers in boxes marked "glassware." That bears vanish. That giraffes disappear. That mountain lions are sent to fictitious wildlife centers. That tiny monkeys are hidden amid a bed of newspaper and claimed as squirrels when passed through airline cargo terminals. That animals travel with no paperwork, bogus paperwork, or paperwork that intentionally obscures details of the transaction.

But root out documents for every legal transfer, and they should presumably form a paper trail that lays bare details of the exotic-animal industry. After all, dealers who move hoofed stock illicitly along back roads likely file at least some paperwork—proof for inquiring regulators and tax collectors that they are legitimate entrepreneurs. The well-known middlemen who launder monkeys and other exotics must also file paperwork, and so too, no doubt, do those who are one transaction removed—the bit players who resell the zoo stock to the pet trade or at auction barns. Because documents often include names, tattoos, or disease-test identifiers, I figured that it should be possible to follow the movement of animals from state to state. What's more, this database of interstate transport could be augmented with annual reports to the U.S. Fish and Wildlife Service, the *AZA Animal Exchange* newsletter, state fish and game permits, USDA inspection reports, zoo inventories, species studbooks, taxidermy reports, game-farm records, and any other cache of documents that chronicled where and when animals were moved.

The trick, of course, would be to collect paperwork from every state, or else trails might be lost at every turn. So I mapped out the assignment: Sift through one state's records, pull the relevant documents for copying, then drive to the next state capital and do exactly the same thing. Raleigh to Columbia, Columbia to Atlanta, Atlanta to Montgomery; Topeka to Lincoln, Lincoln to Des Moines, then on to Pierre, Bismarck, and St. Paul. Two-week loops across five or six sections of the country would give me the documents to prove categorically whether generalizations about the exotic-animal trade were wildly overstated or, perhaps, dramatically underestimated.

But despite liberal open-records laws in most states, collecting health certificates was proving to be difficult, in some cases nearly impossible. My grand scheme was unraveling, and I hadn't even moved off the East Coast.

Despite protests, the North Carolina veterinarian wouldn't budge. He insisted that no one had ever asked to see the documents—a claim made in other capitals as well—and he predicted that because the records contained proprietary business information, the department's general counsel would deny my request.

"These records could give away sensitive information," he said. "You could find out the names of Henry Hampton's business partners."

That was an unfamiliar name at the time, so I made a note of it. Later that evening, at the next stop of the Great Dome Tour, I had a chance to study the North Carolina health certificates that had indeed been made public. Sure enough, Hampton's name appeared on many of the documents, although his only instantly recognizable business partners were some Midwest auctions and Wild Safari, a New Jersey theme park. For the moment, the rest were all just names on a page.

--o--

If you're willing to sift through a hundred thousand or so documents, as you must in Arkansas, Louisiana, and other states that lump together health certificates for cattle, swine, and anything else with wings, paws, hooves, or fins, you can learn a lot about the exotic-animal industry. It's a worthwhile exercise because the letter-size sheets sometimes tell unexpected stories: The Bronx Zoo gives its Mexican gray wolves the antidepressant Prozac for "behavioral problems." The Birmingham Zoo sends tarantulas through the mail. There is a pet market for Madagascar hissing cockroaches. When universities finish their species-survival research, deer and other animals are sometimes sent off to hunting preserves or the dealers who supply these operations.

The certificates also show that although the high-profile flagship animals are often transferred from one AZA-accredited zoo to another, or at least to purportedly respectable dealers, other animals are nothing but seasonal props—disposable exhibits that in no way further the zoos' stated missions of conservation and education. For example, the zoo in Little Rock, Arkansas, which was suspended from AZA in 1998 for an assortment of unsavory activities, leases reindeer for the Christmas season, and the Colorado broker to whom the animals are returned unloads his inventory at auction. The Glen Oak Zoo in Peoria, Illinois, and the San Antonio Zoo, in Texas, have sent exotic birds to the Flamingo Hilton casino, in Las Vegas—hardly a bastion of wildlife preservation. The National Aquarium, in Baltimore, is where individuals and dealers go for their poison-dart frogs, an increasingly popular pet-trade commodity. Bushmaster Reptiles, a Colorado-based pet-trade wholesaler, has counted on the Dallas Zoo and the Oklahoma City Zoo for its yellow-footed tortoises, New Caledonia geckos, reticulated gila monsters, and Pueblan milk snakes. Tom Crutchfield, a high-profile dealer, was convicted in 1992 of smuggling endangered reptiles into the United States, but he could subsequently rely on the Montgomery Zoo for his inventory. In one shipment, the Alabama Zoo sent the disgraced trafficker sixteen Gaboon vipers and fourteen Burmese pythons.

As it turns out, the health certificates often tell only part of the story, because there's no way of immediately knowing who's really on both ends of a transaction. When a certificate reveals that New York's Seneca Park Zoo sent a flock of its unwanted golden pheasants to the Zoological Animal Reproduction Center, for example, the name certainly seems to indicate that the zoo took care in placing the Asian game birds. In truth, however, the so-called reproduction center is nothing but an animal dealer in southern Indiana whose animals sometimes end up in Missouri and Illinois auction rings, other times with a prolific animal dealer in South Florida.

Names on health certificates are often difficult to decipher, providing a convenient smoke screen for those dumping their animals inappropriately. When the Kansas City Zoo rid itself of two geriatric New Guinea singing dogs, the health certificate listed only the recipient's name and post office box, not his Emporia, Kansas, pet-supply business. When the Dakota Zoo, in Bismarck, North Dakota, sent yaks to a man in South Dakota, the paperwork didn't reveal that the recipient's family ran an exotic-animal auction. And when the Bronx Zoo unloaded four of its red-handed tamarins on Small World Zoological Gardens in Wesley Chapel, Florida, it certainly appeared as if the famed conservation park had found a suitable destination for its surplus. In fact, this so-called zoo was licensed by the government as an animal dealer. And seven months after the quartet of South American monkeys went from New York to Florida, Small World Zoo was advertising tamarins—both adults and babies—in *Animal Finders' Guide,* the pet-trade periodical.

Cedar Hollow Breeding Center certainly has the right ring to it, so no one would question Seattle's Woodland Park Zoo for choosing it as a destination for aging South American tapirs or young Angolan spring-bok. But the breeding at this Texas ranch, also a destination for many of the San Diego Wild Animal Park's surplus (the laundering done by dealer Larry Johnson), may not be for purposes that jibe with the zoos' stated mission. Cedar Hollow Ranch, as it's more accurately known, supplies animals to the likes of Y. O. Ranch, home to an exotic-animal auction and world-famous hunting operation, as well as to Priour Ranch, another private Texas hunting ground. Yet another recipient is Little Creek Exotics, in Utopia, Texas, whose Web site boasts of selling surplus exotics to ranchers hoping to "stay out of the limelight."

—◦—

Two hours after the keeper of the Iowa agricultural records welcomed me and my assistant for the day to his warehouse, he announced that he'd soon be leaving for an off-site meeting and suggested that we per-haps should return to the building sometime that afternoon. Shortly thereafter, he ushered us to the Xerox machine and watched impatiently as twenty-one sheets were laid individually atop the machine's glass. Then he went to his 11 A.M. meeting and I went on to Wisconsin.

The search of this musty Des Moines records center had been arranged weeks earlier, and telephone calls confirming the appointment had been made from three or four stops across the Midwest—insurance against a repeat of the Boston and Raleigh snafus, or any of the other horrors on the state capital tour. At a pay phone somewhere between Little Rock and Nashville, I learned that Tennessee attorneys had sud-denly declared the health certificates exempt from the state's Freedom of Information Act and was advised that the following day's appointment should therefore be scratched from my calendar. In Montgomery, an animal-care veterinarian withdrew permission to search the file cabinets and instead handed over all of the Alabama records I presumably wanted—as if he could read my mind. The visit to Bismarck, North Dakota, was set in stone for a Monday morning, but the prior Friday the custodian of the state health certificates decided that it wasn't convenient after all, that she would be taking Monday afternoon off and perhaps I could travel halfway across the country some other time. The curator of the Nebraska records had claimed that the health certificates for exotics were kept segregated from all others, so I trudged through a spring snowstorm to find the zoo-animal paperwork—all sixteen pieces of it—instead buried amid records for a few hundred thousand heads of cattle. Then I was told that to get the documents I wanted, I would have to mail in a Freedom of Information Act request with a check for a dollar per copy. So I left Lincoln empty-handed and pressed on to Des Moines, where two hours was actually all the time I needed. The paperwork for exotics was supposedly lumped together in the monthly collections of certificates, but the bunches never included more than two or three pages. Waiting around for an afternoon go at these records was pointless, so it was off to Madison, Wisconsin.

But for each state that came up bust, there was one like Illinois, Indiana, Michigan, Missouri, or New York, where open-records laws have real meaning and orderly record-keeping systems allowed me to easily retrieve dozens, even hundreds, of health certificates. And with each new state's documents, the big picture began to come into sharper focus. The same dealers kept turning up on the receiving end of transactions; the paper trails could be followed from one state to the next and in turn somewhere else; and the subterfuges became apparent. Dealers list Bengal tigers on the certificates designated for family pets—documents that state wildlife officials rarely examine and that interested outsiders like me presumably would never pore through. Post office boxes are listed as recipients' addresses—a practice frowned on by state veterinarians but one exploited by those eager to keep details of their transactions guarded. Annual reports to the U.S. Fish and Wildlife Service, which detail the movement of endangered species, don't match health-certificate claims: The former states that one male tiger and two females had been moved across state lines, whereas the latter reports that it was one female and three males. The telephone number on a health certificate doesn't belong to the person listed as consignee, so where the animal actually went is uncertain. Health certificates are sent directly to the receiving state's department of agriculture, thereby leaving no paper trail in a dealer's home state. And then there's the sort of practice engaged in by the San Diego Zoo: It has submitted a year's worth of health certificates at once, thumbing its nose at receiving states' requirements for timely notification that animals had crossed their borders.

But the real flaw of health certificates is that they usually track only the movement of animals across state lines. Consequently, when the Denver Zoo files paperwork stating that it sent three pronghorn antelopes to the Endangered Species Propagation, Survival, and Research Center, which seems to be little more than a breeding farm for Texas ranchers and dealers, the animals may then be moved again inside Texas without generating additional certificates—documents that would, of course, reveal their whereabouts.

Another problem with this paperwork is that it sometimes omits critical details. In November 1996, for example, the Denver Zoo sold the three pronghorn antelopes in question to the Mesker Park Zoo & Botanic Garden, in Evansville, Indiana, which at the time was an AZA-accredited facility. According to officials at the Denver Zoo, their counterparts at Mesker Park provided shipping instructions, and the animals were sent to Texas. But the transaction raises questions about the fate of the antelopes: The health certificate shows the recipient to be the Endangered Species Propagation, Survival, and Research Center, which is based in Mertzon, Texas, although the paperwork lists an address in San Marcos, some three hundred miles away. What's more, the San Marcos address doesn't belong to this "survival" center, which has sold animals to the likes of the Forest Ranch, a pay-as-you-go hunting operation, but it's rather the home of a breeder/dealer who recently gained some unwelcome prominence in the zoo community. According to a December

1997 complaint filed with the AZA Ethics Committee, Ronald Young, the director of Mesker Park, contracted with a number of AZA zoos to have lemurs shipped to his institution, then he diverted the animals to this same dealer in San Marcos. (Young told the Ethics Committee that the dealer was merely housing the endangered primates while the zoo built its new lemur exhibit. However, this dealer sold lemurs to the pet trade, sometimes advertising his stock in *Animal Finders' Guide*. Coincidentally, his classified ads also listed pronghorn antelopes for sale.) As a result of the complaint, Young was expelled as an AZA Professional Fellow for two years and Mesker Park's accreditation was suspended. Denver Zoo officials "believe" that their three pronghorns landed in San Marcos, but they can't say for certain. If that's so, the transaction raises even more questions: An official of the Texas Parks & Wildlife department says she can find no evidence that the agency ever issued the dealer the permit required to import the Denver Zoo's antelopes.

This, in fact, is how many zoo animals are made to disappear. They're first sent to a dealer, conservation center, or wildlife propagator with either a formal tie to the AZA or an aura of legitimacy earned by virtue of a name, government license, or days-gone-by dealings with accredited zoos. Judging solely from the paperwork, these transactions seem for the most part to be good deeds, inasmuch as the recipient individuals and organizations seem to do good work. But the paperwork, more often than not, is deceptive, because the animals are destined to be resold to the very individuals and institutions deemed unacceptable by AZA members. In many instances, these animals are transferred elsewhere in-state, whether to backyard breeders or wildlife speculators. Those third parties are then free to move the animals again, and with each transaction it becomes increasingly difficult to trace them to the zoo of origin. There is no paper trail to speak of. In this way, an animal becomes like a used car whose original title long ago disappeared. Even a tattoo won't help identify an animal's origins, because a five-digit number on its lower lip or on the inside of its thigh could have been applied by any owner along the chain.

In like fashion, the middlemen often send the zoo animals across state lines, where the paper trail grows equally cold. For example, in February

1994, the Denver Zoo sent a six-month-old Kirk's dik-dik (a dwarf African antelope) to Jim Fouts, the Kansas animal dealer; six weeks later, Fouts sent it to Dwayne Lake, a Georgia breeder and dealer who advertises in *Animal Finders' Guide*. If Lake then sold the dik-dik in Georgia, no public records would show that it had come, thirdhand, from the Denver Zoo. And even if Lake sold the antelope outside of Georgia, the health certificate filed with the state veterinarian would show only that Lake was its owner.

The situation is only compounded by USDA policies, which substitute secrecy for government in the sunshine. Although federally licensed zoos and dealers must make their disposition records available to USDA inspectors, the department has deemed these documents exempt from release under the Freedom of Information Act. In effect, the USDA has paved the way for the systematic laundering of exotic species. By allowing its licensees—whether AZA zoos or auction houses—to conduct their unsavory commerce in secret, the USDA has made it all but impossible for others to put the puzzle together.

A thin ray of sunshine falls in Kansas, whose record-keeping system is a model for the rest of the nation. When Safari Zoological Park, in Caney, a for-profit, non-AZA facility, sends weeks-old big cats to backyard collectors in Oklahoma, as it does routinely, the health certificates filed in Topeka provide full details of the transactions. When it sends a newborn African lion to Lolli Brothers auction, in Missouri, as it did one autumn, that interstate transfer is also detailed on a Kansas health certificate. This is the standard procedure required of any zoo or dealer when it moves any animal across state lines.

More important, though, Kansas also requires anyone transferring animals within its borders to file the same health certificates. As a result, when Safari Zoological Park consigned a baby African lion to El Dorado Livestock Auction, which is also in Kansas, it was required to disclose that transaction as well. Or when the Lee Richardson Zoo, in Garden City, sent an elk and a bison to dealer Jim Fouts in 1996, this AZA member was similarly required to report the details on a health certificate. By requiring such intrastate transactions to be disclosed, Kansas officials are able to track the movement of animals that may spread disease; in addition, a mechanism exists for monitoring the resale of zoo animals. If other states adopted similar provisions, it would be far more difficult for zoos and their partners to launder surplus animals into obscurity. Thomas Solin, of the Wisconsin Department of Natural Resources, says that dealers in his state have aggressively battled against proposals to require the testing of exotic animals for disease. "They don't want to create a paper trail, because that allows government agencies to track things. If there's no testing required, there's no paper trail. And if they don't create a record, they don't have to report profits."

Similarly, the exotic-animal industry will surely fight other measures that might reveal the fates of their castoffs. They will argue, for example, as they have in the past, that implanting each animal with a microchip—a unique electronic identifier—is an unfair record-keeping burden, that the technology is too costly, that self-regulation works fine, and that the government has no business imposing such heavy-handed regulation. Zoos will further argue, as they have repeatedly, that their own system of tattoos, ear tags, and numbers assigned by the International Species Information System—a not-for-profit global membership organization—provides thoroughly adequate means of tracking animals over their lifetimes.

In reality, these systems are designed to keep the truth from those who are not part of the inner circle. The tattoos and ear tags are just indecipherable jumbles of letters and numbers. The International Species Information System (ISIS) divulges sheer numbers of animals housed at zoos, but the nonprofit organization guards its database of individual-animal transfers as if it held state secrets. Most dealers don't report their sales to ISIS or to the studbook keepers for each species, further obscuring, or even obliterating, the paper trail for individual animals.

Even the species studbooks don't always tell the entire story. For example, the international studbook for the golden lion tamarin shows two of the primates sent by the National Zoo to the University of Nebraska in the late 1980s, but it contains no trace of the sixteen tamarins sent by the zoo to that school's psychology department in 1984. Moreover, the studbooks are in large part indecipherable to those without the mnemonic key to the institutions and individuals who are on the receiving end. The "codebook" is on a CD-ROM published annually by ISIS for its members. Also on the disk—but never published in printed copies—are the studbook keepers' confidential notes about what really happened to some of the animals: how they were never actually delivered to the institution of record, for example, or the true identities of those recipients listed for readers only as "private." Naturally, these disks are not for sale.

—◦—

In November 1996, Henry Hampton, an animal dealer in Mt. Ulla, North Carolina, filed a health certificate testifying that he had delivered thirteen elk to a woman in Hyndman, Pennsylvania. The certificates listed two males and eleven females ranging in age from five months to adult. Matching brucellosis test results, noted on health certificates from both New Jersey and North Carolina, confirmed that the elk came to Hampton and then the woman by way of Six Flags Wild Safari, the drive-through park in Jackson, New Jersey.

The woman who got the elk is not listed as a breeder, dealer, or exhibitor in USDA records. There is no evidence of her having ever violated the Animal Welfare Act. Searches of newspaper archives turned up no mentions of her name. No other documents could be found listing her as a buyer or seller of animals. She is not on a manifest of those licensed in Pennsylvania to sell wildlife or maintain a menagerie open to the public. There was no apparent reason for this delivery of thirteen elk. It was all a mystery.

There were hundreds, perhaps thousands, of similarly unanswerable questions posed by paperwork I collected on my visits to state capitals. In one way or another, personally or with the help of assistants and open-records laws, I collected documents from every state but Alaska and Hawaii—a few thousand pages fished from among a few million.

On their face, the records show only an endless parade of animals— seemingly benign transactions that in most instances hardly warrant a second look. But decipher each one, connect the dots as the animals are moved from one owner to the next, and there's usually more to the story.

For example: A reindeer is sold to a Wisconsin man at a Missouri auction, one of a thousand animals sold during the four-day event. The paperwork contains only the barest details of the transaction; it doesn't reveal that the buyer operates a canned hunt, that his clients sometimes pay to kill animals confined to a five-acre pen, or that the five-year-old caribou, who had passed through this same auction ring a few years earlier, would be slain fourteen days later at that Wisconsin kill-for-a-fee operation. Similarly, a certificate shows that Charles Robbins, a professor of zoology and natural resource science at Washington State University, sent a couple of two-month-old bear cubs to Bear Country U.S.A., a South Dakota drive-through park just down the road from Mount Rushmore. This is not unusual: After Robbins and his colleagues at the university's Bear Research, Education, and Conservation Program finish their projects, they send their unwanted subjects to zoos and sanctuaries. Ironically, animals studied for insights into ensuring the longevity of the species are in this instance sent to an amusement park with a chronic history of flunking Animal Welfare Act inspections. What's more, this drive-through park, which is home to about three hundred sixty bears, has a radical approach to keeping its population stable: Some of those bears are quietly trucked off to South Dakota slaughterhouses, where they're butchered and packaged for the exotic-meat trade. During one recent year, twenty bears in South Dakota were slaughtered under state inspection. The state veterinarian will not say how many of those animals came from Bear Country U.S.A., nor will the park's owners.

The shuffling of animals and the doctoring of paperwork are usually so effective that they preclude anyone from being able to say with certainty whose elk, bear, or caribou was sent to slaughter, sold at auction, or shot in a pen. In fact, even with a comprehensive set of records from forty-eight states, making those definitive connections is usually impossible. The Penn State University Deer Research Center sent eighteen whitetails to a Missouri dealer who six months later trucked nine deer to Larry Barger, of Stuttgart, Arkansas. Barger is a hunting-ranch operator and president of Whitetail Genetic Research Institute, which markets semen from large-antlered deer and breeds "superior" specimens for canned hunts. "The desire for trophy animals is much greater than the supply," Barger told the *Florida Times-Union* in early 1997. "Hunting pressure has gotten greater and greater, and the sport is going to get even bigger as the years go by. The demand for high-fenced [pay-to-hunt] areas is going to increase dramatically." Were those the university's deer that ended up with Barger? If so, what happened to them? If not, where are they?

In March 1995, the Jacksonville Zoo sent a four-year-old oryx antelope to Zoological Animal Exchange, one of the three commercial animal suppliers affiliated with the AZA. Was it the same four-year-old oryx that Zoological Animal Exchange sent to the Woods & Waters auction in Delphos, Ohio, the following November? Was that the Utica Zoo's muntjac deer that the Zoological Animal Exchange was advertising in *Animal Finders' Guide* magazine a few months after the zoo shipped one there? Were those elk sent to the West Virginia game farm the ones that came from New Jersey's Bergen County Zoological Park? The Pittsburgh Zoo? The zoo in Racine, Wisconsin? How about ZooAmerica, in Hershey, Pennsylvania? No one but these animal dealers knows for sure, which is of course the way that they and their clients want it.

But sometimes the point-to-point trails are completely logical. In 1992, for example, the year that Time Warner took over the operation of Six Flags Wild Safari, thirteen of its baboons were sent to Buckshire Corporation, in Perkasie, Pennsylvania, a firm that supplies primates and dogs for biomedical research. That same year, the New Jersey drive-through park sent fifty-three fallow deer to Dixie Wildlife Safaris, a Florida hunting operation that offers fallow deer as part of its standard kill list.

Similarly, it's sometimes possible to connect enough dots to expose the state-to-state laundering schemes. In 1996, for instance, Wild Safari unloaded dozens of animals on Henry Hampton. As in years past, Hampton hauled a diverse inventory of specimens to the first leg of their ultimate disappearance: eight llamas, thirty fallow deer, one beisa oryx, one dorcas gazelle, eight Sicilian donkeys, four zebras, forty-three black-buck antelope, twenty-one elk, one giraffe, six waterbuck antelope, one scimitar-horned oryx, and two dromedary camels. Hampton in turn sent half of the blackbucks, two of the zebras, and all eight donkeys to relatively small exotic-animal auctions in Missouri and Ohio, but no public documents could be found that reveal whether any of them were sold there. In fact, Ohio authorities couldn't find a single health certificate to show what happened to any of the animals walked through the sales ring that year. As far as anyone can determine, they just disappeared.

And then there were the Wild Safari elk delivered to the Pennsylvania woman. Months went by before a clue surfaced about their fates: A two-by-two-inch ad in *Deer & Deer Hunting* magazine for Pennsylvania's Glen Savage Ranch. The eight-hundred-acre ranch, it turns out, which offers deer and elk trophy hunting, is run by the woman and her husband.

5

To Market

The half-page advertisement for Lockmoor Exotics in Great Falls, Virginia, proudly highlights its springtime inventory, some babies already on hand and others on the way: camels, kangaroos, wallabies, zebras, and Patagonian cavies, the long-legged rodents native to the Pampas of central and southern Argentina. Three male nilgai antelope are also for sale. Camel breeding is available. The company, owned by Jack Crippen and managed by Wyatt and Sherry Bentley, a husband-and-wife team, also publicizes its need for a male peccary, whether tame or not, for breeding purposes.

This is typical of the advertisements that fill the newsprint pages of *Animal Finders' Guide,* the eighteen-issues-a-year digest of the private exotic-animal industry. Crippen, the founder of Reston Animal Park (née Pet-a-Pet), is a regular *AFG* advertiser, also hawking the likes of his Watusi cattle—lumbering West African behemoths whose startling horns can each stretch five feet. Crippen has long been fond of exotic animals. Peacocks and a variety of unusual deer were regular fixtures in the yard of his home in Reston, Virginia. He bought and sold animals at the Lolli Brothers auction, in Macon, Missouri, where the World Watusi Association stages its yearly sales. He traveled the country in search of new prizes, sometimes transporting his animals home in a jet helicopter. Crippen owned a young hyena named Joe that his buddy, wildlife evangelist Jim Fowler, showed off to Johnny Carson on *The Tonight Show,* and he once stored a dozen young elephants in his barn for dealer Jurgen Schulz, who later farmed them out across the nation. He delighted in putting a young bear cub in the back seat of his station wagon, then picking up hitchhikers to watch their stunned reactions. His daughter once testified in a deposition that the weirder the animal, the more Crippen liked it, thus his fascination with the Watusi cattle. A longtime favorite of Crippen's is a peccary named Grandma, a bristly porker he posed with in a mouth-to-mouth smooch for an *Animal Finders' Guide* photograph.

Longtime readers of the black-and-white publication, which typically runs about forty pages, probably didn't give the photo a second look. This, after all, is a periodical whose feature stories have included: "Death of an Aoudad," "Llama Birthing," "Raising Elk for Fun and Profit," "The Joy of Keeping Striped Mice," "Homegrown Mealworms," "Prairie Dog Collecting," "Sugar Glider Diet," "Stomach Bloat in Marmosets," "Do Bobcats Make Good Pets?" "Help Build the Rhea Industry," "Springhaas—The 8 Lb. Jerboa?" and "Suggestions on Raising Servals." The magazine reprints news releases and tipsheets from such organizations as the American Camel Club Association and Registry and the International Llama Association. Letters to the *AFG*'s editor vilify animal-rights activists and legislators seeking to impose new restrictions on the sale or ownership of exotic animals. Readers submit gushing poems or sentimental testimonials about their fennec fox or recently deceased wallaby; others send in curious staged photos: a pet coatimundi raiding an Easter egg basket, a pet prairie dog chomping on Froot Loops. Editor Patrick Hoctor, who founded the publication in 1984, is known for his acerbic tirades about an overly intrusive, out-of-control government bent on shutting down the exotic-animal business. On the U.S. Department of

Agriculture: "You must do what they say even if it makes no sense. They are gods and will make sure you know it." On state fish and game departments: "One by one, compound by compound, county by county, state by state, they are attacking your brothers and sisters in this business. We better learn to stand side by side and defend one another or, someday, there will be no private ownership of animals in this country!"

But the editorial copy, whether a husbandry primer or a call to arms, is really just so much filler between the ads. *Animal Finders' Guide* is the place to learn about upcoming auctions and rare-breed shows. More important, the ads reveal who's dealing black-backed jackals, the going price of degus, and whether the tenrec—a hedgehog-like mammal native to Madagascar—will likely find a more conspicuous niche in the pet trade as the sugar glider's star begins to fade. More than one hundred fifty species of mammal, bird, and reptile are advertised in a typical issue of *AFG*, some well known, others only vaguely familiar: addax, binturong, capybara, palm civet, Patagonian cavy, and pygmy zebu.

There are twenty-odd species of primates for sale, including chimpanzees and a half-dozen types of macaque, which can carry a virus potentially fatal to humans. Deer and elk are advertised in unusually great numbers, sometimes as "shooters"—that is, hunting-ranch stock. African lions, which in captivity breed like beagles, go for $200. There are sales galore: a jungle-cat reduction sale, a going-out-of-business caracal sale, an albino-wallaby moving sale. There are ads for custom-made monkey clothing and ads promising quantity discounts for short-tailed opossums and bottle-fed Bennett's wallabies. Someone wants six-legged sheep; someone else is selling a six-footed pig. A one-armed squirrel monkey has been marked down to $1,200. A cow elk with an amputated leg is a bargain, just make an offer. Top dollar paid for bottle-raised otter babies. A skunk herd is available, cages included. Now taking nonrefundable deposits on lions and tigers. There are ligers (lion-tiger crossbreeds) and zeedonks (zebra-donkey hybrids). Wanted: breeding-age male wildebeest. Wanted: pair of Chinese water deer for breeding. Capuchin for sale, canines removed. Coatimundi bottle babies for sale, eye teeth removed. Expecting muntjac babies. Handleable bear cubs, due in January. Coyote pups, due late April. Black spider monkey, very sweet, $2,500. African spur-thighed tortoise, extremely gentle, $750. Eleven-month-old spider monkey, rides in car seat, is good with children and pets, wears diapers and clothes (included), $3,500. Will trade a twelve-week-old declawed Siberian tiger for a baby lynx or cougar. Will sell two-toed sloths for $1,500 or consider trade. Wanted: exotic chipmunks (color mutations or normal). Wanted: albino prairie dogs (must have red eyes). Wanted: white elk. For sale: litter- and leash-trained Canadian lynx. Very tame cougars. Super-tame kinkajous. Super-sweet red-rumped agoutis. A Michigan hunting ranch is for sale, one hundred twenty acres and inventory (500 fallow deer, three or four dozen Corsican, Barbado, Texas Dall and Black Hawaiian sheep). Big 4-Day Spring Exotic Sale. Rare Breed Livestock, Miniature & Small Pet Expo. Bighorn semen for sale. *Miniature Donkey Talk,* a bimonthly magazine. Join the Reindeer Owners and Breeders Association. Fertile emu eggs, $10. Flying squirrels, $25. Sugar glider babies, $40 each. Chinchillas, $75 and up. Tennessee fainting goats, $150 to $250. Bear cubs, $395 each. Blesbok, $1,000. Red kangaroo, $1,750. Breeder baboons, $2,250 for the pair. Sitatunga, $3,000 a pair. Bengal tigers, $3,500 a pair. Green monkey babies, $2,200–$2,400. Bonnet macaque, $2,500. Bongo, $4,000. Grant zebra, $6,000. Chimpanzee, $42,500. Game farms, are your customers tired of hunting the same old castrated black Duroc-crossed potbellied pig? Try a few European boar and see if things get interesting!

The ads are from nearly every state, though a peculiarly large number are from Florida and Texas. Servals, long-legged predators native to central African savannas, are unusually popular, as are white tigers. Lemurs, Amur leopards, Bengal tigers, and other endangered species are offered in great numbers, usually with an in-state sales requirement—a way to exploit a loophole in the Endangered Species Act and make the animals available to any interested buyer, no permits or qualifications required.

Display ads usually list business names and addresses, so it's easy to find Jim Fouts, Earl Tatum, and Larry Johnson, the latter two being the prime movers of "surplus" for the San Diego Zoo and other California wildlife parks (in the 1990s alone, for example, the San Diego Zoo and San Diego Wild Animal Park have relied on Tatum and Johnson to dispose of well over one thousand animals). But the hundreds of three- and four-line classifieds in a typical issue include just a phone number and the seller's home state. The anonymous advertisers include some of the other dealers that AZA zoos routinely use to get rid of unwanted animals, including Edward Novack of Cairo, New York, and Eric Mogensen, the proprietor of the Zoological Animal Exchange, in Natural Bridge, Virginia. Petting zoos and roadside menageries unload their animals via *AFG* ads. So do charlatans pretending to be sanctuary operators, some with tax-exempt status and reputations in their communities for being avowed wildlife conservationists. Some advertise once, and never again, whereas others have long, twisting histories in the exotic-animal business, such as the Ohio man whose two-year-old son was mauled to death by a tiger in 1983. A decade and a half later, he seems intent on passing along the madness: He breeds cougars and bears, then sells the cubs to the public.

Lockmoor Exotics, a regular advertiser in *Animal Finders' Guide,* is an anomaly in its residential neighborhood of Great Falls, Virginia, twenty miles from downtown Washington, D.C. Barns and outdoor pens are situated beside a 500-foot, grass-covered hill. The man-made mound, which is ringed by a tall fence, was previously a landfill that accommodated hundreds of trucks per day. For years, neighbors lobbied the country to close Stump Dump, as it was known. They thought that they had prevailed over Jack Crippen in a 1988 lawsuit, but the gates were only finally shut seven years later.

The landfill, capped with dirt and turf, soon became home to a large private menagerie that included llamas, zebras, elk, oryx, and a variety of other animals, including, of course, Watusi cattle, one of which was beheaded by an intruder. The Department of Animal Control tried to thwart Crippen's plans, accusing him of illegally keeping a pet nilgai antelope. He was later found guilty of a misdemeanor, but a Circuit Court judge considering an appeal gave him a year either to obtain the proper permits or else to remove the exotic antelope. The charges against him were dismissed after the permits were in hand.

Although the county imposed some restrictions on Crippen, he was free to continue amassing his collection of two- and four-legged novelties. And Crippen, who will reclaim Reston Animal Park at the end of 1999 and move his animals there, has an ongoing surplus for sale: Chinese water deer and capybara, nilgai antelope and Patagonian cavies, zebras, camels, and kangaroos. There are conures, macaws, and other birds for sale, including flightless ratites. Here, buying an animal—no matter how unusual—is no more complicated than buying a hamster or a parakeet at a local pet store, although at least one of the species in Crippen's stock is off-limits to Virginians who don't already own one: Recent regulations prohibit prairie dogs as pets, a decision imposed by the state's Department of Game & Inland Fisheries because of worries that the two-pound rodents might infect their owners with Bubonic plague or hantavirus, or that they might escape and create feral colonies that would disturb existing ecosystems. Crippen's prairie dogs, released in a field near his animal barn, built their typically elaborate network of tunnels, then refused to surface. A ferret was brought in to clear them out for recapture, but it stuck its nose in the ground and turned tail. So the ferret was put up for sale, and the prairie dog colony is spreading across the meadow, although so far, at least, not in the direction of the unsuspecting neighbors.

—◦—

Not long after the young mountain lion showed up in the pet-shop window, complaints started flooding the police and the humane society of Albemarle County, Virginia. Once or twice a week, the owner of the pet store would transport the cougar from his home and place the animal in an eight-by-ten-foot Plexiglas cage, where it would spend the day pacing or lying motionless. After visiting the pet store a dozen times, animal-control officers finally began telling angry passersby that there was nothing they could do. Because the U.S. Department of Agriculture had licensed the pet store as an exhibitor (the same designation accorded a zoo), and because the cage complied with federal standards, the cougar could remain in the store window. The community's displeasure, callers were told, was immaterial.

There are believed to be several privately held cougars in Albemarle County, although no one has an exact census. One couple keeps a pair of the big cats to show off at county fairs. Some keep the mountain lions as house pets, which requires no federal, state, or local permits. In this enclave at the foothills of the Blue Ridge Mountains, as in much of the nation, one person's pets are nobody else's business.

Such a laissez-faire approach isn't universally tolerated. A few years ago, Georgia granted licenses to the owners of monkeys and other exotic pets but barred others from acquiring them. Some states prohibit the ownership of indigenous animals, whereas others outlaw raccoon dogs, red deer, and a host of species that might pose a threat to human health or livestock. Some states require the owners of dangerous animals to pay an annual permit fee, whereas others, such as Utah, grant ownership licenses only after conservation officers inspect the facilities. In Rhode Island, would-be owners of dangerous animals not only must withstand the harangues of the state veterinarian about the inappropriateness of keeping such pets but also must offer advance proof that a qualified local veterinarian will provide the animal care. New York requires a license to own black bears or other native species, as well as a handful of species deemed dangerous, although anyone not prohibited by local statute is free to keep a pet dingo or just about anything else not classified as endangered. As a result, the number of New Yorkers keeping African lions as pets is anyone's guess.

Florida has the nation's most stringent requirements for wildlife ownership. The 1974 law that created the state's permit system was spawned by attacks—some fatal—on pet owners by their big cats or other dangerous animals. A Personal Pet Council composed of state officials and exotic-animal owners created a licensing system—subsequently added to fish and game regulations—based on three classes of wildlife species. Lions, chimpanzees, bears, and other especially dangerous animals (Class I) were declared inappropriate as personal pets and their ownership limited to zoos or research facilities. Animals such as cougars, coyotes, and macaques (Class II) were okayed for pet ownership, although the permit carries a $100 annual fee and requires either a thousand hours of care and husbandry experience or, alternatively, one hundred hours of animal-care experience and a passing score in a state-administered test. Owning raccoons, skunks, squirrel monkeys, and other small animals (Class III) requires only a no-cost permit.

Other states have looked to adopt parts of Florida's regulations, or tried to come up with their own, only to be shot down by the exotic-animal lobby. In state after state, legislative deals have unraveled when exotic-animal breeders and dealers unleashed aggressive lobbying campaigns, tying up bills before House or Senate committees and scuttling agreements that had taken months, even years, to craft. In many instances, the dealers, breeders, and ranchers have been uncompromising in their insistence that no regulations of any sort be enacted—that the rights of animal owners take precedence over the state's right to protect wildlife or to protect the population from disease or accident. Dealers in some states have even argued that more-humane cage sizes represent an unwarranted intrusion by government. If animals need more room or a different diet, they say, dealers—not office-bound bureaucrats—would know that.

Although the exotic-animal industry is relatively small, it makes do with political muscle in some states and with attitude in others. In Texas, where the business of raising exotic species has been flourishing since the 1930s, ranchers and game-preserve owners don't leave their political battles to chance. For years, State Representative Harvey Hilderbran served as the executive director of the Exotic Wildlife Association, a three-decade-old coalition of exotic hoofed stock breeders and game ranchers intent on protecting the rights of their members to raise animals and the rights of their paying customers to kill them. Hilderbran was also a member of the House Committee on State Recreational Resources, whose responsibilities include the regulation of Texas wildlife; witnesses before the committee included the chairman of the organization he directed.

In 1997, after the news media gave considerable attention to a spate of vicious attacks by large cats, the Texas Senate passed a bill that would have prohibited the private ownership of some dangerous wild animals. But the measure died in a House committee, where the opposition was headed by two former Speakers of the Texas House, including one big-game hunter who lobbies on behalf of the National Rifle Association. For good measure, the chairman of the Texas Parks and Wildlife Commission, which regulates hunting statewide, is Fort Worth businessman Lee Bass, who breeds rhinoceros on his spread. Although Bass did not publicly oppose a ban on the ownership of dangerous animals, the bill's proponents maintain that he privately engineered the measure's defeat. After the legislation passed the Texas Senate, the powerful exotic-game ranchers helped kill it in the House. The result was that each of Texas's two hundred fifty-four counties were left to decide whether—and how— to regulate the ownership of these wild animals. The Texas Humane Legislation Network, which led the effort to get the ban enacted, more or less conceded defeat. "Short of one of the lead opponent's family members being mauled by one of these wild animals, we're not going to get strong regulations in this state," Cile Holloway, the organization's president, says.

By contrast, the tactics in some states are more about bullying than they are about political brainstorming. "They tend to be a pretty rough crowd," says an Indiana official. "They can be physically intimidating. We have a USDA inspector whose life was threatened by a guy."

In Ohio, where there is virtually no state regulation of the personal ownership of nonnative species, lawmakers and animal-welfare organizations pushing for controls have proved to be no match for the Ohio Association of Animal Owners. Spearheaded by a husband-and-wife team, Polly and Gary Ward, the association lacks the high-profile, big-money interests of its Texas counterparts, but it successfully wages aggressive campaigns against any legislative proposal deemed a threat to the rights of those who own or sell animals.

Making this a free-enterprise issue—a favored tactic of like-minded groups in other states—has resonated with enough lawmakers to ensure that the Wards and their constituents are free to buy, sell, and own wild animals. As a result, it's hard to find an Ohio county where someone doesn't have a full-grown cougar chained to a backyard tree or a tiger living alongside his children.

In many states, new laws or regulations have come about only in the wake of human tragedies or health threats to the traditional livestock industry. And municipalities across the country have changed zoning laws or enacted local ordinances against dangerous pets after discovering that someone was breeding leopards on his farm or keeping a lion penned in a residential neighborhood. The mere possibility of escape provided the impetus to rewrite the law.

But these patchwork changes to local statutes sometimes only result in the animals—and the threats they pose—being moved elsewhere, where the complaints and community meetings begin anew. For example, when Catawba County, North Carolina, adopted an ordinance prohibiting residents from keeping dangerous animals, the target of the regulation—a pair of brothers preparing to open a sanctuary—packed up their two big cats and headed across the county line. Officials there enacted similar restrictions, but David and Eric Holm were able to exploit a loophole that permitted them to raise exotic animals for "educational uses." So now their nonprofit SHEA (Safe Haven for Endangered Animals) Park is home to so-called Animal Ambassadors, a collection of "rescued" beasts that are marched before the public as a means, the Holms claim, of highlighting threats to vanishing species.

Coincidentally, a serval was spotted at a nearby farm following the relocation, where for weeks the animal raided the chicken houses. The aggrieved farmer finally killed the marauding African cat with a .22-caliber bullet, but the Holm brothers insisted that the long-legged predator belonged to someone else; their serval, they assured local officials, had been sent to an unnamed Georgian.

—◦—

Regulations of the U.S. Department of Agriculture also provide many exotic-animal owners with the means to circumvent local laws and maintain their private menageries. In 1996, for instance, a young white tiger owned by Timothy Hart, a lawyer in Palmyra, Ohio, broke through a window screen and briefly ran free before being corralled by a neighbor and the county sheriff. A series of community meetings followed, during which townspeople complained that Hart was ill-equipped to keep animals. Hart's tiger, cougar, and other wild animals constituted a danger to the community, neighbors insisted, and should therefore be removed.

Hart's white Bengal tiger had come to him from Rolling Valley Exotic Animal Farm in Ravenna, Ohio, a federally licensed animal-dealing operation mistakenly thought of by some as a wildlife refuge. The Cincinnati-area SPCA once sent Rolling Valley a female lion that had been seized in an animal-cruelty case—a rescue that the animal welfare organization's general manager today recalls as a real triumph, since the big cat was relocated to a safe haven. But just four years earlier, Rolling Valley's owner, James Witchey, Sr., had been cited for numerous animal-welfare violations by USDA inspectors, including a failure to provide his primates, bears, and large cats suitable food or shelter. About the time that the lion was on its way from Cincinnati to Ravenna, the so-called refuge was advertising the availability of Bengal tigers in *Animal Finders' Guide* and shipping the big cats around the Midwest. In the years that followed, Witchey sold or loaned more tigers to roadside zoos and private individuals, including boxer Mike Tyson, whose local zoning board also tried to bar him from owning a white tiger.

The residents and township trustees of Palmyra, Ohio, also sought a way to render Hart's menagerie illegal. But Hart employed a frequently used scheme to frustrate his neighbors: He applied for and was granted a USDA dealer's license, giving him the right to breed and sell animals. Because Ohio law decrees that a township can't zone out animal husbandry, Palmyra officials couldn't stop Hart from keeping his dangerous animals or in fact from accumulating more. Meanwhile, Mike Tyson had the USDA declare his backyard cages a zoological park, frustrating his neighbors as well—a tactic that the animal dealers are happy to share with their prospective clients.

The Agriculture Department's Office of Inspector General studied this loophole and found that pet owners were routinely being issued licenses presumably reserved for zoos and other bona fide exhibitors. In fact, the inspector general's office discovered that nearly two-thirds of the exhibitors it audited had received federal licenses as a way to sidestep state or local laws that would have otherwise prohibited them from keeping potentially dangerous animals.

The 1996 audit, which was tucked away in the Agriculture Department's archives, scolded USDA's Animal and Plant Health Inspection Service for its propensity to shower licenses on so-called exhibitors. The government investigators reported:

> Since APHIS does not have guidelines to evaluate applicants' qualifications in handling animals, we found that licensees were not always experienced in handling or caring for the animals they were licensed to exhibit; in some cases, this jeopardized both the animals and the public. Once licensed, an individual may obtain any number or type of animals desired, without further approval by APHIS; individuals who were initially licensed to exhibit common domestic animals, such as rabbits, subsequently obtained wild or exotic animals which were not present when the prelicensing inspections were performed.

The inspector general's report soberly documented APHIS's ineptitude—the near-universal view of most on the outside and many, even, on the inside. The audit noted, for example, that as the number of licensed breeders, dealers, and exhibitors continued to rise, the number of animal-care inspectors declined (since then, the number of inspectors has dropped even further, along with the budget to enforce the Animal Welfare Act). This made it even less likely that the agency could, as the Animal Welfare Act requires it to do, conduct annual inspections of more than two thousand exhibitors and thousands of other licensees.

But APHIS nonetheless kept acting as a license mill. When the inspector general's investigators visited some of the backyard collectors who had billed themselves as zoo operators, they found individuals with no knowledge or experience maintaining wild animals; in some instances, pet owners kept more than thirty large cats in cages obviously inadequate to contain them, jeopardizing the safety of the owners, the community, and the animals themselves. In other cases, the Agriculture Department's Animal and Plant Health Inspection Service issued permits to "zoo operators" whose exhibits included lone cougars kept caged in an owner's trailer or basement. Communities hoping to rid themselves of potentially dangerous animals have found themselves powerless to do so, as the federal license has given bogus exhibitors the wherewithal to keep their animals. And with these loopholes so easily—and frequently—exploited, the exotic-animal dealers continue doing as they wish.

—◦—

The sign on the driveway to L Cross Ranch in Okeechobee, Florida, says "Brokers, Dealers, Traders, and Merchants. No Pests." Mark Pearce, the owner of the ranch, uses the word "pests" as shorthand for animal-rights activists, whom he insists are nothing but troublemakers—misguided souls who incorrectly accuse him of wrongdoing. Pearce has little tolerance for these and other undesirables and wants them kept away from his exotic-animal auctions, which he's run at the ranch since 1991. And so Pearce stations a man with a sidearm halfway up his long gravel driveway. The sentry gives you the once-over, eyeballs the car seats for cameras or tape recorders, and if convinced you're not a pest, takes your twenty bucks. He hands you coupons for lunch and dinner and makes small talk about the weather. Then he sends you on to the sale barn.

Not all the troublemakers are kept away from Pearce's twice-monthly auction, however. A couple of inspectors for the USDA's Animal and Plant Health Inspection Service, which licenses Pearce's operation, had a car tire sliced at one of his sales. They didn't suspect Pearce, but neither did they ask the local authorities to investigate this destruction of federal property. As everyone around Okeechobee knows, what goes on at Mark Pearce's auction is only his business.

At L Cross, two hundred to three hundred people fill metal folding chairs and the barn's high-rise bleachers for a single day of bidding. A half-dozen ostriches are ushered into the ten-sided ring, and when the bidding ends the flightless birds are chased through an exit door, their place taken by a baby zebra. It goes on like that in a nonstop, daylong procession: Goats and bison calves, then hedgehogs and llamas. There's a litter-box-trained skunk for sale, then a declawed otter that will eat from your hand, a burlap bag filled with turtles, Easter baskets with emu eggs, a tame flying squirrel, a box of baby chicks, a variety of exotic pigeons. Someone has consigned a common ground squirrel. "Hell," an onlooker jokes, "I shoot those things in my backyard." It nonetheless sells for twenty-five dollars. When a pair of wallabies is brought into the ring, the auctioneer says: "You can't reach in the cage, but the male will take a potato from your hand." That brings an appreciative buzz from the mostly male, nearly all-white crowd. For those shut out in the bidding, there are five-dollar zebra-skin hatbands for sale. On the lawn outside the barn, a man parades back and forth with a five-year-old leashed iguana. He's got another for sale, which he says will grow to six feet, just like his buddy's pet. A young boy pleads with his father, but to no avail. Instead, the bed of a pickup is loaded with exotic birds bought earlier that morning and the family heads for the exit.

◄o►

Getting through the doors at the North Carolina Reptile and Exotic Animal Show requires a half-hour wait, but those queued up at the state fairgrounds, in Raleigh, don't seem to mind. It's a warm Saturday morning, and would-be buyers—many of them drawn to the sale by a promotional radio campaign—look on in rapt attention as those leaving the expo show off their newly acquired snakes, birds, and lizards.

Inside the building, a couple is selling red-handed tamarins, $2,000 for a male and $2,300 for a female. They know little about the lineage of these small, South American primates—they came from an unidentified lady in Texas, who supposedly got them from someone in Florida—and know even less about their proper care, but they happily announce that more babies are on the way and that interested buyers can reserve one with a phone call. Someone is selling capybaras, someone else pygmy goats. A vendor from nearby Wake Forest, who also sells his animals at the big auctions in Ohio and Missouri, has brought a three-week-old camel. A man from Statesville, North Carolina, one hundred fifty miles to the west, has for sale a pair of beautiful black-winged peacocks that he crammed into a cage barely large enough to hold them. When a teenage girl inquires about the small size of the cage, the birds' owner says: "At 4 A.M. last night that was the only thing I could get hold of. Things look bigger at 4 A.M."

Some vendors sell tomato frogs, Madagascar hissing cockroaches, or rose-hair tarantulas, their inventory displayed in endless rows of Tupperware containers lined up on long tables. Much of the show is devoted to the sale of reptiles: water snakes and Nile monitors, leopard geckos, and baby ball pythons. Reptiles, in fact, constitute an increasing percentage of the exotic-animal trade—a trend of concern to public-health officials because some of the imported animals harbor infectious-disease-carrying ticks and other insects. State and federal agriculture officials are concerned about the imports for another reason: Foreign reptile exporters fill shipping containers with flora-killing feeder insects, many of which are still alive when the cargo arrives here. Conservationists are concerned because entire ecosystems are being ravaged to supply the trade. And veterinarians are troubled by the boom for another reason: Reptiles are not covered by the Animal Welfare Act, and this lack of regulation has doomed many of the creatures to abuse. "They don't scream and they're not pushy, and nobody cares about the poor things," a veterinarian says. "But boy do they suffer."

Some vendors at the North Carolina show are selling hedgehogs, prairie dogs, sugar gliders, and dormice. Interest in these so-called pocket pets is cyclical, and after being out of favor they are making a strong comeback. The reason, some speculate, is that these small, low-maintenance animals require little space or investment, don't make noise, and don't have to be walked. And when the owners tire of a pocket pet, they can simply haul the cage or terrarium to the backyard and tip it over. The animal will likely die, although it just may adapt to its new habitat, much like Jack Crippen's prairie dogs or the ostriches and emus released into the wild by Texas farmers unable to capitalize on their investments. Some newcomers adapt so well to their new environments, in fact, that they kill off or force out native species.

The exotic-pet industry relies on a never-ending stream of new animals as a means of enticing those who have tired of their degu, tenrec, or whatever else is in vogue. In early 1995, the rage—albeit brief—was bats that dealers in the United States imported from the Middle East. Egyptian fruit bats by the hundreds found their way into private hands, although most soon died from improper care. The Centers for Disease Control and Prevention was unaware of the bats' newfound popularity and was tipped off only by reports from USDA and U.S. Fish and Wildlife port-of-entry inspectors that the winged mammals were streaming into the country. Because the bats carry troublesome viruses, the CDC immediately limited ownership to diagnostic laboratories, zoological collections, and scientific researchers. With the bats banished, the fennec fox and Bennett's wallabies rose to newfound prominence. After that, there was money to be made in chinchillas and short-tailed opossums.

—◦—

If you want to buy an exotic animal, your must-read list might include *Rare Breeds Journal*, *Wings & Hooves*, *Farm & Country Market Place*, *Animals Exotic & Small*, and, of course, *Animal Finders' Guide*, whose heft, breadth, and following is unrivaled. Then there are the exotic-animal swap meets and expos, and the Internet, which is awash with exotic-animal sites. But auctions such as the one at L Cross Ranch are where much of the trade in exotic animals is conducted. This bimonthly sale—like dozens of others across the country—attracts primarily a local clientele, including would-be owners of exotic animals and wholesalers looking both to unload inventory and to pick up bargains for resale at the huge out-of-state auctions. But because Florida is a hub of the nationwide exotic-animal network, the L Cross sale barn typically draws a cavalcade of big-name breeders and dealers. Their ranks include the proprietor of nearby Otter Creek Exotics, whose longtime poster pet was a wallaroo named Arnold—a red, freakishly muscular stud that was memorialized in *Animal Finders' Guide* with a quarter-page photo and a fitting tribute: "It was an honor and a privilege to have been your friend." Otter Creek's owner has also sold South American short-tailed opossums, prairie dogs and a variety of other pocket pets. A Florida wildlife officer says that she sometimes blocks the sale of one of her animals rather than entrust it to someone whom she suspects won't provide adequate care.

Tim Wise patronizes the L Cross auction. He and his wife, Denise, operate The Wise Monkeys, one of the many primate-dealing operations that pose as "sanctuaries" for unwanted animals. Although the couple insists that they provide their monkeys with lifetime care, some are advertised for sale before they're even born: "Baby weeper capuchin born 5-13-98, sex unknown, $3,500. Cinnamon capuchin babies due July & August. Black & white capuchin male breeder, 8 years old. Black & white capuchin male juvenile, 2 1/2 years old, will consider trade. Red-handed tamarin babies due June. Cotton top tamarin male, 2 years old, $1000, Florida only."

Dr. Richard Miller, a Fort Lauderdale animal dealer whose suppliers include the Bronx Zoo and Central Florida Zoological Park, an AZA member in Lake Monroe, Florida, has been spotted on the videotapes that secretly record everyone entering the L Cross sales ring. Miller, who operates a veterinary clinic, has a private menagerie that includes extremely rare red pandas. These Asian omnivores, native to the temperate forests of the Himalayas, are fast disappearing from the wild. There are so few in captivity that zoo directors in the United States who hope to acquire them have to exploit their connections, lobbying the AZA Species Survival Plan coordinator for a chance to add a pair to their collection. Many zoos fail in their efforts to acquire the animals, and those that do succeed sometimes must wait years. And yet Miller has managed to acquire three pairs of red pandas, courtesy, in part, of the Cincinnati Zoo—a gift omitted from the official species studbook. Miller keeps the rare animals hidden in buildings and cages behind "Miller World Zoo," which is nothing but a few unsightly, primate-filled cages situated next to his veterinary office.

Michael Powell, a dealer who does business under the name Miami Reptiles, also patronizes the L Cross auction. He sells everything from fennec foxes to primates and South American opossums. "If it doesn't sell, Powell will just release them," a Florida wildlife officer says. "I've seen him knock over a trough of turtles. He releases snakes. It's a commodity—you buy and sell it." A few years ago, when Sylvia Taylor, a veterinarian for USDA's Animal and Plant Health Inspection Service, examined Powell's records, she noted a particularly grisly ten-month period. March 10: A red-bellied tamarin sold to an unlicensed individual in Miami died. April 29: One striped opossum, two sugar gliders, and two palm civets imported from Indonesia died, with no record of veterinary care given. May 5: Two sugar gliders died from "stress." May 8: One striped opossum died. June 8: Six "surplus" squirrel monkeys were sent to Powell by Dr. Roger Broderson, the director of Animal Care and Use at the University of Georgia; one soon died from "stress," but no records exist to show that veterinary care was given ten-year-old "Marvin." June 15: Two rock cavies were received from another dealer with back wounds, apparently from fighting, and were dead by week's end. June 20: Nine civets (cat-like mammals) died. June 20: Two more civets "looked bad," but no veterinary care was given and they apparently died later. June 22: Eight Indonesian tri-colored squirrels died of unknown causes. July 14: A green squirrel monkey died of heat stress. July 28: Seven squirrels from an Indonesian shipment were dead on arrival; no veterinary care was given to the others, eleven of which died within eight hours and eight more of which died within five days. October 16: Powell shipped out eighteen New World primates, five of which died shortly afterward. December 1: Seven squirrels died in shipment to Powell, and two surviving opossums died within three days. December 13: Four striped weasels shipped to another animal dealer in South Florida were dead on arrival. January 19: Six opossums that Powell shipped to Belgium were dead on arrival. "The body count from the above," Dr. Taylor wrote, "is 82."

Yet another familiar face at the L Cross auction is Robert Crowe, who does business as Ashby Acres Wildlife Park. Although Crowe and Ralph Bedell, the co-owner, like to portray their ten-acre facility, which is an hour north of Cape Canaveral, as a zoo, it is really just a private menagerie—open to visitors by appointment only—from which the two conduct their trade in everything from domestic waterfowl to ocelots, Amur leopards, and other endangered species. Crowe was busted by the Florida Game and Fresh Water Fish Commission in 1990 for illegally maintaining wildlife—including a variety of primates—for commercial purposes. Crowe stated at the time his intention to breed and sell exotic animals as pets, but still the Bronx Zoo and AZA zoos in Cincinnati; Houston; Little Rock, Arkansas; Utica, New York; West Palm Beach, Florida; and other cities kept sending him their "surplus." Crowe also sells endangered big cats to individual collectors—another practice publicly condemned by AZA zoo directors—but the Mesker Park Zoo in Evansville, Indiana, and the Columbus Zoo in Ohio nonetheless have supplied him with snow leopards. Even Zoo Atlanta, whose director, Terry Maple, is coeditor of a book about zoo ethics, sent the primate dealer rare mona monkeys. (Maple now says that dealing with Crowe was an oversight by curators, and the zoo hopes to retrieve the animals.) About the same time, Crowe was nabbed for selling a cotton-top tamarin—an endangered species—to an individual who lacked the required permit. He was also cited for failing to maintain an accurate record of the transfer of wildlife.

In October 1995, the Florida Game and Fresh Water Fish Commission gave Crowe nine cougars that had been used to study the feasibility of reintroducing endangered Florida panthers to the northern part of the state. A state biologist reported that he called Crowe beforehand and asked, "Is there any chance that you would sell these animals to someone who would use them for hunting, a hunting or shooting preserve, for example, or for animal experimentation?"

"No, none whatsoever," Crowe replied. "I do not do things like that."

Despite such assurances, Crowe picked up the cougars at a state research laboratory and transported them directly to a big-cat breeder and dealer in South Carolina. One cougar died en route, another died at the dealer's facility, and the remaining seven were shipped to a Missouri "exhibitor," who in turn sent them to the operator of a Texas canned hunt. The U.S. Fish and Wildlife Service later rescued "Waldo," who was believed to be a true Florida panther, and a Sarasota-based animal-welfare organization raised $11,000 through public appeals to buy three survivors and relocate them to a Texas sanctuary. But three of the cougars entrusted to Crowe disappeared with the canned-hunt operator, who also uses the big cats as targets for hunting-dogs-in-training.

Crowe is particularly adept at getting university researchers to entrust him with their unwanted primates—a skill that has earned him the envy (as well as the scorn) of other dealers vying for the same lucrative prizes.

Like many of his monkey-dealing competitors, Crowe searches out animals in a newsletter published by the Primate Supply Information Clearinghouse. The PSIC, a project of the University of Washington's Regional Primate Research Center that's funded by the National Institutes of Health, is the mother lode of used university monkeys—six photocopied pages with ads for the likes of eighty owl monkeys at one university and one hundred ninety-five rhesus macaques at another, the latest entries identified by a prominent "NEW" banner to help Crowe and his ilk quickly and easily identify potential targets.

Among those on the receiving end of a Crowe solicitation was Jeanette Ward, a professor of psychology at the University of Memphis. Faced with a sudden cutback in support funding, Ward was forced to sell some of the hundred-plus bushbabies—small, nocturnal African primates—used in her research. Crowe beat Powell and other dealers to the punch, and Ward agreed to sell him some of her breeding colony for $350 each. So impressed were Ward and the university's lab-animal veterinarian with Crowe's transport cages and interest in the animals that they let him have three additional pairs of bushbabies. For a decade, Ward had cared for the world's only captive colony of bushbabies, never subjecting them to any invasive research, and this seemed like a fitting finalé for some of those animals: They would be displayed in a private zoo.

A week or two later, however, Ward received a telephone call from someone who had been offered the bushbabies for $2,500 a pair. Before that, Ward was told, Crowe had tried to unload her primates at a Texas auction. Shortly thereafter, Crowe reportedly surfaced at the Lolli Brothers auction, in Missouri, trying to peddle what remained of his bushbaby collection. "I think an auction is horrible," Ward says. "It takes into account no consideration of where the animals are going."

Ward was furious for other reasons: Crowe had told her that he didn't indiscriminately sell animals, though he said that he occasionally peddled one to an individual with the knowledge and resources to provide it care. He told her he was licensed only as a breeder/retailer and never sold wholesale, which, she complained, also isn't true.

Where the bushbabies went is uncertain, but by the following year only a few of them remained at Ashby Acres. Ward is still enraged by the 1995 incident, although she says she can take some solace in the fact that some of the other bushbabies she sold were not consigned to such unhappy fates. By way of example, she donated two to the Memphis Zoo and sold some to the Kansas City Zoo. In addition, Ward points to New Jersey's Animal Kingdom Zoo, whose owner, Burton Sipp, sends occasional postcards to keep her apprised of the ten breeding pairs and two babies that he took in July 1996.

What Ward didn't know, however, was that nine months after she sent Sipp the bushbabies, he in turn consigned a pair of the primates to the Woods & Waters auction, in Ohio. And early in 1998, a "Reduction Sale!" ad with a New Jersey phone number appeared in *Animal Finders' Guide*. Along with squirrel monkeys, spider monkeys, and olive baboons, Burton Sipp was offering a breeding pair of bushbabies. Price: $2,500. He also had a newborn bushbaby up for grabs ($1,500). Sipp had found another profit center.

6

Unholy Alliances

Twenty-eight years after the U.S. Fish and Wildlife Service designated the peregrine falcon an endangered species, thereby affording it government protection, the agency decreed that enough of the swift birds were thriving across the nation to warrant their formal removal from the endangered list. The service's proposal to "delist" the peregrine falcon, published in the August 26, 1998, edition of the *Federal Register,* was accompanied by a triumphant statement from Interior Secretary Bruce Babbitt. "Every American should be proud," Babbitt had proclaimed during a visit to Stone Mountain Park, just east of Atlanta. "In twenty-five years, the people of the United States have rescued this awesome raptor from the brink of extinction. We have proved that a strong Endangered Species Act can make a difference. We don't have to stand idly by and watch our wildlife go extinct. We can bring species back. We have proved it with the peregrine falcon."

By no means was there universal agreement that the peregrine falcon's outlook was secure enough to warrant its removal from the endangered list. But the government-led effort to ensure the bird's survival, bolstered by help from the Peregrine Fund and two other conservation organizations, certainly produced a dramatic recovery. In 1970, when the swift bird of prey was added to the endangered list, its population in some parts of the United States had declined by as much as 90 percent below historical levels. Five years later, a census showed a scant three hundred twenty-four nesting pairs in North America—the bird having fallen victim to the pesticide DDT, which caused its eggshells to thin so dramatically that they broke during incubation.

The Environmental Protection Agency's 1972 ban on the use of DDT provided the peregrine falcon hope of recovery, as did the Endangered Species Act, which makes it illegal to harm protected species. Captive breeding and release programs, conducted by the federal government in concert with state agencies, independent researchers, and private conservation organizations, sent thousands of peregrines back into the wild. By the time the Fish and Wildlife Service proposed delisting the bird, ornithologists and government agencies in Canada and the United States were able to document at least 1,593 breeding pairs—far above the recovery goal of 631 pairs. "It would have been hard to imagine this day back in the 1970s when there were so few peregrines left," Babbitt proclaimed, "but it shows how effective a law the Endangered Species Act is when allowed to work as it was intended."

But not all provisions of this controversial law provide wildlife the sort of protection that Congress intended, that the public envisioned, or that Babbitt would tout before the cameras. By artfully exploiting loopholes in the Endangered Species Act, exotic-animal dealers have rendered some parts of the law virtually meaningless, turning protected species like tigers, snow leopards, and lemurs into just more pet-trade fodder. And the dealers have done so with an unlikely set of partners: the nation's zoos, research centers, and universities, which keep them well stocked with their endangered surplus.

Consider the case of the New England Regional Primate Research Center, which is affiliated with the Harvard University Medical School. Supported by the National Institutes of Health, NERPRC is one of seven regional primate centers established by Congress. The center's research, which has focused on AIDS and other infectious diseases, drug addiction, and chronic neurological disorders, is conducted by some five dozen doctoral-level scientists and more than one hundred technical and support staff. In addition to performing biomedical research aimed at cures for human health problems, the institution's stated mission includes the study of nonhuman primates "to enhance their scientific utility, health, and well-being."

The center houses approximately fourteen hundred primates, including baboons, squirrel monkeys, common marmosets, and rhesus monkeys. It also maintains the nation's largest colony of cotton-top tamarins, squirrel-size monkeys native to parts of northern Colombia. The U.S. government added the arboreal primate to the endangered list in October 1976, and recent estimates put the number remaining in the wild at only two thousand to three thousand. As deforestation accelerates, the tamarin's future becomes increasingly perilous.

Each year, approximately two hundred monkeys are born at the New England Regional Primate Research Center, and about four dozen are euthanized for reasons of poor health—typically, from stress associated with the research. Like the nation's other primate centers, NERPRC also sells or donates animals to a variety of facilities, including hospitals, medical schools, and, on rare occasions, zoos. In 1997, the center sold nineteen monkeys; the year before that, fifty-nine.

But in 1995, the Harvard-affiliated research center sold more than three hundred primates, half of which were cotton-top tamarins. Because of this monkey's endangered status, the center could sell its unwanted surplus only to those granted special permits by the U.S. Fish and Wildlife Service. This provision of the Endangered Species Act is supposed to protect threatened and endangered animals from ending up in the hands of unscrupulous dealers and others who may not be committed to the enhancement or propagation of the species. Furthermore, this section of the law is intended as a statement that the United States will cooperate with global efforts to protect a wide array of endangered species, no matter where their historic range or current distribution.

But finding buyers for large numbers of cotton-top tamarins can be problematic. AZA zoos are the most likely outlets, since they participate in a Species Survival Plan for cotton-tops. But of the fifty or so AZA institutions that display the one-pound primates, about two-thirds keep three or fewer. Faced with the prospects, then, of having to provide its endangered monkeys long-term care, the New England Regional Primate Research Center petitioned the U.S. Fish and Wildlife Service to exempt captive-born cotton-tops and their progeny from the provisions of the Endangered Species Act, a change in the law that would have freed the university to sell its unwanted cotton-tops to anyone, or even euthanize them. Precedent under this special rule had already been established with chimpanzees, Japanese macaques, and twelve other primates. The impetus for this dual status had come from the research community, which persuaded the government that their captive-born primates didn't need as much legal protection as those caught in the wild. As a result, chimps and Japanese macaques born in captivity, along with their progeny, may be sold at exotic-animal auctions, or just about anywhere else not prohibited by local law, without regard for the buyer's qualifications.

The U.S. Fish and Wildlife Service ultimately denied Harvard's petition, but the primate center managed with the status quo: In May 1995, it began ridding itself of the unwanted cotton-top tamarins, selling seventy-four that month to a facility that had the required federal permit. By late October, one hundred fifty-one of the endangered primates were gone, all shipped to "Tanganyika Wildlife Park," near Wichita, Kansas. Thirty-one common marmosets—nonendangered primates—also went to Tanganyika Wildlife Park, according to the primate center's annual report to the U.S. Fish and Wildlife Service.

The real name of this operation is actually Tanganyika Wildlife Company. It is not a zoo or a park, nor is it classified by the government as an exhibitor of any sort. Rather, it's the place from which Jim Fouts— one of the dealers exposed by *60 Minutes* in 1990 for reselling zoo animals at auction—conducts his animal-dealing operation. Fouts's facilities are described by visitors as first-rate: There is ample space, the grounds and buildings are well maintained, the animals are humanely treated.

Unlike many other dealers, Fouts receives high marks from government inspectors for his compliance with Animal Welfare Act standards. But his business is dealing animals, whether to backyard collectors, roadside attractions, or auction barns, and before long he was advertising the availability of Harvard's cotton-top tamarins and common marmosets in *Animal Finders' Guide,* the pet-trade magazine. Shortly thereafter, the monkeys were being shipped across the country.

Of the one hundred fifty-one cotton-top tamarins sent to Fouts by NERPRC, it appears that only a single male was subsequently transferred to an AZA zoo. By the following February, thirty-two of the endangered monkeys at Fouts's facility had died from bacterial infections, fights among themselves, and the stress of shipment. Some of the others were sent to dealers, a Pennsylvania roadside zoo, and individuals without dealer or exhibitor licenses—all legal transactions, because of loopholes in the Endangered Species Act. Although endangered species such as cotton-top tamarins may be sold across state lines only to individuals or institutions with a federal permit, those same animals may be sold in-state to virtually anyone, whether a bona fide zoological park or a backyard collector. In essence, any transaction that does not entail interstate or foreign commerce falls through a gaping crack in the Endangered Species Act. The recipient is not required to educate the public about the conservation needs of the endangered species in question, for example, or help in any other way to enhance its propagation or survival. What's more, the law allows those same cotton-top tamarins, like any endangered species, to be legally shipped across state lines if no money changes hands—a loophole literally big enough to drive a truck through. In other words, "donate" the animals or make them available on a "breeding loan," and they can be hauled across state lines to the individual or institution of your choosing. The recipient may then sell the animals at an in-state auction, give them away, or cage them in his basement. And as a thank-you, he may return the favor with a "donation" of his own.

Although Fouts paid an undisclosed amount for the one hundred fifty-one cotton-top tamarins (they typically sell for about $1,500 apiece in the pet trade), he claims to have given away more than one hundred of them. He sent one pair of the cotton-top tamarins to Susan Kriz, a collector in Shueyville, Iowa. Three months later, sheriff's deputies removed from Kriz's residence fifty pet monkeys, many of them suffering from malnutrition and dehydration. Veterinarians who inspected the property found deplorable conditions, resulting in civil proceedings alleging animal neglect. "The stench of feces was so strong that the people removing the primates were also negatively affected," Judge Larry Conmey later wrote in his ruling. "Live and dead rats were observed in the premises. Litter, debris, and garbage was strewn about the inside of the premises. A prairie dog was permitted to run at large in the home, burrowing holes in the sheet rock and running through the walls of the home." The neglect was so severe, the judge ruled, that it contributed to the death of two monkeys. Although Kriz hoped to reclaim her pets, including an endangered lemur, eight spider monkeys, and four cotton-top tamarins (Fouts had given another cotton-top to Kriz a year earlier), the court denied her request and ordered that the animals instead be sent to zoos or sanctuaries.

Fouts sent most of Harvard's cotton-top tamarins—ninety-one in all—to James Anderson, an animal dealer in Fort Lauderdale, Florida, who did business as Exotic Pets and Zoological Animal Exchange, Inc. Anderson was sent his first shipment of eighteen "imperfects" (animals with missing fingers or shortened tails, for example) on September 2, 1995. Four weeks later, the U.S. Department of Agriculture, which had been investigating Anderson for suspected violations of the Animal Welfare Act, took away his dealer's license for a month.

One area of the government's inquiry stemmed from Anderson's sale of a female squirrel monkey to an Illinois woman. The buyer, who learned of the monkey's availability through an advertisement in *Animal Finders' Guide,* wired Anderson a thousand dollars plus shipping fees, then went to Chicago O'Hare International Airport to claim her new pet, which she hoped would be a suitable companion for her six-month-old male squirrel monkey. When the Pet Taxi door was opened later that evening, Emily emerged: She was missing two-thirds of her tail and a finger on her left hand. Two fingers on her right hand were paralyzed. A toe on her left foot was paralyzed. There was a wound on her face. She was covered with an unidentifiable hard, sticky substance. The pads on her hands and feet were burnt raw, apparently from standing in her own urine for four days. Parts of her were covered with excrement. Her eyes were glazed and watery. Her front teeth had been filed down. Her breathing was labored. She had diarrhea. No health certificate accompanied the shipment, as the law requires. Her chest was tattooed with blue letters and numbers, which is the standard practice of research laboratories. She was, in the parlance of the pet trade, an imperfect.

Florida wildlife officers say that Anderson, one of South Florida's major dealers, has been repeatedly cited for transferring animals throughout the state to those without the required permits. Anderson earned some public notoriety for reportedly plucking monkeys from two free-roaming colonies, where descendants of refugees from shut-down tourist attractions had lived for decades, then selling or trading them. The U.S. Fish and Wildlife Service, which monitored Anderson's activities for years, finally seized his records in 1998, but the longtime dealer is still in business.

Anderson helped make the cotton-top tamarin an increasingly familiar exotic pet, an unfortunate achievement for any number of reasons. Because the small monkeys are unusually fragile and susceptible to colon cancer, poor animal husbandry can doom them. What's more, should the demand for them in the United States escalate, poachers and smugglers will undoubtedly further decimate the remaining wild population. That's precisely why the United States and other nations offer international treaty protection to nonnative animals that are rapidly disappearing: Removed from the stream of legal commerce, these species are, it's hoped, less vulnerable to those who might exploit them for profit. Ironically, however, it is the Endangered Species Act itself that has made the cotton-top tamarin's status even more precarious: In October 1976, just before the monkey's addition to the list of endangered species, dealers rushing to beat the deadline imported nearly eight hundred of the vanishing primates into the United States. None of them were from their native Colombia, but rather from other countries in Central and South America—a clear indication that the monkeys had been illegally poached. This was on top of the estimated twenty thousand to thirty thousand that had already been imported for use at Harvard and other research institutions, decimating the wild population.

—◦—

Fouts's enterprise, Tanganyika Wildlife Company, is licensed by the government as a Class B animal dealer, a designation indicating that its primary business is the brokering of animals. If that alone weren't enough to raise a red flag at Harvard, officials of the primate center could have taken the obvious step of contacting the Kansas Animal Health Department, whose estimable record-keeping system would have turned up for them one document after another revealing that Fouts's clients include roadside zoos, exotic-animal auctions, dealers such as Anderson, and even individual pet owners. Tanganyika Wildlife Company's annual reports to the U.S. Fish and Wildlife Service show more or less the same thing.

But performing such honest-to-goodness due diligence is exactly what primate centers, as well as zoos and other institutions with unwanted animals, aim to avoid. Knowing the truth about where a dealer resells his animals could have serious financial consequences—namely, the institution might not be able to continue doing business with that middleman. If the Harvard Medical School couldn't plausibly deny knowledge of Fouts's involvement in the pet trade, it might have been stuck caring for the endangered cotton-top tamarins.

NERPRC has a strict policy against selling endangered species to dealers who would redistribute them to the pet trade—a prohibition that's stipulated in every contract, according to Don Gibbons, the director of the medical school's office of public affairs. (He declined, however, to provide a copy of the contract with Fouts.) Then how did the monkeys end up being sold throughout South Florida? "We can't help it," Gibbons says, "if someone does that."

The sale and subsequent redistribution of the cotton-top tamarins show just how anemic the provisions of the Endangered Species Act are. And to grasp how the system has warped the thinking of just about everyone in it, consider the view from Harvard's end of the pipeline. Gibbons, for instance, points with pride to the huge colony of cotton-tops housed at the medical school, where the only research performed, he says—seemingly oblivious to the irony of his own words—is aimed at keeping the monkeys alive.

—◦—

The policies of the New England Regional Primate Research Center are hardly in keeping with the spirit of the Endangered Species Act, which was first enacted in 1966 as the Endangered Species Preservation Act. In its original form, the law allowed the Secretary of the Interior to compile a list of endangered native species and to provide them limited protection—the acquisition of habitat, for example. In 1969, the passage of the Endangered Species Conservation Act offered additional protection to species in danger of "worldwide extinction" by prohibiting their importation, as well as their subsequent sale within the United States. That rewrite of the law also called for an international summit to adopt a convention on the conservation of endangered species.

A 1973 conference in Washington, D.C., led to the adoption of the Convention on International Trade in Endangered Species of Wild Fauna and Flora, a global treaty designed to protect the world's wildlife from exploitative trade. On the heels of this landmark agreement, a near-unanimous Congress, urged on by the Nixon Administration, passed the Endangered Species Act of 1973. The amended act made the protection of both threatened and endangered species—as well as their habitats—a bona fide government priority, combining U.S. and foreign endangered-species lists, for example, and creating uniform provisions that applied to the species listed on either. By so doing, the U.S. government decreed that nonnative species such as the cotton-top tamarin could enjoy the same protected status as the peregrine falcon, which can now be found nesting both on American cliff-sides and atop big-city skyscrapers.

The Endangered Species Act is aimed chiefly at the import, export, sale, and "taking" (hunting, collecting, or even harassing, for example) of endangered and threatened species. (Species in danger of extinction are listed as endangered; species likely to become endangered in the fore-seeable future are listed as threatened.) The wide-ranging conservation law makes it unlawful to import or export any listed species without the proper permits, and it also requires permits for interstate or foreign commerce involving protected species. But there is a problem. Because the law regulates only commerce, those issued permits by the U.S. Fish and Wildlife Service are free to "donate" their animals to friends, pet-trade breeders, or virtually anyone else. For example, dealers with captive-bred wildlife registration permits, which authorize the sale and purchase of nonnative listed species that have been born in the United States, know that they can freely mislabel and otherwise lie about their transactions, and they do so with a vengeance. The sham—a dare-you-to-prove-otherwise fixture in the annual reports that permit-holders must file—frustrates officials of the U.S. Fish and Wildlife Service, who can only watch helplessly as it is carried out. "To prove that it really wasn't a donation, you'd have to put all kinds of staff power into some kind of undercover investigation," an endangered-species specialist at the agency says. With limited resources, agency officials add, such investigations are rare. And so the dealers and roadside-zoo operators, who need only fill out a relatively simple application to get a captive-bred wildlife registration permit, write "donation" or "gratis" on their annual reports and continue to commit their crimes with impunity.

What's more, the Endangered Species Act allows anything from a Siberian tiger to a swamp deer—both classified by the government as endangered—to be sold in-state, resold, bred and sold again, with no credentials or federal permits required of the buyers. As a result, the original intent of the law—that even nonnative animals be protected from commercial exploitation—has been warped almost beyond recognition.

For example, there are thousands of pet tigers in the United States, the great predators having been turned into seven-foot lapdogs for status-seeking owners, profiteering charlatans posing as conservationists, and those delusional enough to believe that their backyard or basement cages are somehow contributing to the enhancement and protection of the species. So overbred, inbred, and crossbred are tigers in the United States that in October 1998 the U.S. Fish and Wildlife Service gave in and declared that anyone is free to buy and sell "generic" tigers—that is, those that can't be identified as purebred members of Bengal, Sumatran, Siberian, or Indochinese subspecies. Since then, patrons of exotic-animal auctions have been free to buy crossbred tigers and cart them across state lines. Such buyers must be prepared only to say that their purchase was for purposes of breeding, should the authorities come knocking—which they almost never do. Dealers are also free to sell pure-bred tigers at auction and claim they're "generics"; after all, no one will order DNA testing. What's more, *Animal Finders' Guide* advertisers are now free to sell their cubs to out-of-state buyers without U.S. Fish and Wildlife Service permits.

In short, the United States celebrated the year of the tiger by removing the only major impediment to the great cat becoming an even more prominent fixture of the exploitative pet trade. And six months after that rule change, it appeared that tigers were already heading the way of African lions, which today sell for a few hundred dollars live (assuming a buyer can be found) and fetch about a buck a pound from exotic-meat dealers. At the Lolli Brothers auction, in April 1999, a male tiger cub sold for about $350 and a female fetched even less. In fact, there are now so many tigers in the United States—for every tiger in an AZA zoo there are, by some estimates, twenty in private hands—that it may not be long before the Asian medicinal trade turns to America for its tiger bones, penises, and other body parts. The entrepreneurs who found profit in slaughtering bears for their paws, teeth, and gall bladders will then, of course, diversify.

◄○►

Sadly, the tiger's fate, like that of the cotton-top tamarin, is nothing more than history repeating itself. Although some exhibitors have worked diligently to protect endangered species—participating in inter-zoo exchange programs designed to head off inbreeding, for instance—others have simply shipped their unwanted animals out the back door. The animals trucked off from accredited zoos rarely, if ever, find their way back, so their removal means that they no longer have any role to play in the preservation of their species. Banished from the AZA community, which keeps close tabs on lineage, the animals are of no use to bona fide conservation efforts. They're just pets, castoffs, and curiosities.

Lemurs are a prime example. When Dr. Stephanie Ostrowski, of the Centers for Disease Control and Prevention, studied primate transfers from AZA zoos over two decades, she documented more than eight hundred lemurs "lost to follow-up." Finding lemurs, however, is not at all difficult: They're for sale every month in *Animal Finders' Guide,* including babies, adults, and proven breeding pairs. Robert Crowe maintains a breeding colony of lemurs that provides him with "product" for the exotic-animal auctions, sales to buyers in Florida, and "donations" to dealers and others outside of Florida. He donated a female ring-tailed lemur, for example, to Marvin and Linda LaFrentz, who are USDA-licensed dealers in Lorena, Texas, just south of Waco. Not long ago, Linda LaFrentz penned a tribute to "Precious," a ringtail that now prefers Dairy Queen cheeseburgers and fries to her old fruit-and-biscuit diet and, in what unquestionably must be a first for her species, has started to speak English. "One day, to our shock and amazement, when Marvin stuck his head in the door she [Precious] said, 'Hi,'" LaFrentz wrote. "When it is time for her to come in the house (for now she stays with the other lemurs some) if she isn't ready to come in she says 'No.' She means it, too."

Crowe, who in the spring of 1998 was stripped of his captive-bred wildlife registration permit for not filing an annual report and failing USDA animal-welfare inspections, built his lemur colony with surplus from, among others, the AZA-accredited zoo in Racine, Wisconsin, and the highly regarded Duke University Primate Center in Durham, North Carolina.

It's hardly surprising that the Racine Zoological Gardens would send Crowe its lemurs. This, after all, is the zoo that has supplied Mark Schoebel with aoudads, elk, and lions, showing once again why the cornerstone of the AZA's code of professional ethics—that animals will not be handed over to those not qualified to care for them properly—is an empty oath. That an institution as highly regarded as Duke University would have dealt with a Robert Crowe, however, lays bare the extremes to which some go in getting rid of unwanted animals. For many dealers, in fact, the supply pipeline starts at some of the nation's most prestigious research facilities.

Duke, for example, also sent lemurs to Thomas Nichols a year and a half before the high-profile Georgia dealer was indicted on primate-trafficking charges and to Northland Wildlife, another party to the federal indictment. Another destination was Finser Exotics, in Umatilla, Florida, a breeding farm whose lemurs and other primates are regularly advertised in *Animal Finders' Guide*. Through its "Adopt-a-Lemur" program, Duke University solicits contributions of up to $1,000 a year to help ensure a "bright future" for these endangered animals, although many of its donors undoubtedly would be shocked to learn the track record of the institution they are supporting.

The record of many AZA zoos is no better. Central Florida Zoological Park, an AZA member in Monroe, Florida, has sent a lemur to Nichols. Antonio Alentado, one of Nichols's co-defendants in the primate-trafficking case, got lemurs from the Miami MetroZoo and the San Diego Zoo. In the late 1980s, Southwick Wild Animal Farm, a roadside attraction and animal dealer in Mendon, Massachusetts, got more than a half-dozen lemurs from Beardsley Zoological Gardens, in nearby Bridgeport, Connecticut. The Greater Baton Rouge Zoo sent a lemur to Smoky Mountain Zoological Park, in Pigeon Forge, Tennessee, an unaccredited operation that has never been open to the public and whose owner buys and sells exotic animals at the big auctions. (Among them are binturongs, which have come to Pigeon Forge from Baton Rouge and from the Cleveland Metroparks Zoo, another AZA member.) Highwater Farms of Kipling, North Carolina, whose stock of pet marmosets has come at least partly from the research labs of drug company Bristol-Myers Squibb, got one of its lemurs from the Nashville Zoo, which is not a member of the AZA. The lemur in question actually was on loan from St. Catherine's Wildlife Conservation Center, in Georgia, a breeding facility for rare and endangered species that's an arm of the Bronx

Zoo, which is a member of the AZA. And so while the Bronx Zoo rightly trumpets its hundreds of admirable field projects—tracking snow leopards in Nepal, for instance, and helping to reduce the illicit trade in rhinoceros horn—its curators, like so many of their AZA colleagues, show a pitifully limited sense of responsibility for animals no longer deemed "useful" to their global conservation projects.

Some exhibitors, such as Lion Country Safari, in Loxahatchee, Florida, will hand their endangered species to just about anyone. One recent year, for example, the drive-through park noted on its annual report to the U.S. Fish and Wildlife Service that it had sent three Brazilian tapirs to "Florida Sanctuary." This so-called sanctuary is actually Ashby Acres Wildlife Park, Robert Crowe's animal-dealing operation. In May 1995, Lion Country Safari sold three chimpanzees to an animal dealer in northern Florida. In late 1998, even though his USDA license had lapsed, this dealer advertised the sale of "proven breeder" chimps in *Animal Finders' Guide;* subsequently, these chimps apparently landed at a roadside zoo in Georgia. Among those to whom Lion Country Safari sent gibbons was an Arizona man who, months earlier, was featured in news stories after he sneaked another of his pet gibbons on a commercial airliner, in violation of federal regulations. (The gibbon that Lion Country Safari sent this private collector, who also had been stopped trying to bring one of these apes into the U.S. Capitol, was actually "on loan" from the San Antonio Zoo.) That same year, Lion Country Safari sent four endangered Indian pythons to Strictly Reptiles, in nearby Broward County, one of the nation's largest reptile importers and pet-trade wholesalers. Among its other distinctions, Strictly Reptiles used to frequently throw injured snakes and reptiles in its dumpster rather than provide them with veterinary care. Schoolchildren in the neighborhood took to fishing the half-dead creatures from among the garbage and walking them to nearby exotic-animal veterinarian Terri Parrott—an afternoon ritual that ended only after a Florida wildlife officer, acting on the complaints of both neighbors and Parrott, padlocked the dumpster. In the summer of 1997, the owner of Strictly Reptiles, Michael Van Nostrand, was fined $250,000 and sentenced to eight months in prison, to be followed by eight months of home confinement, after he pleaded guilty to smuggling more than fifteen hundred rare animals into the United States. The following February, the U.S. Fish and Wildlife Service revoked his company's import-export license for five years.

In 1996, Lion Country Safari sent a Brazilian tapir to Charles "Buddy" Jordan, the owner of NBJ Ranch, in Bulverde, Texas. Although Jordan refers to his two-hundred-acre spread as a zoological park, it's really just a private menagerie that's classified by the government as an animal-dealing operation. The collection is maintained by Jordan and his wife, Nancy, who have posted signs around their property that say: "Guard on duty. Surviving trespassers will be prosecuted."

Jordan has built his collection of fifteen hundred animals mostly with "surplus" from AZA zoos, some of which can't seem to breed their stock fast enough for the Texas dealer. In 1996 alone, in six separate transactions, the Montgomery Zoo sent Jordan forty-five animals, including endangered Eld's brow-antlered deer and slender-horned gazelles. Busch Gardens Tampa Bay, the theme park that's owned by Anheuser-Busch Companies, sent Jordan nineteen animals one year and followed the next spring with four impalas and three Grant's gazelles. Later that summer, Jordan trucked away another three dozen animals from Busch Gardens, including a ring-tailed lemur. Among the animals Jordan got from the Jacksonville Zoo were a pair of ruffed lemurs and a siamang (a member of the gibbon group), all endangered species.

More than two dozen AZA zoos have continued to send animals to Jordan, even though they may have good reason not to. In the summer of 1994, after a two-year investigation, the Humane Society of the United States reported that zoos across the United States had either sold animals directly to hunting ranches or to dealers who had done business with auctions or hunts. Jordan was among the board members of the San Antonio Zoo who, the Humane Society said, bought surplus animals from the zoo and who owned ranches "where hunting occurs." Jordan, the secretary-treasurer of the Exotic Wildlife Association, the Texas-based hunting lobby, adamantly denied the charges, and in fact denied any direct involvement with so-called canned hunts. "There's no hunting of any kind of animal on this place," he told a reporter for the Associated Press. "As far as that's concerned, I do not sell them direct to a hunting range." But in May 1996 Jordan sent nineteen adult elk to Heartland Wildlife Company, in Bucklin, Missouri. "Trophy elk hunters thoroughly enjoy their hunts here at Heartland," a promotional letter for the hunting ranch says. "These are extraordinary animals and this is a great opportunity to add a spectacular trophy to your collection."

In 1998, it was controversy of an entirely different sort that dogged Jordan. When the California Department of Fish and Game ordered a couple in Alamo Oaks, fifty miles east of San Francisco, to dispose of seven capuchin monkeys and a male-female pair of adult chimpanzees, animal-welfare organizations tried to find a sanctuary willing to take the longtime pets. But the California authorities preempted the effort and gave the entire group to Jordan, who trucked the animals to what he described for a local newspaper as a "primate preserve for rare, endangered species."

Jordan went on to say that he collected animals as a hobby, not for money. "We're going to keep them," he told Michael Peña, a reporter for the Contra Costa *Times,* before he took the nine primates to Texas. "We enjoy having animals." That was February 11. The female chimp died on March 14 from blood clots in her pulmonary arteries, and on April 25 Jordan sent fifteen-year-old Jimmy Joe (who was rumored to have been born at the St. Louis Zoo and sold as an infant) to an animal dealer in southwestern Kansas whose preferred sale venues include auctions in Missouri and Texas.

Jordan's NBJ Ranch is a high-volume operation that sometimes trucks animals across the border to Mexico. Endangered species account for a substantial number of Jordan's sales. Over a three-year period ending in 1996, for example, Jordan reported to the U.S. Fish and Wildlife Service that he sold more than one hundred endangered species. He sold twenty-six lemurs to pet owners, exotic-animal dealers, and Noah's Land, a drive-through park/animal-dealing outfit in Harwood, Texas, whose inventory was auctioned in 1997 after the business went under. In the same period, Jordan sold eland to Castleberry Triple 7, a family-operated animal-dealing enterprise that once included a low-rent auction where animals were sometimes trampled in the holding areas. Jordan sold Eld's deer and Arabian oryx to Y.O. Ranch, a hunting operation that also runs an annual exotic-animal auction. He sold four Arabian oryx and one Grevy's zebra to the owners of Chulagua Ranch, who also own an exotic-animal auction called Showplace Hill. He sold a pair of Arabian oryx to Kifaru, an exotic-animal auction run by canned-hunt supplier Jurgen Schulz, the co-owner of Catskill Game Farm. He sold Grevy's zebras to a Missouri dealer who advertises zebras and other mammals in *Animal Finders' Guide*. He sold hog deer to Forest Exotics, the hunting ranch and exotic-game breeder to which Wild Safari's addax were sent. And he sold Eld's deer and hog deer to Parker Creek Ranch, one of about a dozen ranches, mainly in Texas, that have "cull" permits from the U.S. Fish and Wildlife Service. These permits, which authorize the hunting of excess male hoofed stock for "enhancement of survival of the species," are essentially licenses to conduct government-sanctioned canned hunts. Hunter Schuehle, a San Antonio lawyer who owns Parker Creek Ranch, was authorized by U.S. Fish and Wildlife to "take"— whether by sport-hunting or other means—excess male red lechwes, dama gazelles, barasingha deer, Arabian oryx, and Eld's deer. In 1992, when Schuehle's permit to cull endangered species was held up by biologists at the agency, he flew to Washington to make his case in person; when that proved ineffective, he pressed members of Congress to intervene on his behalf. In one of his letters to the U.S. Fish and Wildlife Service, Schuehle explained that he was trying to beat the clock. "I am tired of them looking bad and standing around like they are dead due to no teeth," he wrote, "and having them fall over from starvation and old age." Schuehle got the permit.

Jordan also sells Brazilian tapirs, a disappearing species native to the Amazon rain forest, some of which came from AZA zoos in Cleveland, Houston, Seattle, and Garden City, Kansas. The Cleveland Metroparks Zoo's two tapirs, Molly and Little John, came to Jordan via a circuitous route: In July 1992, the Cleveland zoo entrusted the animals to Northland Wildlife, of Grand Rapids, Minnesota, whose owner, Robert

Troumbly, had been indicted just weeks earlier on federal primate-trafficking charges. Zoo officials say they thought the tapirs were going to Bohn's Ark, an unaccredited zoo in Hinckley, Minnesota, but Troumbly actually transported them to Jordan. Unfortunately, one of the tapirs died not long after the fifteen-hundred-mile truck ride to Jordan's ranch.

The tapirs leaving Jordan's property sometimes don't fare much better. A couple of them, for example, went to a Texas dealer who at the time lived in a compound that one visitor has likened to an illegal dump. Three olive baboons were confined to a filthy three-by-four-foot cage, with almost no protection from the elements. Beside it were cages filled with rattlesnakes and lizards. The grounds were littered from one end to the other with empty cat-food cans. The tapirs were housed in a hundred-year-old barn made of river rock. Their water source was an old, rusted washtub. Two twenty-foot-long pythons were housed in the next stall. The dealer, who had let her permits to trade in animals lapse, tried to unload her inventory before she and a companion moved from the squalid compound to an assisted-living facility. But before she could do so the male tapir ate one of the plastic garbage bags littering the property and died.

◄○►

Jordan's sale of endangered species to such buyers is not surprising, since he is, after all, an animal dealer. What's surprising is that so many zoos and other avowed conservationists dispose of their endangered species in much the same way. White Oak Conservation Center, in the northernmost part of Florida, is a prime example. The six-hundred-acre retreat, which is on land owned by Gilman Paper Company, is home to a diverse collection of endangered and threatened species. One of only two dozen AZA "Related Organizations," the center breeds vanishing animals, provides veterinary training, and sponsors various global efforts to boost the survival chances of threatened species. It is the place that the Florida Game and Fresh Water Fish Commission sometimes sends rescued or abandoned exotics, and it occasionally hosts international gath-

Lolli (or is it Macon?), shortly before Reston Animal Park's bears were trucked to Ohio (or was it Wisconsin?). When police officers arrived at Susan Kriz's Iowa home, they found a trash-filled living room overrun with caged monkeys and makeshift cages. She kept endangered cotton-top tamarins, castoffs from the Harvard University Medical School, in another living-room cage at the far left.

Dumping grounds: Ashby Acres "Wildlife Park" (top) got mona monkeys from Zoo Atlanta and "surplus" macaques from zoos in Milwaukee, Pittsburgh, and Syracuse. The now-defunct Scotch Plains Zoo (center), which Seattle's Woodland Park Zoo deemed appropriate for two unwanted orangutans. (Photo credit: New Jersey Division of Fish, Game & Wildlife) Animal Kingdom Pet Store & Zoo (bottom), where the National Zoo's young giraffe, Michael, died in a fight. This New Jersey zoo gets rid of its unwanted animals through ads in *Animal Finders' Guide*.

Reduction Sale!

White bearded WILDEBEEST male, 3 years old,	$ 1500
Reticulated GIRAFFE female, 19 years old,	$ 17,500
ZEBRA female, 5 years old, with ZEEDONK female at side,	$ 7500
BUSHBABY breeding pair,	$ 2500 pair
SPIDER MONKEYS, 1.1,	$ 5800 pair
SQUIRREL MONKEYS, 5 males,	$ 3000 group
North American PORCUPINE,	$ 250
Nilgai ANTELOPE, 1.2,	$ 2000 trio
White faced CAPUCHINS, 2 males,	$ 1500 both
Toco TOUCAN,	$ 1250
PATAS MONKEYS pair with female baby,	$ 7500 group
GRIVET MONKEYS, 2 males,	$ 500 each
Japanese SNOW MACAQUES, 3.2,	$ 6000 group

Mountain lions have become increasingly popular as pets. A now-grown Buffy (top), once owned as a cub by baseball star Jose Canseco, was brought to Dr. Terri Parrott's veterinary clinic after being seized by wildlife officers. After Catherine Twiss and her husband trucked their menagerie to a Mississippi farm, one of the couple's full-grown cougars was confined for months in an oil drum. The owner of this adult cougar (left), kept as a pet in an Illinois basement, is licensed by the USDA as an "exhibitor," the same designation given to zoos. (Photo credit: Doll Stanley/IDA)

The bidding gets underway (top) at the Lolli Brothers Alternative Livestock and Bird Sale, in Macon, Missouri. The program for the spring 1999 sale boasts animals large and small (live or mounted). A crush of animals (bottom) wait their turn in the auction ring at L Cross Ranch, in Okeechobee, Florida.

At Buckhorn Flats Game Farm, in Wisconsin, the carcass of a "full-curl" bighorn sheep is loaded into a pickup and driven to the nearby woods, where the paying "hunter" can pose with his kill. After Buckhorn Flats owner Stanley Hall dismembers the sheep, he and a local taxidermist prepare the "trophy" for mounting. "Health certificates" show the possible origins of the slain sheep, including a South Dakota game farmer whose bighorns have come by way of the Buffalo Zoo.

Are pet macaques, which can carry the herpes B virus, living time bombs? Ringo (top) landed at Dr. Terri Parrott's veterinary clinic after being confiscated from his owner. Spock (center), another rhesus macaque, was bought as an infant from a roadside attraction and relegated as an adult to a filthy enclosure behind a commercial building. Spock was rescued and sent to a sanctuary, but was euthanized after a medical exam revealed that he was herpes B-positive and suffered from chronic medical problems. At a street festival (bottom), a woman cradles a baby rhesus macaque that has earrings in its pierced ears.

28

The "Dahlonega Five" shared two ten-by-ten-foot cubicles (above), their only source of daylight two small, grimy windows. Like the four other adult chimpanzees, Vicky (center) underwent a physical examination after being removed from the horrific cages. Her hair loss—since reversed—was the result of over-grooming by her companions, poor diet, and lack of sunlight. Emily (bottom) was "rescued" from an abusive owner by the operator of an Ohio puppy mill, who fed her such treats as Pepsi-Cola and butterscotch candies. After Emily attacked family members trying to change her diaper, the puppy-mill operator sought a new home for her pet spider monkey.

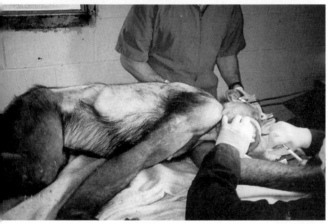

Emily and another four dozen monkeys and apes now live at the Primate Rescue Center, in Kentucky. Indoor/outdoor environments (above) give them access to sunlight and heated nighttime quarters. The thirty-by-sixty-foot enclosure and attached building (center) is home to both the Dahlonega Five and seven chimpanzees from a New York University laboratory. Four-year-old Ike (bottom), one of the former NYU chimps, has room to roam for the first time in his life.

erings on key conservation issues. When conservationists talk about White Oak, their admiration for its work is usually unrestrained.

White Oak Conservation Center also breeds a large number of animals it apparently has no use for, and its staff disposes of them accordingly: They have sent their unwanted nyala antelopes and dama gazelles to Henry Hampton. In light of White Oak's commitment to endangered species, the idea of sending Hampton dama gazelles seems especially misguided: The small, graceful antelope is on the verge of extinction in its North African habitat, with perhaps as few as twenty-five hundred remaining in the wild. Several dama subspecies have in fact already disappeared from the desert and bushland that was once their home. The IUCN–The World Conservation Union, one of the three global wildlife monitoring agencies, categorizes the dama gazelle as "endangered" on its *Red List of Threatened Animals;* some subspecies of dama gazelles are on the U.S. endangered species list as well. Sending five of its dama gazelles—three of them just nine months old—to an auction and canned-hunt supplier hardly seems to jibe with White Oak's mission of species conservation.

The Asian banteng, whose population has been decimated, in part, by the illicit trade in the wild cattle's horns, is classified by the U.S. government as endangered. The Grevy's zebra, native to the grasslands of Ethiopia and Kenya, is designated by U.S. Fish and Wildlife as threatened and is protected by international treaty. The Brazilian tapir is also classified by the U.S. government as endangered. Despite such threats to these animals, all are among the leftovers that White Oak either sold or "loaned" to Bob Brackett, an Illinois dealer with a private menagerie. The sales—but not the "loans"—appear to be improper, according to a biologist with the U.S. Fish and Wildlife service, since Brackett does not possess a captive-bred wildlife registration permit.

Brackett, who also gets animals from zoos in Kansas City, Little Rock, and other cities, buys and sells animals at auctions across the country, moving them around like pieces on a game board. He and his wife are also proprietors of the Little Ponderosa Sale, an auction where bidders can pick up the likes of fallow deer, zebras, and four-horned sheep. On occasion, the animals bought there are reconsigned to auctions elsewhere. White Oak also supplied Brackett with scimitar-horned oryx (listed as "critically endangered" on the IUCN *Red List*), as well as such nonnative mammals as nyala, greater kudu, and a roan antelope. Among others receiving animals from White Oak was Exotic Resort, a Texas drive-through park that deals animals from its facility. The "donations" included thirteen bantengs and six gaurs, large Asian cattle facing extinction in the wild. White Oak also sold two bonteboks to Oregon Wildlife Foundation, an AZA "Related Organization" whose permit from the Fish and Wildlife Service did not cover these endangered South African antelopes. Oregon Wildlife Foundation's client list includes a supplier of Big Velvet Ranch, outside of Darby, Montana, whose canned hunts were singled out for ridicule in 1998 by *Field & Stream* magazine.

—◄o►—

For all its indiscretions, however, White Oak is by no means the worst in its disregard of the spirit of the nation's endangered species laws. That distinction goes to the Tulane Regional Primate Research Center in Covington, Louisiana, for its handling of a troupe of mangabeys, monkeys native to Ghana, Togo, and other nations in western and central Africa.

Tulane, which is affiliated with the university of the same name, is the largest of the nation's seven regional primate centers supported by the National Institutes of Health. Its specialties are the study of AIDS, hepatitis, malaria, and other infectious diseases.

In the early 1980s, when the institution was still known as the Delta Center, Robert J. Gormus, a staff biologist, developed a particular interest in leprosy and for a time collaborated on his research with the Yerkes Regional Primate Research Center, at Atlanta's Emory University. The appeal of Yerkes for Gormus was the research community's only breeding colony of mangabeys, which were deemed physiologically well suited to the leprosy inquiries.

In the late 1980s, Gormus was promised federal grants to continue his work at Tulane, provided he could put together his own collection of mangabeys. But there was a problem, as journalist Deborah Blum, a winner of the Pulitzer Prize, chronicled in her 1994 book, *The Monkey Wars*. When Tulane asked the U.S. Fish and Wildlife Service about the legality of importing sooty mangabeys, which Gormus sought for his research, the agency ruled, in keeping with widely held scientific and zoological opinion, that the sooty was a subspecies of the endangered white-collared mangabey. As a result, it decreed that the sooty mangabeys could not be imported for Gormus's research purposes.

Adroit lobbying and the exploiting of connections at the National Institutes of Health, Blum writes, earned Gormus a special permit to import the mangabeys, although the agreement carried such requirements as the establishment of a mangabey breeding colony at Tulane. After assenting to the conditions, Gormus set out to round up his one hundred fifty mangabeys, a process that took him on harrowing treks to Africa. Blum vividly portrays Gormus's search for the monkeys, which brought him into contact with con men, wildlife smugglers, and African tribesmen who trapped mangabeys by placing nets on the ground and then burning down the trees in which the primates nested. After four trips to Africa, and having spent a small fortune of federal dollars, Gormus managed to round up only forty-nine of the one hundred fifty mangabeys he sought, some plucked from restaurant kitchens before their pending date with the stew pot. He bought another thirty-five mangabeys from Yerkes, reports Blum, along with fifty rhesus macaques from China, and began this new phase of his research.

But Gormus soon faced a problem: In the summer of 1993, the National Institutes of Health withdrew its funding for the leprosy project. Peter Gerone, the director of the Tulane primate center, agreed to support the mangabey colony from general funds for at least a year. Gormus was determined to continue the study, which he believed had shown early promise, and appealed to the government. In April 1994, Blum reports, Gormus learned that NIH was likely to provide enough money to finish the leprosy vaccine tests. A reprieve was in the offing.

But the money wasn't forthcoming, and Tulane immediately set about disposing of the mangabeys. There was, however, a potentially thornier problem: Because the U.S. Fish and Wildlife Service had declared these monkeys an endangered species—a ruling Tulane had accepted, and one to which it was presumably legally (and ethically) bound—the primate center could sell the unwanted animals only to individuals or institutions with the proper permits. And because the monkeys were designated endangered, Tulane did not have the option of euthanizing them.

Gerone says today that the reasons for discontinuing the leprosy research weren't financial: Not only were forty-nine monkeys too few for the experimental protocol, he says, but the imported specimens were actually found to be a different subspecies of the white-collared mangabey—a subspecies, it turned out, that could not be used for Tulane's research. At that point, Gerone says, the primate center began searching for institutions that would take them.

Gerone says that Tulane contacted at least six AZA zoos—including the zoo in Sacramento, California—in the hope of finding the mangabeys a new home. But Leslie Field, the lead keeper at the Sacramento Zoo, says that, to her knowledge, Tulane never contacted anyone there. In fact, adds Field, who is the official mangabey studbook keeper and who tracks the fate of these primates more closely than anyone in North America, "I don't know of a single zoo that was contacted."

In the end, Tulane "donated" sixteen of the monkeys to Grindstone Valley Zoo, in Chatham, Illinois, an unaccredited roadside operation whose owner, Brad Reynolds, has received large numbers of "surplus" primates from the National Zoo and other AZA members and then resold them outside the legitimate zoo community. (Reynolds shut down his place in the summer of 1998, leaving the fate of the mangabeys and his other animals in doubt.) And five weeks later, on July 20, 1994, Tulane "donated" twenty-two more mangabeys to "Tanganyika Zoo." That would be Tanganyika Wildlife Company, Jim Fouts's animal-dealing enterprise.

Just two days later, Fouts in turn "donated" ten of these breeding pairs to Mark Schoebel. This is the same Mark Schoebel who, a decade earlier, had supplied more than two dozen bears to a game farmer caught shipping decapitated, dismembered carcasses to Korea for their organs. Schoebel sells animals to canned hunts, to pet owners, to auction houses, and to anyone else he can make a buck off of. Ironically, the reason that Fouts came up with for reconsigning these endangered species to Schoebel was: "Helping Tulane find good homes for mangabeys."

How could Gerone ever justify sending the mangabeys to Tanganyika Wildlife Company, a government-licensed animal dealer that fuels the trade in pet primates? Like all the others who would trash the intent of the Endangered Species Act, Gerone exploited one of the oft-used loopholes: He "donated" the monkeys to Jim Fouts. "It was our understanding of the Endangered Species Act," Gerone writes, "that, although we were prohibited from selling the monkeys, there was nothing that prevented us from giving them away."

Gerone's interpretation of the Endangered Species Act may or may not hold water (the mangabey "donations" raised so many red flags that the U.S. Fish and Wildlife Service launched an investigation). But Gerone's reading of the Foreign Quarantine Regulations—the declaration that imported primates not be sold to dealers for use as pets, hobby, or an avocation—is both inaccurate and, it would seem, a potential source of trouble for his institution.

The regulations, which were adopted to protect human health, do not merely say that primates can't be sold to dealers for use as pets; rather, they say that live primates may be imported into the United States and sold, resold, "or otherwise distributed" only for bona fide scientific, educational, or exhibition purposes. "The maintenance of nonhuman primates as pets, hobby, or an avocation with occasional display to the general public," the regulations go on to say, "is not a permissible use." Only primates imported before October 10, 1975, as well as their progeny, are legitimately "grandfathered" as pets.

In the judgment of many state and federal public-health officials, the wording can be interpreted in only one way: Since the 1975 cutoff date, any imported monkeys or their offspring may not be sold or donated to dealers such as Jim Fouts or Mark Schoebel for redistribution to the pet trade. But the Centers for Disease Control and Prevention, which oversees the foreign quarantine regulations, has chosen to interpret the regulations more narrowly; in fact, officials of the agency have essentially decided to look the other way and allow monkeys imported after the 1975 date to be freely sent to those seeking them for their pet collections, hobbies, or avocations—in short, all the uses that even some CDC officials insist are specifically prohibited by law. Tom Demarcus, who is the assistant branch chief in charge of nonhuman primate quarantine activities, says that from a public-health standpoint, the specific diseases mentioned in the regulations—most notably, the Ebola virus—are addressed during the thirty-one-day quarantine period that follows the importation of primates. "Instead of interpreting the regulations to prevent redistribution," Demarcus says, "the major intent is to contain infectious diseases at the importers, and to prevent the animals from being imported and distributed for use as pets." The regulations, he adds, are not intended to monitor the cradle-to-grave chain of custody for every animal.

But what if monkeys imported in 1990 are used in leprosy-vaccine research, for example, and then sent to a dealer, and then another dealer for possible resale to the public? "Onward distributions do present some health and safety concerns," Demarcus says, "but they go beyond the quarantine mission." In other words, let the regulations be damned and let the state public-health officials deal with the consequences.

The fate of Tulane's mangabeys is difficult to determine. Schoebel sent some to a low-rent roadside zoo in the Wisconsin Dells, an operation that in one recent year returned the favor by sending the longtime dealer four dozen exotic deer. One of the mangabeys bit a child at the roadside zoo, and before long the rare monkeys were on the move again. Some of the mangabeys shipped by Tulane to Grindstone Valley Zoo, in Illinois, were in turn sent to an unaccredited Indiana menagerie. Despite a federal-agency dragnet, their whereabouts also remain uncertain.

As Gormus described the mangabey ordeal to Deborah Blum, he rejected the charges heaped on him by those opposed to the use of primates in medical research, such as Shirley McGreal of the International Primate Protection League. Every monkey he acquired from Africa, he told Blum, was destined to be killed there, and by purchasing them for research he spared their lives. "What really gets me is people passing judgment on this without knowing anything about it," he told Blum. "And you can't know anything about it unless you've been there. You can't imagine what it's like for those people and those animals. I don't think the people at NIH really understand. I don't think Shirley McGreal understands. And I'll tell you what the bottom line is here. The bottom line is that I saved the lives of those mangabeys."

And here's what Gormus's institution saved them for: Mangabeys grow to about thirty pounds and, if given the opportunity, will do great harm to humans. It's possible to hybridize a mangabey with a macaque (crossbreeding macaques with anything now is in vogue), thereby creating a genetic combination that would not otherwise exist in nature. Some subspecies of mangabeys are known hosts of simian immunodeficiency virus, which can jump the "species barrier" and infect humans. The endangered monkeys are reaching breeding age—an opportunity that the nation's dealers will undoubtedly exploit. In fact, two young mangabeys turned up at the Lolli Brothers sale in April 1999—a first, say auction regulars. In short, Tulane has handed the nation's profit-minded animal dealers another commodity for their inventory, thereby creating the likelihood that yet another pet-trade novelty will be established and another endangered species will be edged even further toward its ultimate demise.

7

AN EXALTATION OF LIES

For generations of schoolchildren in the New York City metropolitan area, the class-trip roster invariably included Catskill Game Farm. Founded as a private menagerie in 1933 and opened to the public eight years later, Roland Lindemann's thousand-acre spread was the place where city and suburban kids got their first close contact with both farm animals and exotic species. It was also the standard by which other petting zoos came to be measured—a successful business venture whose proprietor was well regarded by the zoo community for his high professional standards of animal care.

A German immigrant who made his money in banking, Lindemann built the game farm on his Catskill Mountains retreat, one hundred twenty miles north of Manhattan. The farm was eventually home to some two thousand animals, many of which Lindemann collected on trips to Africa and other parts of the globe. In addition to the now-familiar petting-zoo inventory of llamas, goats, and deer, which visitors could walk among and feed, Catskill Game Farm also became known throughout the world for its collections of threatened and endangered species, including addax, white rhinos, and Przewalski horses.

But the game farm did more than just display these rare animals for the public, which year after year descended on the zoo in great numbers. Lindemann also inaugurated ambitious breeding programs to help bolster captive populations. He was even credited with reintroducing animals in habitats from which they had virtually disappeared—an operation not yet attempted by most major zoos at the time.

Lindemann's pioneering work in animal husbandry and his dedication to wildlife conservation brought him widespread recognition. His success breeding the king vulture, for example, earned him an award from President Lyndon Johnson and recognition from the American Zoo and Aquarium Association (known at the time as the American Association of Zoological Parks and Aquariums). Many of the nation's major zoos, including the San Diego Zoo and the National Zoo, bought animals from Lindemann and sent him their surplus animals. Zoo directors and curators in search of better captive-breeding techniques sought his counsel. Even animal-welfare groups thought highly of him: When a deplorable roadside menagerie in southern Virginia was shut down in late 1977 and its animals put up for auction, on hand to monitor the day's events was a staff zoologist for the Humane Society of the United States. She spotted one of Lindemann's daughters among the animal dealers in attendance that morning and, in a memo, wrote of the game farm: "If all the animals went there I would be delighted."

Roland Lindemann's most notable achievement was undoubtedly his work with the Przewalski horse. The short, stocky equine is extinct in the wild, having been exterminated by humans bent on eliminating their livestock's grazing competition. Lindemann devoted considerable resources to breeding the so-called Mongolian wild horse—whose numbers at one time were believed to be fewer than a hundred—and his efforts helped pull the species from the brink of extinction. In fact, the international studbook of the Przewalski horse, which tracks the lineage of captive-bred stock back to 1899, is filled with references to animals both born at Catskill Game Farm and descended from those once stabled there.

But neither the studbook nor the laudatory newspaper articles reveal the most illuminating aspects of Lindemann's work with this critically endangered species. Two decades later, however, one former game-farm employee recalled these details vividly: A few of the zoo's Przewalski horses were relegated to a yard behind a concrete wall, away from public view. Because most zoos keep some of their animals off-exhibit, whether for breeding, quarantine, or lack of space, the attendant didn't pay much attention to the horses. But one day he noticed that some of these animals' hooves were splayed and cracked, and he asked the park's second-in-command why they weren't being given veterinary attention.

"There's no need to bother," the keeper was told. "They're going to be killed anyway."

"For what reason?" he asked, stunned by the reply.

"Lion food," the zoo official answered matter-of-factly.

As this former game-farm employee learned, slaying the critically endangered horses was simply about supply and demand: Lindemann controlled the U.S. market for the Przewalski horse, and his breeding success had produced a temporary glut. By reducing inventory, he could presumably head off a price decline and maintain his profit margins.

Lindemann's colleagues and supporters would no doubt call this story garbage, an apocryphal affront to his memory and outstanding conservation work. But this sort of unseemly profiteering was certainly in keeping with the game-farm owner's less publicized activities. For example, Lindemann routinely moved animals from Catskill Game Farm to his Rare Animal Survival Center, in Ocala, Florida. From there, exotics like impalas, sika deer, and African lechwes were dumped off on private hunting preserves and the middlemen who supply them. Among Lindemann's clients: Forest Ranch, the same Texas hunting ground on the receiving end of Wild Safari's addax and, via a middleman, the National Zoo's oryx.

Even more telling, though, was a transaction in the summer of 1987, two years before Lindemann sold Catskill Game Farm to his daughter and son-in-law, Jurgen Schulz, whose firm, J.C. Schulz, Inc., is one of the nation's largest exotic-animal dealerships. It was a one-sentence letter from Lindemann's renowned petting zoo to the Special Licenses Unit of the New York State Department of Environmental Conservation. It said simply: "We kindly request the permission to slaughter 10 captive born American black bear for human consumption." Permission was granted because horrified New York State officials could find no applicable statutes to preclude the killing of the bears that the kids on class trips so gleefully fed. Permission was extended to the next year as well.

—◄○►—

Four years after Margaret Cook finally gave up her fight against the animal-disposal policies of the Kansas City Zoo, her voice occasionally still crackles with the sort of anger and frustration that first motivated her to undertake the decade-long battle. For the most part, however, Cook talks almost dispassionately, even good-naturedly, about her travails, having long since resigned herself to the near futility of opposing an institution so able to manipulate public opinion, deflect criticism, and bury ethical misdeeds under claims that its actions not only were legal but conformed to the stringent professional guidelines of the American Zoo and Aquarium Association. "It took me a while to find out these things," Cook says. "I was so naïve."

These things, which Cook learned over a decade at her hometown zoo, included revelations that the animals for which she cared—including primates she raised from birth in the zoo's nursery—were sent off to substandard roadside zoos, unqualified pet owners, entertainment-industry trainers, and dealers intent on keeping the details of their subsequent transactions secret. What's more, Cook discovered that criticizing an AZA zoo—no matter how compelling the evidence against it—is often pointless because ethics complaints are routinely dismissed by clubmates intent on guaranteeing that malfeasance is never acknowledged outside the association's ranks.

This is typical of the exotic-animal business, which is populated by those who behave like Roland Lindemann: Publicly, they're all dedicated to the survival of the species, the welfare of their charges, the repatriation of the endangered, the education of the masses about the sorry plight of the world's threatened, vanishing, and exploited wildlife. Privately, however, their commitment is often selective, transient, and influenced only by such bottom-line considerations as cage space, or lack thereof. In one instance after another, conscience gives way to expediency.

Margaret Cook first learned about the zoo business in the early 1970s, when she signed on as a volunteer docent at Kansas City's municipal park. In 1977 she was elevated to a staff position in the zoo's nursery, where she cared for newborn chimpanzees, gorillas, and orangutans, along with the likes of baby hippos. She enjoyed the work, particularly the bonds she developed with the infant primates, but before long she grew disillusioned. "It was bittersweet," she recalls. "I loved the animals but couldn't take what was going on."

It was what happened to the zoo's animals that so troubled Cook. A pair of three-year-old chimpanzees was sold to a roadside zoo in Guatemala. A young orangutan named Pumpkin was sold to a German animal dealer, who in turn shipped him back to a Hollywood trainer who was unwilling to disclose details of the animal's condition or whereabouts. Cook delivered a three-week-old orangutan to a Miami animal dealer who, visitors reported, dressed his young apes as children and who talked about ways of binding their feet so they would walk upright. A year-old chimp named Mikey was sent to an animal trainer whose firm was under investigation by the U.S. Department of Agriculture for mistreating numerous animals, including an orangutan who was beaten with a cane and an ax handle (he was later fined and stripped of his federal exhibitor's license). A chimp named Chobe, whom Cook raised for two years as a surrogate mother, tending to the animal both day and night, was sold to International Animal Exchange. IAE planned to sell Chobe to Buckshire Corporation, a supplier of primates to biomedical research, whose client, pharmaceutical company Merck Sharp & Dohme, wanted the chimp for use in hepatitis-vaccine testing. When Cook learned of this in a chance phone call from an employee of Buckshire Corporation, who wanted blood drawn from the chimp, keepers pressured the zoo's director to intervene, and Chobe was instead transferred to IAE's drive-through park in Grand Prairie,

Texas. For saving Chobe, Cook was rewarded with an admonishment to never again answer the phone in the zoo's nursery.

Dumping primates in such fashion was not unusual during the 1970s and early 1980s, whether from zoos directly or via the dealers to whom zoo surplus was entrusted. Orangutans from the San Diego Zoo and Chicago's Lincoln Park Zoo were laundered through a Miami dealer to Las Vegas showman Bobby Berosini (later accused by an animal-rights group of beating an orangutan). The Memphis Zoo sold two orangutans to William Vergis, a wrestling-bear showman who was subsequently run out of Florida. Chimps from zoos in Knoxville, Tennessee, and Jacksonville, Florida, were also sold to Merck Sharpe & Dohme, while chimps from Baton Rouge, Louisiana, and Philadelphia were sent to a biomedical research facility in New Iberia, Louisiana. Some surplus zoo primates landed at university cancer labs or the Coulston Foundation, in Alamogordo, New Mexico, a chimpanzee warehouse whose director has proposed farming the great apes for their blood and organs. Like Pet-a-Pet's chimp, Mario, who was disposed of when owner Jack Crippen shut the gates, chimpanzees from zoos in Detroit; St. Louis; San Diego; Syracuse, New York; and other cities were consigned to New York University's Laboratory for Experimental Medicine and Surgery in Primates, which subjected animals to decades of human hepatitis research. The fate of some of the lab's chimps was detailed in a research paper a few years after San Diego Zoo and the others consigned their animals to the New York facility. "Two of these anemic chimpanzees died in hypoglycemic shock, and we can speculate that the death of a third may have been precipitated by this condition," the paper stated. "From the clinical standpoint, the most striking features, common to all of this group in some degree, have been failure to grow properly and development of the pot-bellied, thin-limbed, sunken-eyed appearance of malnutrition."

Cook feared that the animals she helped raise might be similarly doomed, although details were nearly impossible to come by. So in 1984 she quit her zoo job and mounted a campaign to learn their whereabouts. She contacted federal agencies and local newspapers. She enlisted the aid of a Humane Society investigator. And Cook detailed her concerns for the chairman of the AZA's ethics board, at the time the director of the Denver Zoo.

Although formal complaints are typically filed by members of the AZA, the ethics committee deemed Cook's charges serious enough to warrant consideration. "I hope you understand our position here as one of being helpless in trying to correct the circumstances that have placed 6 primates from the zoo in places that hold their mental and physical life in jeopardy," Cook said in her letter. "Your organization is the only one that would carry any influence with the director of the zoo." But Ed Schmitt, the chairman of the ethics board, had reason not to be overly harsh with his colleague. After all, while Cook was fretting about Kansas City's primates being sent to unsuitable places, the Denver Zoo was sending a gibbon—an ape classified as endangered—to the biomedical research lab in New Iberia, Louisiana.

—◄o►—

In a 1997 interview with his hometown *Enquirer* about his institution's policy regarding the disposition of surplus animals, Edward Maruska, the executive director of the Cincinnati Zoo, said: "We're very selective on where [animals] go. We have to have a lot of background information on private individuals before we deal with them."

Apparently, Maruska's staff isn't collecting nearly enough information, because the Cincinnati Zoo is among those that have sent bongos to animal dealer Earl Tatum, who has supplied these rare antelopes to a Texas rancher who advertises his stock in the newsletter of the Exotic Wildlife Association, the hunting lobby. It has supplied leopard cats and sand cats to a husband-and-wife team of breeders in Tarzana, California, who fuel the private trade in exotic cats. It has sent primates and large felines to Robert Crowe, the Florida dealer who unloads animals at auctions around the United States. Cincinnati—along with zoos in Denver, St. Louis, and other cities—routinely sends snow leopards and other big cats to the Oakhill Center for Rare & Endangered Species, in Luther, Oklahoma. Oakhill's founder and director is John Aynes, formerly the proprietor of Animal Actors of Oklahoma, an operation that was shut down by the federal government after Aynes was charged with buying and selling exotic animals without a license. Aynes was also charged with providing miserable care to his animals: A zebra without sufficient shelter died of pneumonia. A jaguar escaped and was shot to death by local police. Aynes's lions, tigers, and leopards were all housed in cages that federal inspectors deemed too small, too filthy, or too decrepit to offer the animals a buffer against rain, snow, and cold. During a photo-taking session, a chained tiger under Aynes's control bit the head of a two-year-old girl.

The Oakhill Center for Rare & Endangered Species, one of two dozen organizations granted "Related Organization" status by the American Zoo and Aquarium Association, is a fitting sequel for Aynes. Although he bills his organization as a nonprofit "conservation center" that does not sell offspring as pets, he has advertised not-yet-born snow leopards, Bengal tigers, and servals in *Animal Finders' Guide*. He trades big cats with groups that use lectures and live-animal presentations as a smoke screen for their animal breeding and dealing, including Bridgeport Nature Center, the Texas operation that breeds big cats by the dozen for photo shoots and sale to the pet trade; Noah's Land, a defunct Texas drive-through park that supplied tigers to hobbyists and dealers; and Center for Endangered Cats, the "sanctuary" whose founder left a neighboring state after being convicted on animal-cruelty charges. On its 1996 report to the U.S. Fish and Wildlife Service, Oakhill Center reported the donation of a month-old snow leopard to a Texas sanctuary. In a series of articles, the *Dallas Observer* filled in the missing details: A wealthy patron of the sanctuary, whose pets have included a wolf and a leopard that was shot and killed after chewing off part of the man's face, wanted to buy a snow leopard from Aynes but he lacked the proper permit. So Aynes fashioned a compromise: He could "donate" $6,000 to Oakhill Center, and Aynes in turn would "donate" the snow leopard to the Texas sanctuary, which this donor reportedly used as a "glorified kennel."

A Persian leopard that escaped its cage in 1997 mauled a woman to death at Oakhill and was later killed by sheriff's deputies. Aynes's animal dealing has been so prolific that over a two-year period in the early 1990s, he sent into private hands seventeen mountain lions, most just a month old. The list of buyers included the operator of a Texas-based canned hunt. Although the AZA's code of professional ethics decrees that members should make every effort to assure that animals do not find their way to "those not qualified to care for them properly," it's clear that the Cincinnati Zoo and many of its peers play by their own rules.

--◦--

After resigning her job at the Kansas City Zoo, Margaret Cook devoted herself full-time to piecing together the stories and fates of the animals once under her care, including the chimpanzees Chobe and Mikey. The U.S. Department of the Interior explained to her that although chimps are listed by international treaty as endangered, U.S. law exempts those born of parents in captivity, and she should therefore contact the Centers for Disease Control and Prevention in Atlanta for help in finding her animals. CDC monitors only compliance with laws governing the quarantine of imported primates, however, and therefore referred her to the U.S. Department of Agriculture. But the USDA told Cook that she was wasting her time, that it would not be able to help.

Cook should have expected as much. The USDA's Animal and Plant Health Inspection Service, which is charged with overseeing/regulating exhibitors, dealers, transporters, and research laboratories, is viewed as a worthless bureaucracy by state fish and game personnel, federal wildlife officers, and even by many of its own employees, who have seen their calls to investigate corrupt traffickers repeatedly ignored by higher-ups. A field staff of only sixty-four veterinary medical officers and animal-care inspectors is charged with monitoring more than ten thousand licensees for compliance with the federal Animal Welfare Act—an impossible task, some of those inspectors privately admit.

But Cook's mission was hampered by the Animal Welfare Act itself, which merely lays out minimum standards for the humane care and treatment of certain warm-blooded species. As long as dealers and exhibitors maintain records of their transactions—paperwork that APHIS exempts from release under the Freedom of Information Act—zoo animals may be sold to medical laboratories, slaughterhouses, or just about anywhere else. And those not required to be licensed under the law—pet owners, sanctuaries, or private hunting ranches, for example—are beyond the reach of APHIS inspectors, bound only by state or local humane laws. Consequently, tracking the whereabouts of a zoo animal is usually an exercise in futility. After one or more transactions, it's inevitably lost to follow-up.

In this instance, however, sympathetic caseworkers in the offices of Cook's U.S. senators, John Danforth and Thomas Eagleton, helped her develop leads. The chimp Chobe, given a last-minute reprieve from biomedical research, was bought by International Animal Exchange for $5,000 and, seven months later, resold to a Texas businessman for $12,000. His new owner dressed three-year-old Chobe in a suit and dragged him along to amuse clients. But by the following spring, however, the novelty had apparently worn off, and the chimp was again for sale, this time for $10,000. Cook spearheaded a fund-raising drive that brought in $9,000, and Chobe was purchased and sent to a sanctuary in Texas. Ernest Hagler, the director of the Kansas City Zoo, expressed reservations about the sanctuary, claiming it was a dead-end street for the chimp. But he nonetheless refused to reclaim Chobe and provide the animal care.

It wasn't just Chobe who was in trouble. The chimp Mikey, whom the zoo had sent to Ralph Helfer, a California animal trainer, had allegedly been stolen and sold to a Houston-area petting zoo—the chimp's whereabouts revealed in an anonymous telephone tip to police. A Texas justice of the peace ruled that Helfer, not the petting zoo, was Mikey's rightful owner. After the court hearing, Helfer told a reporter for the *Houston Chronicle* that Mikey received excellent care and was subjected only to affection training. "Talk about tears, we cried when we lost Mikey," he said. "I've worked with animals for 33 years and never heard of an animal being kidnapped. He's been gone a month and a half, and we don't know if he has suffered any emotional damage." Helfer's company, Gentle Jungle, Inc., was under investigation at the time for allegedly violating the Animal Welfare Act. APHIS charged that Helfer's firm repeatedly violated standards for the care and handling of its animals; in one instance, for example, the government charged that the head trainer of Gentle Jungle beat a juvenile orangutan with a cane and an ax to make it more submissive on a movie set. Following this and other incidents, including the abuse of a tiger that was dyed black to portray a panther in a movie, the USDA fined Gentle Jungle $15,300 and revoked its animal exhibitor license.

Cook thought this information important enough to pass along to the AZA ethics committee, whose investigation of the Kansas City Zoo was continuing. She also sought to debunk the claims of the zoo's director that, to his knowledge, the chimp was merely sold to International Animal Exchange, thereby relieving him of any responsibility for later transactions. In truth, Cook explained, she personally flew Mikey to California and, on orders of her boss, delivered the chimp to the Hollywood trainer.

"The picture still remains the same," Cook argued. "A zoo director was a willing participant in placing a threatened species in a facility not approved of by the American Association of Zoological Parks and Aquariums. I hope someone in your association will care about the fate of the animals sold to show people to be exploited for money."

—◦—

In May 1992, and again in July, police in Orange County, California, arrested twenty-three-year-old Eric Jarvies after he had attempted to sell big cats without a permit. In the first instance, Jarvies had placed a newspaper ad offering for sale seven declawed African lions, ages four to fifteen months, which were being held at a health-food store in San Clemente that he had once co-owned. Jarvies told a reporter for the *Los Angeles Times* that he rented animals for commercials and films, and that he'd placed the newspaper ad not to actually sell the animals but merely to gauge the public's interest in owning lions. That July, Jarvies was charged with the illegal possession and mistreatment of wild animals after a pair of uncaged six-week-old tiger cubs, were spotted in his unattended car. He later pleaded guilty to illegal possession.

The seven lions were seized by police and taken to the San Clemente Animal Shelter. Four days later the California Department of Fish and Game ordered that they be returned to their breeder, Circle 3 Buffalo Ranch, in Longford, Kansas, which is operated by Ray Smith and his sons. (The Smith family still cranks out baby lions and, more recently, has been dumping bear cubs into the pet trade.) The lions were loaded into crates and put on a truck driven by Jarvies, then escorted by California officials to the state line. The relocation effort received considerable news-media coverage in both California and Kansas, with fish and game officers in both states lamenting the boom in exotic-pet ownership. Also weighing in with comments about this trend was Ron Tilson, the director of conservation at the Minnesota Zoo, who told a reporter for the *Los Angeles Times:* "I'm disgusted by it. These animals end up living rather miserable lives."

Tilson was correct, and the same could probably be said for the male-female pair of pronghorn antelope that his own zoo had sent to Mark Hemker, the owner of a private zoo in Freeport, Minnesota, in late 1996. Hemker, whose fourteen-acre park is not accredited by the AZA, is exactly the sort of middleman that Tilson's more high-minded colleagues insist is an inappropriate trading partner for accredited zoos. Hemker frequents exotic-animal auctions, a means of commerce that the AZA is on record as strongly opposing: In 1981, the association decreed that members offering wildlife for sale at such auctions would be in violation of its code of professional ethics, because AZA members should "make every effort to assure that exotic animals do not find their way into the hands of people not qualified to care for them properly." Hemker sells animals to the pet trade via classified ads, such as this one that appeared—with his phone number, but no name—months after he got the Minnesota Zoo's pronghorn antelope: "3.3 mule deer; 1.1 pronghorn antelope; 7.0 whitetail deer, bottle babies; 3.0 woodland caribou; 1.1 llama; 1.1 stone sheep." (The numerical designations are standard animal-business shorthand: 3.3, for example, means three males, three females.) Hemker sells deer to animal dealers whose clients include Larry Barger, the Arkansas purveyor of trophy-buck semen. Hemker has also rented animals to the likes of William

Vergis, the disgraced wrestling-bear trainer whose props have also come by way of the National Zoo, the Miami MetroZoo, and more recently, the Columbus Zoological Gardens—a sure prescription for the miserable lives that so concern Tilson.

Hemker, in fact, sued Vergis after Vergis leased a couple of moose for an appearance in a Poland Spring bottled-water commercial and the deal went sour. According to a complaint filed in a Minnesota district court, Vergis provided the animals such inadequate care during their trip to and from Maine that both developed pneumonia and, as a result, one died. The suit maintained that Vergis illegally transported the animals to the Poland Spring photo shoot and then falsely claimed he was there on behalf of Hemker, saddling the latter with a fine and, Hemker claimed, irreparably harming his reputation. What's more, the suit alleged, Vergis stopped payment on two checks totaling $9,000, and owed another $4,000 for returning the moose four days late.

Hemker obtained a judgment and had Vergis's animals seized. These included an African lion, a mandrill baboon, two white wolves, a Kodiak bear, and a mountain lion (coincidentally, the Columbus Zoo had supplied Vergis with a puma just a few years earlier). The animals were sent to a roadside zoo for safekeeping, and within days Vergis filed for bankruptcy. In his 1996 bankruptcy petition, Vergis claimed that all of these animals were co-owned by Sam Mazzola, of Ohio, who travels the country staging wrestling-bear matches at bars and outdoors shows; pin Caesar's shoulders to the mat, and you can turn your $20 entry fee into a cash prize of a thousand. The weak or timid can instead pay to merely pose with one of Mazzola's smaller bears.

The Vergis/Mazzola menagerie became part of a complicated legal entanglement that for months left the fate of the animals in limbo. In the end, the animals were returned to Vergis.

◄○►

Although Margaret Cook was most concerned about the fates of the primates she had raised, she also investigated the sale of the Kansas City

Zoo's other animals. Cook's interest was prompted by the disappearance of the zoo's hoofed stock, which in many cases ended up with Earl Tatum, who has probably received more AZA "surplus" than anyone else. Cook knew Tatum from her years working in the zoo's nursery: He'd stroll through looking for animals, and sometimes, she says, he'd later return to retrieve them. It was as if the Kansas City Zoo was Tatum's private breeding facility.

The whispered word among the zoo's staff, Cook says, was that Tatum sold the zoo's surplus hoofed animals to hunting ranches, and she learned that his clients included a game farm in the Ozark Mountains, a no-kill/no-fee canned hunt whose animal suppliers, it turns out, also included Jurgen Schulz. "The zoo had just sold Earl a bunch of gemsboks," she says. "I called this game farm and said I wanted to give my husband a birthday present and he wanted to shoot an exotic animal; what do you have? He said, 'We can get anything you want.' He said, 'You need to let us know ahead of time so we can have it here. We can't keep them here because they can't live on the fescue in southern Missouri.' So I asked about a gemsbok, and he said, Yeah, he can get a gemsbok. He gets them from the dealer who was always at the Kansas City Zoo."

Cook again turned to her U.S. senators for help, and through Danforth's office she learned that her former employer had sent Tatum seven gemsboks eight months earlier. Tatum claimed to still have four of the African antelopes, while two had been sent to a Texas dealer and another to an unnamed Missouri man. Because the latter was not licensed to sell animals, the USDA would not release his name.

Presumably, this sort of resale would have troubled Ernest Hagler, the Kansas City Zoo's since-retired director. After all, his institution's placement policy for surplus animals dictated that private individuals must have the knowledge, experience, and proper facilities for animal care before the completion of any transaction. "In all cases," the policy decreed, "the Curator must approve placement of any animal to a private party." No matter that Tatum had resold the zoo's animals to private individuals quite probably lacking such knowledge, experience, and facilities. Because his zoo had nothing to do with Tatum's reselling of its animals, Hagler told Cook, it could not be responsible for the end result.

This no-mea-culpa reasoning has always been the zoo community's most trusted line of defense against charges that its animals land in inappropriate places, such as hunting ranches. In early 1993, in the midst of a year-long debate about ethics and responsibilities, the AZA's board of directors proposed a revision in the organization's charter to more forcefully acknowledge that zoo animals are seen as "the people's animals," held in public trust. The proposed revision stated that the AZA "strongly opposes the sale, trade, or transfer of animals from zoos and aquariums to organizations or individuals which allow (or will transfer animals to another organization or individual which allows) the hunting or the breeding of animals for hunting."

Later that spring, however, the AZA's board of directors ignored public sentiment, abandoned its collective conscience, and approved a watered-down version of the guidelines: Gone was the parenthetical phrase opposing the secondary transfer of animals to hunting operations. Once again, the nation's zoos proclaimed that their moral obligation ended when an animal left their grounds, making it likely—if not inevitable—that "the people's animals" would suffer fates entirely inconsistent with that public trust in which they were once held.

Any zoo director who wishes to know more about the dealers who haul off unwanted surplus could, in most cases, do so with a few letters or telephone calls. If zoos are in fact trustees of valued public treasures, as their curators would have us believe, then presumably they can devote adequate resources to ensuring that the animals under their care and supervision are not in any way compromised.

Instead, Wildlife Safari, an AZA member in Winston, Oregon, sends dozens of its "surplus" blackbuck antelopes, Rocky Mountain goats, nilgai antelopes, sika deer, elk, and other animals to Paul Drake, a dealer one hundred fifty miles away in Sublimity, Oregon. And where does Drake unload animals? He sells large numbers of sika deer and Rocky

Mountain goats at the Lolli Brothers auction, in Missouri. He sells blackbuck and nilgai antelopes at Kifaru, Jurgen Schulz's Texas auction. He sells dozens of fallow deer to a Louisiana man with no USDA license who loads up on elk, antelopes, exotic goats, and other animals at the Missouri auction barns.

Chicago's Lincoln Park Zoo, along with AZA zoos in Knoxville, Tennessee, and Fort Worth, Texas, send Mouflon sheep to Hidden View Farm, in New Market, Tennessee. Anyone with Internet access can find the owner's classified ads for Mouflon and other species, as well this blurb about his exotic-animal business: "We also deal in exotics and have established connections with the most legitimate and reputable public and private zoos in the country. We can locate quality animals of nearly any breed or species and have it delivered by USDA certified transporters." The Dakota Zoo, an AZA member in Bismarck, sent nine elk to a Minnesota animal dealer; readily available Minnesota records reveal that this dealer—an official of the North American Elk Breeders Association—routinely unloads his inventory at auctions in Colorado and North Dakota. Tampa's Lowry Park Zoo sent eight-month-old Bactrian camels to Hostetler Wildlife Farms, in Buffalo, Missouri; the park's operator sells any interested parties the drive-through park's surplus animals, including, his advertisements announce, Bactrian camels. The Lincoln Park Zoo sent monkeys to a roadside zoo in New Braunfels, Texas, with no affiliation to the AZA. Texas records show that the owner of the so-called Snake Farm supplies large numbers of young primates to Randy Davies of Peoria, Arizona, a well-known monkey dealer who, years earlier, used classified ads in *USA Today* and the *National Enquirer* to flood the pet trade with baby monkeys from his Cincinnati-area warehouse; these days, his ads appear in Phoenix-area newspapers, much to the dismay of state health officials. Zoos in the Bronx, Cincinnati, Pittsburgh, and Syracuse, New York, dump monkeys on Ashby Acres Wildlife Park. And Mark Schoebel may have pleaded guilty to providing bears for slaughter, and he may unload animals at auction, and he may sell deer to a Wisconsin canned hunt, but none of that appears to concern the Racine Zoo, an AZA member in his home state.

Not only has it supplied Schoebel with lions, elk, and other common zoo animals, but a notation buried in the official orangutan studbook, to which the public would never have access, reveals that the Racine Zoo also secretly loaned Schoebel a pair of these great apes for a year.

Zoo directors like to insist that such activities represent a bygone era, but all these transactions are in fact recent. The inappropriateness of such trade has been discussed for decades among the AZA membership, as increasingly successful captive breeding weaned zoos from their reliance on dealers—at least for the acquisition of their collections. Some zoo directors have even suggested that their peers may want to completely sever their ties to dealers—an idea akin to heresy, in light of the dealers' role in removing unwanted surplus.

Among those taking such a moral stance was Stefan Graham, the former director of the Detroit Zoo. Graham was a controversial figure because he insisted on putting issues before the public that others would have preferred to keep entirely within the club. For example, he warned of a population explosion that would overwhelm the nation's zoos, and as a solution he advocated the widespread use of euthanasia, whether culling the least genetically desirable hoofed stock for carnivore food or euthanizing healthy Siberian tigers (as he once did) when homes at other accredited zoos were impossible to find.

Graham lambasted his colleagues at the AZA's 1987 convention, as the surplus issue was becoming increasingly troublesome. He criticized zoos for their surplus policies, which, he said, were subjecting animals to auctions, pet shops, roadside menageries, and the exotic-meat trade. And Graham went so far as to suggest that zoos either sever their ties with animal dealers or else place animals with them on loan only, with a requirement that subsequent transactions be reported to the originating zoo. As for the practice of sending animals to unaccredited zoos, Graham told his colleagues, "Some would say this is acceptable; I say it is not."

These, however, were empty words. Not long before his plea for ethical transformation, Graham's zoo sent surplus oryx to an unaccredited exotic-animal dealer and a Missouri drive-through safari park so wretched that a few years earlier, the director of a nearby AZA-member zoo had asked the Humane Society to investigate the place. What's more, just months before the AZA convention, Graham's zoo sent a three-year-old snow leopard to a California breeder/dealer, who in turn sent the endangered cat to an Oregon dealer. A decade later, this dealer's pet-trade inventory includes not only Bengal tigers and North American cougars but also endangered snow leopards.

Even the nation's leading animal-welfare organization has, like Graham and his brethren at the AZA, let principle give way to expediency. In late 1997, the Humane Society of the United States lobbied the U.S. Fish and Wildlife Service for permission to relocate two hundred eighty Canada geese that had been trapped by a Minnesota wildlife agency near the Minneapolis–St. Paul Airport. The migratory birds, which were said to pose a potential safety threat to airplane traffic, were tabbed for slaughter and processing under a controversial program that provides food to the needy. The Humane Society and two allied organizations sued the U.S. Fish and Wildlife Service, successfully forestalling the killing. A court ultimately sided with the government, but agency officials nonetheless agreed to let the Humane Society relocate the geese to another state.

After a difficult search, a home was found for the birds with the Choctaw Nation, a Native American tribe in Oklahoma. The Humane Society agreed to pay the full costs of transporting the waterfowl and, with a government relocation deadline looming, hastily made arrangements. The move was carried out just before Christmas, and weary Humane Society officials roundly congratulated themselves and trumpeted their success to the news media and their nearly seven million constituents.

But they failed to ever publicly disclose one important detail: The relocation was handled by International Animal Exchange, a company that the Humane Society of the United States has long ridiculed, monitored, and vilified for its role in laundering animals for AZA zoos. In fact, at the AZA's 1984 convention, in Miami, the director of the Humane Society's Captive Wildlife Protection Division presented a paper that criticized zoos for using middlemen/dealers. By way of example, she pointed to the Kansas City Zoo's chimpanzee, Mikey, whom International Animal Exchange had sold to a Texas pet owner. "It is only self-deceiving if you believe that by putting them into the hands of AAZPA-member dealers, all is well," she told the gathering. "Time after time, the animals we encounter in roadside menageries or other equally abhorrent situations have been supplied by the very dealers who ought also to be upholding your code of ethics."

—◁o▷—

In the summer of 1992, Margaret Cook petitioned the Kansas City Zoo to contribute to a fund to buy the orangutan Pumpkin, so that the great ape could be transferred to a sanctuary. In 1979 Pumpkin had been sent to an animal dealer in Germany, and after three years in a German zoo had been sold to a Hollywood trainer, who prepared him for TV appearances. Pumpkin apparently became difficult to handle and was sold again—this time to a Texas roadside zoo, where he was stricken with a near-fatal case of pneumonia. Cook, still battling a decade later to find satisfactory homes for the primates she once cared for, hoped to raise enough money to pay for the great ape's retirement at a Texas sanctuary.

The zoo's new director, Mark Wourms, expressed his dismay over Pumpkin's fate and applauded Cook's efforts but informed her that the institution's limited resources were needed to maintain its own collection. Pumpkin's overseas sale, Wourms wrote Cook, was in keeping with practices of another era, and he admitted his uneasiness over this or any other animal being moved from place to place and, as a result, receiving substandard care.

Eight years earlier, the AZA's ethics board, acting on Margaret Cook's complaint, had shown no concern at all for the orangutan's well-being. Pumpkin had been sold in a legal, appropriate, and acceptable manner, it concluded, and zoo officials certainly couldn't be held responsible indefinitely for the disposition of "specimens" or for the actions of others. Likewise, the transactions involving the chimps Mikey and Chobe were conducted in a legal, appropriate, and acceptable manner, and therefore no ethics-related charges were warranted. The only villain, according to

Ed Schmitt, the chairman of the ethics board, was Cook herself. Schmitt castigated Cook for relaying her concerns about the welfare of the great apes to the news media and the Kansas City Parks Board, which oversees the zoo's operation. And then Schmitt added a single sentence that would, in its twisted brazenness, be difficult to match: "Had you been a member of our Association, we would have had no recourse but to file ethics charges against you, for you have violated the confidentiality of processing an ethics charge and in doing so compromised the integrity of the Board and all others involved in this matter."

Mark Wourms was far more sympathetic, and he noted that much had changed in the thirteen years since Pumpkin had left the zoo. For example, the AZA code of ethics prohibited sending animals to any institution lacking the proper facilities. Programs had been instituted to reduce the breeding of surplus animals. And policy dictated that his zoo deal only with accredited institutions as its primary sources for acquisitions and dispositions. "We do care about animals as species and as individuals; that is part of the Kansas City Zoological Garden's mission," he wrote.

But when a listing in the *AZA Animal Exchange* brought no takers for a couple of Bennett's wallabies, the Kansas City Zoo dropped its asking price from $750 to $500 apiece and, in late 1995, sent them—along with some unwanted birds—to a roadside zoo in Illinois. Two and a half years later the Illinois zoo closed its doors, leaving the fate of these and all its other animals in doubt.

When an *Animal Exchange* listing for one of the zoo's unwanted Ankole cattle generated no interest from AZA members, Kansas City entrusted the lumbering, long-horned animal to Larry Johnson, the dealer able to make giraffes disappear. A young male impala, along with a sable antelope, a greater kudu, and a beisa oryx weren't even offered to AZA members, but in the spring of 1995 were simply given to dealer Earl Tatum. (Three years earlier, Tatum delivered a kudu from Florida's Busch Gardens, a blesbok born at the Memphis Zoo, and a sable antelope from the Mesker Park Zoo, in Indiana, to Jack Moore Ranch, outside Val Verde, Texas, a private hunting operation, according to the

Hunters-Breeders Directory of the Exotic Wildlife Association.) The zoo sent elk, impalas, kangaroos, sable antelopes, and other animals to Little Ponderosa Animal Company, the Illinois dealer and auction. It sent impala and other hoofed stock to Jim Fouts. It sent a serval to an animal dealer in Raywick, Kentucky, who in turn sent a serval to a dealer in New York who had a history of run-ins with state and federal wildlife authorities. In the summer of 1998, it sent a two-year-old Masai giraffe to International Animal Exchange's compound in Texas, the site from which it exports many of its cast-off giraffes and other zoo animals. And the zoo dumped an aging pair of New Guinea singing dogs that had never been offered to the AZA community. Chances are, there wouldn't have been takers anyway: Only five member zoos display the small wild dogs, and they're not much of a draw. So Kansas City simply shipped the pair to a pet dealer in Emporia, Kansas, who operates a puppy mill from his backyard. Although the AZA frowns on zoo animals being sent into the pet trade, there is nothing in its charter or code of professional ethics specifically prohibiting this. As a result, the transaction was legal, acceptable, and appropriate.

8

UNFAIR GAME

Don't ask Ray Hanson for a look inside his pole barn, because you're not invited. He once admitted a business associate, but no one else, he insists, is ever getting through those doors. Hanson has a sizable investment tied up in that building, and he's not inclined to share the secret of his success.

Hanson is a deer farmer, and he's got plenty of competition. Although the nation's suburbs are overrun with whitetails and mule deer, leaving shrub-shorn communities searching desperately for ways to rid themselves of the long-legged pests, thousands of hobbyists and full-time farmers are nonetheless raising lots more.

The promoters of deer farming proclaim that elk and other deer, which are sometimes farmed in tandem, are ideal substitutes for beef: Elk meat is lean and mild, not at all gamy, while venison is low in fat and cholesterol, high in protein. The elk industry says that farming the 600-to 900-pound ruminants is another way for downtrodden cattle ranchers to earn a living, since three wapiti (a Shawnee Indian name that means "white rump") can make do with the grazing land of a single cow, and when the masses finally kick the beef habit their meat will become as popular as ground round. So far, however, elk ranching is just another incarnation of the pyramid scheme that played out with other exotic species, including, most recently, ostriches and emus: Those pioneers who sold eggs—sometimes for as much as $10,000 apiece—turned a profit, whereas many of the latecomers took a financial beating, went belly up, and in some cases turned their birds out on public lands to compete with native wildlife. This time around, the folks who are peddling breeder elk have made money, while their customers wait expectantly for the ever-impending boom.

The real market for elk and deer isn't the flesh. Both animals are staples of private hunting preserves, which fuel much of the commerce. In addition, elk and some other deer species, including the European red deer, are raised for their antlers—a multimillion-dollar trade intended primarily for the Asian medicinal market, whose practitioners attribute numerous healing powers to the deciduous bony growths. Beginning at age two, elk bulls produce "commercial-quality" antlers (those developing antlers covered by furry skin called "velvet") that can be sawed off annually. Although some producers administer an anesthetic, others simply cut the antlers off the physically restrained animal—a bloody process that traumatizes and may even kill the deer. Because many Asians take velvet-antler capsules and potions to cure everything from anemia and diabetes to memory loss and impotence, there is a ready market for American deer and elk farmers to exploit.

But Ray Hanson isn't interested in powdered antlers or newfangled meat products. His niche is urine: the liquid gold that hunters use in the hope of attracting monster bucks.

And it's a big business, even if the evidence of its effectiveness is only anecdotal and even if its use poses such hazards to humans as infection from brucellosis, which can cause everything from headaches to death. Hunters are always looking for an edge, and if sprinkling a little urine-based cocktail on one's camo might lure a ten-point trophy into the cross-hairs, then it's certainly worth the expense. The bottlers and marketers, who have turned adulterated piss into a $15 million-a-year industry, rely on entrepreneurs like Hanson for their raw material. He, too, has found a lucrative profit stream: Plain doe urine can bring up to $40 per gallon, while the doe-in-heat variety—guaranteed to bring a hunter more buck for his bang—can fetch as much as $70.

Given the spread, the latter is obviously the way to go. But because breeding-age females come into estrus only once a year, Hanson uses artificial means to keep that more lucrative flow going: His does are administered biweekly injections of Estradiol cypionate, a reproductive hormone available from chemical-supply houses. These deer may be in "false" heat, but as long as the would-be suitors fall for the ruse, the hunters aren't apt to complain.

Of course, collecting the urine before it hits the earth is the real trick, and that's why Hanson steers visitors away from his pole barn: He wants the design of his unique collection system kept secret. But if you did find your way into the building, here's what you'd see: thirty-four box stalls, each about four by eight feet, with solid plywood on all sides. The compartments are three feet above the ground. The floor is a diamond-shaped metal grate, much like that of a fire escape. There is cheesecloth under the grating and on some days a buildup of feces atop it. The urine cascades through the grate into a slanted trough. From there it flows into five-gallon buckets. It is hardly an engineering breakthrough.

Hanson keeps about one hundred twenty-five deer at the pole barn and a nearby deer farm, including one whose urine is collected in quart jars for a particularly finicky client. Two deer are housed in each four-by-eight stall; they stand there for thirty days at a stretch to deliver about two quarts of urine daily. Because the deer are unable to walk, their hooves are not subjected to the abrasion that otherwise would keep them filed, and they sometimes grow an inch or two longer than normal. Dirt and other matter may then get impacted in the overgrown hooves, which may result in infection. That in turn may become systemic and bring about other health problems, some of them life-threatening. Coupled with the ongoing hormone injections and the stress of being confined for so long, the animals typically live only about three years, not the ten or so that petting-zoo deer might last.

But even three years' worth of urine makes a deer a worthwhile investment: Two quarts a day amounts to more than one hundred eighty gallons a year, which at forty to seventy dollars per gallon means that Hanson can afford to let his deer die prematurely. After all, at going market rates, he can replace them for about two hundred dollars apiece. And the successors don't need gargantuan antlers, nor do they have to be tame, healthy, or potentially good breeding stock. They just have to be female and thirsty.

◄○►

There was plenty of decent merchandise at the Noah's Land Wildlife Park auction in October 1997, including zebras, monkeys, and a variety of carnivores. The owners of the five-hundred-acre drive-through park and animal-dealing enterprise, seventy miles east of San Antonio, had consigned their inventory to a going-out-of-business sale, and interested buyers flocked to the Saturday event from across Texas and surrounding states.

Noah's Land was flush with exotics, including lemurs bought from Texas animal dealer Buddy Jordan and tigers bought from Oakhill Center for Rare & Endangered Species, the AZA-affiliated large-cat dealer. In Texas, where exotics are as common as jackrabbits, the huge goodbye auction generated little media attention. Some newspapers carried a brief item from the Associated Press that turned the sale into a quirky human-interest story: Zebras were among the day's top sellers; a deer farmer was considering adding llama breeding to his repertoire; a local wildlife rehabilitator hoped to buy a wallaby she had once cared for.

Other news from the auction, however, went entirely unreported. For example, a woman with no animal-care experience emerged as the high bidder for a quartet of adult bears. The animals were housed in a chain-link enclosure, and following her triumphant bid the winner reached in to pet one of the bears on the head—a gesture that was accompanied by the sort of high-pitched *wooowooowooowooo* that an appreciative master might direct at her cherished pooch. But the bear apparently wasn't enamored of its new landlady, because the shaggy mammal jerked its head and, in a flash, bit at her hand. The terrified woman—too stunned even to scream—yanked her arm from the cage, and as she did a companion got an unanticipated close-up of the ghastly damage: Two middle fingers had been bitten off. After the onlooker fainted, the stunned victim glanced down at her mangled hand and then conked out as well. A search ensued for the severed digits, in the hope they could be reattached, but the bear had eaten them. Later that night, someone called on behalf of the hospitalized woman to say that she had changed her mind about owning the bears and therefore was withdrawing her winning bid.

The Associated Press story also noted that the giraffes, among the last of the Noah's Land animals to go on the auction block, were expected to fetch as much as $10,000 each. One of those giraffes was ultimately bid higher, but the whispers about its fate among the crowd's intelligentsia never made the AP wire: The buyer, it was rumored, had presold the long-necked animal as a taxidermy mount for $50,000. He apparently was unconcerned that the giraffe was pregnant.

Depraved as that action may have been, it was nonetheless legal. That's because state and federal laws regard animals as property: They may be sold, given away, killed, or used for any purpose not prohibited by anticruelty statutes. Cockfighting is illegal in most states, for example, but deer farmers like Ray Hanson are free to sabotage their animals' biorhythms with hormonal booster shots (Estradiol cypionate is not a controlled substance), confine them for weeks (laws don't address this), and watch them die prematurely in the name of profit. Similarly, there's nothing in most local statutes to prohibit the spectacles of boxing kangaroos, high-diving mules, or the Banana Derby, which puts macaque monkeys in harnesses atop miniature horses for three terrifying laps around a small oval track. The Reverend James Lavender, a Virginia-based Methodist minister, USDA-licensed exhibitor, and *Animal Finders' Guide* advertiser, conducts a traveling tent-revival show called Thank God for Kids Ministries that features an African lion lying down beside what must be the world's most terrified lamb. In Illinois, there are at least two facilities—

Eickman's Processing, in Seward, and Rodosky Meats, in Kinsman—where live bears have been led in for slaughter like swine and cattle.

You can, in fact, kill your animals for food, fun, or just about any other purpose, provided you do it by the book. Months before the Noah's Land auction, for example, Stephen Vinson, a Texas physician, used an aluminum baseball bat to club to death twenty-two of his emus. Vinson, a hobbyist breeder, was upset by his financial losses in a tanking emu market, and when efforts to herd his flightless birds failed one day, Vinson used them for batting practice. It appeared to be an open-and-shut case of cruelty, but Texas law allows owners to kill their animals, provided they don't inflict unnecessary suffering. "His intent was to kill the birds, not torture them," Richard Alpert, a prosecutor with the Tarrant County district attorney's office, told a reporter for the Reuters news service. "I certainly don't like the way he did it, but he didn't cross that line. I just don't have a law I can use against him to prosecute him."

There is no law against killing an exotic pet after it harms a person—an event so commonplace that a highlight map would scarcely have room for all the pushpins. Most of these tragedies have similar circumstances, while all have the same outcome. Robie Creek, Idaho: A pet mountain lion mauls a seven-year-old boy outside his grandfather's isolated home and drags him, bleeding, for about a hundred feet. The animal is shot to death. Luther, Oklahoma: A Persian leopard escapes from its cage at Oakhill Center for Rare & Endangered Species and fatally mauls a fifty-two-year-old woman who was visiting her son, a caretaker at the AZA-affiliated "sanctuary." A sheriff's tactical team shoots the leopard. Center Hill, Florida: A Siberian tiger escapes from its unlocked pen at Savage Kingdom, a private ranch that breeds big cats, and mauls the leg of an unsuspecting worker. Sheriff's deputies shoot and kill the tiger. Lubbock, Texas: A man who planned to breed tigers is mauled by a seven-hundred-pound animal as he works in its cage. His son and a friend shoot the tiger twice in the head. Bellfountain, Oregon: A woman who owns three African lions has them shot to death after the mauled remains of a man believed to be her husband are found in the animals' fenced-in compound. Anderson, South Carolina: A pet lion bursts into a neighbor's mobile home and mauls a five-year-old girl and her grandmother. The owner later arrives and shoots it to death. The list is without end.

In one state after another, game farmers have pressed legislators to reclassify a growing list of animals as agricultural products, much like apples, alfalfa, and other cash crops—a change that allows them to raise, sell, and slaughter exotics without the hassle of fish-and-game-department inspections or other government intrusions. Many game-farm associations have successfully persuaded lawmakers to put deer, elk, and bison under the agricultural umbrella, along with ostriches and other ratites. But the politically well-connected Exotic Wildlife Association helped give its Texas constituents an even bigger edge: In 1997, the association persuaded John Sharp, the state's comptroller, to add zebras and camels to the list of animals qualifying for agricultural exemptions. "It's smart business for the state's tax code to keep pace with the rapid changes in the food industry, from range to restaurant," Sharp declared after approving the regulatory change. "Texas agribusinesses are meeting their customers' demand for lean meat products by offering a variety of alternatives."

A handful of exotic-meat merchants in the United States do in fact offer camel loins and zebra sausage, but it's unlikely that either delicacy will ever find counter space beside chicken breasts and sirloin tips. The Exotic Wildlife Association lobbied to have two more animals exempted from the regulatory meddling of such agencies as the Texas Parks and Wildlife department, freeing game farmers from such unpopular forms of government oversight as wildlife possession permits and allowing them to breed zebras like goats or hogs, for their hides, meat, and taxidermy souvenirs.

Camels and zebras will likely be followed by addax and other African antelopes, perhaps kangaroo after that, and then someday the list will grow to include lions, bears, and the like. Some in the industry go so far as to suggest that the only way to stave off extinction of the planet's besieged wild tigers is through the genius of the free-enterprise system: The threat to the species could be mitigated, the reasoning goes, by farming captive tigers to supply bones and penises for the Asian medicinal markets. It's a model that the Chinese have already perfected: Some five hundred farms sequester thousands of bears in warehouses. Each is outfitted with a metal girdle that contains a pouch to collect bile—the substance coveted by those in the East without ready access to Dristan, Viagra, or hemorrhoid potions. According to the Chinese government, the bile production from the seven or eight thousand bears that are caged helps relieve the threats to the remaining free-roaming bears, which would likely face slaughter for their gall bladders. This way, Chinese officials argue, the imperiled bear species are being saved.

Although it's unlikely that the American public will ever permit similar enterprises to operate here, wildlife investigators have some indications that North American cougars, which have become so abundant in the pet trade, are being killed for their bones and penises—knockoffs for (what else?) the Asian tiger-part market. "My assumption is that it's always been a two-level trade," an expert in wildlife forensics says. "The wealthy, powerful individuals get the real thing and the other 99 percent of the world gets the fakes and the placebos." He includes the parts of cougars and other big cats in the category of "genuine." For those unable to afford such luxuries, he says, *caveat emptor:* "There's a pretty huge trade in fake tiger penises. They carve the bull penis to fake tiger."

—◁o▷—

On the evening of June 23, 1994, an auxiliary police officer peering through the window of a white-concrete warehouse in Poplarville, Mississippi, the self-proclaimed Blueberry Capital of the World, spied a dead bird. The investigation of the one-story building—the home of Purrfect Parakeet, an exotic-animal wholesaler—had been prompted by a tip from the owners of a pet shop in Grenada, Mississippi, two hundred fifty miles to the north. They had ordered animals from James Bates, the proprietor of Purrfect Parakeet, and when the promised delivery didn't arrive they drove to Bates's home. He in turn brought the couple to the warehouse in Poplarville to retrieve their animals.

The couple, horrified by what they saw in the warehouse, later contacted the regional office of In Defense of Animals. Representatives of the animal-welfare organization met with a Poplarville sheriff's deputy, who declared that the couple's accusations, which were spelled out in a letter, were not sufficient cause for a search warrant. That evening, the auxiliary police officer visited the Purrfect Parakeet warehouse and saw the dead bird through the window. But that, police determined, was probably still not adequate evidence for a search warrant.

The following morning, David Barnett, an officer with the Mississippi Department of Wildlife, Fisheries, and Parks, found a snake slithering along the road beside the Purrfect Parakeet warehouse—one of many that had been spotted there by local residents. After retrieving the snake, Barnett and local police then signed affidavits requesting a warrant to search the pet-dealer's warehouse. A local judge complied, and authorities then attempted to contact Bates. When that effort proved futile, police cut the lock and, accompanied by a wildlife expert, entered his warehouse.

The stench inside was so overpowering that some of the officers turned and fled the warehouse. When the search finally got underway, police found cardboard boxes—some of them taped shut—filled with dead and dying reptiles. There were baby iguanas covered with maggots. There were piles of dead savanna monitors. Some snakes were swimming in their own urine and rotting. So many baby ball pythons were crammed into one box that they appeared to be a tangled mass of wires, with those barely alive wrapped around those already dead. Six cockatiels were crammed into a small cage; a seventh was face down on the cage floor. Some birds had been dead so long that their bodies were nothing but rotted shells, the feathers congealed. Parakeet carcasses were covered with ants. Other birds were in further states of decomposition, their heads rotted off their frames. There was no food or water for many of the animals; for others, the water was coffee-colored, the bowls filled with feces. In all, police counted six hundred eighty-three animals. Of those, one hundred forty-two were dead, including twenty-eight iguanas, twenty-five Nile monitors, and sixteen ball pythons. Three more animals were in such bad shape that they had to be euthanized.

The police left receipts for Bates indicating that his property had been confiscated. The animals were entrusted to a wildlife rehabilitator, who in turn passed along some of the injured to foster homes. Most of the snakes that were taken out of the warehouse later died—lab tests showed they were infected with *Salmonella* and *E. coli*—although the birds and some species of lizard fared better.

The following week, Bates was charged with six hundred eighty-three counts of animal cruelty and was held in the Pearl River County jail under a $30,000 bond. The misdemeanor charges carried the potential for stiff fines and years of incarceration. Receipts collected during the investigation showed that Bates had bought the snakes and lizards from Strictly Reptiles, the South Florida wholesaler that consigned sick and injured reptiles to the dumpster.

Two months after being charged, Bates, as part of a deal with prosecutors, pleaded no contest to three of the six hundred eight-three counts, an arrangement that earned him a suspended ninety-day jail sentence and a fine of $3,000 plus $111 in court costs. In fashioning the plea bargain, Poplarville took good care of itself: The agreement stipulated that Bates would release the city from all claims resulting from the seizure of his property. The only losers were the animals: The order of conviction decreed that the surviving snakes and birds could be returned to Bates, provided that he kept them out of Poplarville.

The next day, one of Bates's attorneys began calling the volunteers who had been caring for the injured birds and reptiles and demanding that they be turned over to him. He then drove to each person's home to get the animals. In some cases, however, the lawyer instead sold the rehabilitated animals back to their foster-care providers, who were concerned about their fates. He told one volunteer that he planned to sell the other animals to local pet shops.

In the end, it was a hollow victory for In Defense of Animals and its volunteer foster-care providers. Not only had so many of the birds and reptiles died, but most of those nursed back to health had been dumped right back into the pet trade. What's more, reports filtered back to those who had cared for Bates's animals that he was listed as a vendor at exotic-animal shows in Alabama and Georgia. "The day I had to return the snakes and iguanas in a sack to Bates's attorney," one of the volunteers says, "was one of the saddest days I've ever known."

But if she was saddened by the outcome of the saga, she shouldn't have been surprised. There is almost nothing to stop someone like Bates from getting back into the exotic-animal business. He does not need a USDA license to deal in birds and reptiles; in fact, because they are not even covered by the Animal Welfare Act, he's immune from USDA inspection. When the raid on his warehouse took place, Bates had more birds at his house, and those weren't confiscated. His plea bargain imposed no restrictions on his commercial activities. Even for someone charged with more than six hundred counts of animal cruelty, who subjected his charges to death and torture, getting back in the business is as easy as renting table space at an exotic-animal show. Similarly, collectors cited for abusing their animals invariably seem to acquire more. The exotic-animal habit apparently is a tough one to kick, its practitioners urged on by their quest to rescue besieged species or, as some insist, to do the Lord's work.

Take Susan Kriz, the Iowa woman who ended up with some of the Harvard Medical School's cotton-top tamarins. She unsuccessfully petitioned the state's supreme court to overturn the ruling that had resulted in the confiscation of her fifty monkeys. During hearings to assess Kriz's ability to care for her animals, sheriff's deputies testified that she had summoned them to her home because she believed there were people hiding in the walls of her house and she was convinced that someone was poisoning her cigarettes. Although deputies testified that floor drains were plugged with monkey feces and the house was so filthy that the stench burned their eyes, Kriz's friends insisted that she loved her pets and took good care of them. By court order, the animals were distributed to sanctuaries and zoos, but that wasn't enough to stop this collector: Fifteen months after deputies seized the malnourished, dehydrated primates, which Kriz had rounded up over a half-decade, the USDA issued her a Class B animal dealer's license. Operating under the name RTR Ranch, Kriz could now buy and sell monkeys.

Charles Hess, an Ohio wolf breeder, has been cited repeatedly for animal-cruelty and other violations, moving on to another county after his run-ins with the law. In one incident, police freed four chained animals (three of them wolf-dog hybrids) from the feces-encrusted station wagon in which they had been living for weeks. Authorities were tipped off by someone who'd noticed a pair of bloody cow legs—the canines' food—strapped to the roof of the car. Hess's Oregon counterpart is Jayson Wollander, a wolf-dog breeder who served jail time for keeping forty-one animals in inhumane conditions. Wollander's attorney acknowledged problems with the feces-filled chicken coop that was home to some of the animals, but he maintained that Wollander loved his animals and would change his ways if they were returned. After the county euthanized his forty-one wolf-dogs, Wollander declared, "When they killed my dogs, they killed a part of me." Four months after a jury found Wollander guilty of animal neglect, another two dozen wolf-dogs belonging to him—their fur matted, some of their bodies covered with bites from other animals—were seized in a neighboring county. Sheriff's deputies there described the house in which they were kept as unsuitable for animals.

Another such Oregonian is Robert Fieber. In 1985, Oregon State Police raided Fieber's game ranch, where he was keeping one hundred fifty animals, including lions, cougars, and other carnivores. Fieber, who was charged with fifty-four counts of cruelty to animals, pleaded no contest to four misdemeanor counts and additional allegations of food-safety violations. Fieber then complained to newspaper reporters that some of the animals that had been seized in the raid were being mistreated, that they were being kept in substandard pens, for example. His animals had suffered enough, Fieber declared, and with legislation pending that might have limited his ability to collect more exotics, he moved his menagerie to Lava Hot Springs, Idaho.

A decade later, Fieber and a companion, Dotti Martin, were convicted of animal cruelty and incarcerated after nineteen lions escaped from "Ligertown," their Idaho compound. The judge in the case likened the place to a garbage dump. Sheriff's deputies and armed citizens had taken to the woods and killed all the runaway lions. Prosecutors argued that Fieber and Martin suffered from "collectors' syndrome," an obsessive compulsion to acquire more animals than they could care for. "The paradox is that for people who have such great love for animals," Magistrate Mark Beebe told Fieber at his sentencing hearing, "you ended up creating an animal ghetto."

Catherine Twiss is another such compulsive collector. In the mid-1980s, when she was legally known as Catherine Gordon and informally known as the "Critter Mama" of Crawford County, Indiana, Twiss kept more than one hundred fifty animals at her property, including cougars, lions, and bears. Twiss had repeated run-ins with the authorities, who charged, for instance, that she was illegally hauling dead livestock to her compound to use as feed for her tigers, coyotes, and other animals. During one visit, an inspector with the Indiana State Board of Animal Health counted a half-dozen Holstein cow heads in a cage. Twiss was also investigated by the USDA, and she relinquished her dealer's license only to avoid having her animals confiscated.

Twiss continued to deal animals, the USDA later charged in a complaint filed against her, and she subsequently fled with her menagerie to Arkansas. She was soon on the move again, however, this time to a Texas farm. A few months later, she fled that state after the local authorities, concerned about the well-being of her animals, reportedly threatened to seize them. She returned to another Arkansas locale, transporting forty-two large cats in cattle trailers. The animals were deposited on a ranch, but the owners locked her off the property three months later, accusing her of neglect. She sued her benefactors and regained custody of the animals. The ranch owners, so distraught by the plight of big cats, founded Turpentine Creek Wildlife Refuge on their property.

In 1995, Twiss and her husband, Lawrence, were charged with three counts of cruelty to animals after authorities found fifty-eight lions and tigers, five bears, thirty-seven dogs, and various other animals living in crowded pens filled with portions of animal carcasses. They fled Arkansas for Mississippi, where Manuel and Geraldine Goforth offered some of their farmland for a private zoo. But the animals were kept in wretched conditions. For five months, an adult cougar was confined to a feces-filled oil drum, the large cat barely able to turn around. Thirty domestic cats were crammed into part of a cattle trailer. Lions and tigers were relegated to cramped, urine-soaked coops with no water, piles of cattle bones stacked in a corner, and muddy floors that were not covered with sawdust to help keep them dry. Ten dogs, one of them hobbled by a broken leg, roamed the area. Five bears were confined in a dirty enclosure with only wooden pallets to lie on. A putrid odor emanated from the cages. There was no water for many of the animals; for others, the water buckets were muddied tubs. Plastic tarps covered the tops of the cages, scarcely protecting the animals from inclement weather. A leopard spent months in a wooden box. Some of the animals were emaciated, their food supply cut off after the health department ordered the Twisses to stop hauling in dead cows from area farms and chickens from local processing plants. Some were too weak to move. Others had no sheen to their coats, as if they were covered with fake fur. The faces of some of the cats were visibly scarred from fights. One tiger apparently had an abscessed tooth and was unable to eat. A pair of lion cubs were so malnourished that they had stopped growing. After the Goforths served the Twisses with eviction papers, the Twisses sued them for $3 million, charging that they had reneged on promises to build the private zoo and had inflicted pain and suffering. In the midst of the legal battle, Catherine Twiss told a reporter that it was God's will for her to own so many animals.

The Twisses were charged with seventy-seven counts of animal cruelty (they were later convicted on seventy-three), and in May 1996 dozens of their big cats were put up for sale in a bankruptcy proceeding. Catherine Twiss reportedly fled Mississippi with some of her animals in a livestock trailer, and later that same month she was arrested in Boone County, Arkansas, on eleven counts of cruelty to animals. Sheriff's deputies found two livestock trailers hidden in the woods behind a rented house. There were nine big cats and a llama in one of the trailers; in a nearby barn, a cougar was found in a cramped cage. Nine months later, following a no-contest plea, Catherine Twiss was convicted on animal-cruelty charges. She was fined and placed on probation.

But little changed. Prior to that no-contest plea, Hilda Jackson, the curator of Turpentine Creek sanctuary, reported that Twiss once again seemed to be collecting cats. "My daughter saw her hauling sawdust," Jackson said. "And when she hauls sawdust, she has cats."

◄○►

After hours of spinning tales about the goings-on in South Florida, Lieutenant Pat Reynolds still has plenty more in his repertoire. There is the story about the doctor who sent his illegally imported monkeys to Texas, where an accomplice concocted paperwork to make it appear as if the monkeys had been born there. Then the primates were returned to Florida with Texas health certificates, letting the doctor claim, falsely, that he had acquired them legally. There is the story about the brazen crony of a high-profile dealer who, after getting into it with someone at the L Cross exotic-animal auction, took the dispute to a busy Miami street, where gunfire erupted. There is the story about a man who beat a lion with a two-by-four and another about someone who imported endangered rhino iguanas from the Dominican Republic on a bogus international-treaty permit. Reynolds has a story about a guy whose thousand hours of animal-care experience—a requirement to earn his state-mandated permit to keep dangerous pets—was actually spent stuffing envelopes, not learning about husbandry and handling, as the law requires. He tells of escaped monkeys running wild near an aquifer pumping station, boa constrictors arriving at the airport with drugs stuffed inside them, and a sanctuary getting money from one state agency while his employer of two decades, the Florida Game and Fresh Water Fish Commission, was on the verge of revoking its license.

Reynolds could undoubtedly keep the stories coming until the sun drops from the cloudless Miami sky, but someone who needs some cages inspected keeps punching up Reynolds's number on his pager. Finally, the veteran wildlife officer, deciding that he's kept the persistent caller waiting long enough, answers the page and then begins packing up his gear. But before heading to his truck, Reynolds has one last tale to tell—the one about the guy who "put money on the street" in the hope of retrieving three stolen white fallow deer. The investigation, he says, eventually led to an area near the Florida's Turnpike that is populated with squatters, murderers, and an assortment of dangerous lowlifes. Reynolds knew it wasn't the type of place to go alone, but he had a tip that some white animals were in a horse trailer there. Besides, he had one of the perks that goes with being granted peace-officer status: a shotgun, which sits on prominent, upright display beside his vehicle's front seat.

Reynolds's search turned up chickens, goats, pigs, and parrots in cages, but no deer. He caught a break, however, when one of the boarders at the encampment said that he knew someone who knew someone else who could supposedly get his hands on virtually any animal. And so Reynolds's volunteer contacted the mystery dealer, who checked his computer and offered the good news: He had just received a male, a female, and a baby white deer—coincidentally, exactly what had been stolen. The shill said that he wanted the deer, and, as long as they were doing business, what about other animals? Anything from lions to elephants was available, the dealer replied: His people scouted out zoo animals, then they either bought them or stole them. For example, he had just gotten someone a tiger from a well-known Florida zoo.

Reynolds called the zoo to ask if it was in fact missing a tiger, but the park's curator said that, to his knowledge, all the animals were accounted for. That left Reynolds wondering whether the dealer was for real, but a trailer arrived on the arranged date, at the appointed time, carrying three fallow deer. But the animals were cream-colored, not pure white. The dealer had the wrong hot deer.

When Reynolds finally runs out of stories, his colleagues pick up where he left off. Nine enforcement officers police Florida's thousands of exotic-animal owners, including three (Reynolds among them) whose territories stretch from the Keys to north of the Palm Beaches. It's an area that includes members of a group that the feds have dubbed "the monkey mafia." There are dealers in those hundreds of square miles whose crimes have earned them jail time or home confinement. There are collectors getting baby animals from impossible-to-trace sources. A woman without a wildlife possession permit showed up at a restaurant recently with a monkey in tow. Someone reportedly has a jaguar, but people who may know something about its whereabouts aren't talking. A pet lion escaped near Lake Okeechobee. Dealers are cramming reptiles along with anesthetized birds and primates into boxes labeled "glassware" and shipping them by parcel post. A stakeout at an airport cargo area helps the authorities nab someone illegally importing a cougar from Missouri. There's a big, secretive voodoo trade, but some of the officers tapped for undercover investigations are too frightened of black magic to accept the assignments.

Wildlife officers in other regions of Florida have their own tales of vice and turpitude, as do their counterparts in other states and in federal agencies. It takes little prompting to deal them into a never-ending game of one-upmanship, as their stories relate ever-escalating levels of brazenness, depravity, and sheer stupidity. But if these enforcement officers and animal-care inspectors can talk for a dog's age about a failed system, one question invariably is met with a long and uncomfortable pause: How would you fix it?

Many agree that solutions are hopelessly complicated by a mélange of disjointed interests. Health matters are regulated by state veterinarians. Some dealers are licensed by the USDA; others are not. State fish and game agencies have oversight responsibility for some animals whereas agriculture departments monitor others. The U.S. Fish and Wildlife Service regulates interstate—but not intrastate—sales of endangered species. State agencies regulate game farmers, but violations of law may be referred to local sheriffs, who in turn insist that game farms are the state's responsibility. The Centers for Disease Control and Prevention oversees the importation of primates and, presumably, their resale as pets, which in some cases is legal and in others is not. Agricultural inspection stations in some states record the importation of exotics, but they don't share that information with the department of natural resources, which licenses the importers and tries to keep tabs on their activities. State and federal agencies are often at such odds about what information should be shared that the former sometimes have to file Freedom of Information Act requests to pry documents from the latter, even though they're both trying to bring the same individuals to justice. What's more, so little priority is given to regulating the sale and possession of exotic animals that neither state nor federal agencies devote enough resources to do the job well. It is, in short, a mess, as many freely acknowledge.

"You've got many agencies doing the same thing and many agencies not knowing what the others are doing," Lieutenant John West, a colleague of Pat Reynolds, says. "Some agencies don't have the ability to do what they've been charged to do. And the biggest problem is that there is no clearinghouse for this paperwork. We have paperwork, the National Marine Fisheries Service has paperwork, so does the USDA and the Fish and Wildlife Service. Everyone has paperwork, but it never connects."

Thomas Solin, chief of the Special Investigations Section of the Wisconsin Department of Natural Resources, says that merging data held by state and federal agencies may sometimes be the only way to identify inconsistencies in reports filed by zoos, dealers, and game farms and, therefore, the only way to nab lawbreakers. But, Solin adds, getting the USDA and U.S. Fish and Wildlife to cooperate with a state agriculture department and wildlife agency is a long shot. "I've never been successful at getting everybody to sit down together to form a joint investigation," he says. "That's really what's needed to focus either on an individual species or on an individual. You have to do one of the two, because if you try to shoot at it all, it's too big of a dart board."

Complicating matters, frequently, is the antagonism among agencies. In some states, for example, the agriculture department is at odds with the department of natural resources over which animals should be available for private ownership, while the health department may have its own ideas (which are often ignored). There are also rifts between state and federal agencies. "U.S. Fish and Wildlife won't tell me where they place [confiscated] animals," a state wildlife officer says. "I need to know if [the recipients] are permitted, but they won't tell me. They say, 'Rest assured, everything is perfectly legal.' They're always pumping me for information, but they won't tell us anything."

Perhaps the only thing that nearly everyone can agree on is a disdain for USDA's Animal and Plant Health Inspection Service, which regulates zoos and exotic-animal dealers. APHIS is the object of endless ridicule, most notably for its anemic enforcement efforts. Even some of the service's own animal-care specialists ridicule the agency's policies and procedures. They note, for example, a quiet directive from officials of the agency to omit from their reports any mention of photographs taken during inspections—a convenient means of keeping potentially damaging evidence hidden from the public and other agencies. Although APHIS inspectors often turn up what they believe to be egregious examples of wrongdoing, their pleas for follow-up investigations or prosecution are routinely ignored. "Sometimes I feel that the people upstairs don't want us to make waves," an inspector with more than a decade of service says. "Part of it is political. Part of it is that maybe they don't know what to do. Then you'll get, 'Well, we don't want to refer too many cases to the Office of Investigative and Enforcement Services. They're overloaded.' That's probably true; they are overloaded. But we can bring in good material and pictures, work really hard, and try really hard to get something initiated, and then it just sort of disappears."

State and federal investigators are also hampered by what is often the near-impossible task of gathering credible evidence. When someone writes "donation" on an annual report to the U.S. Fish and Wildlife Service, for example, the agency has no way of proving whether cash actually changed hands.

Similarly, the theft of native wildlife is usually done far from public view, and proving that an animal was wild-caught rather than pen-raised is problematic. A game farmer near Gardiner, Montana, for instance, cut the power from his electrified fence when elk were migrating out of Yellowstone National Park, then turned the juice back on when enough animals had wandered onto his land. He then sold the pilfered wildlife to would-be elk breeders, pulling identifying ear tags from dead animals and reattaching them to the native elk.

Only a costly and painstaking investigation by the Montana Department of Fish, Wildlife, and Parks managed to expose the crime. But that same agency has had to ignore other matters, such as the revelation that bears were being kicked out of trailers at one game farm in the state so that waiting "hunters" could shoot them. "It was inhumane, but we don't have laws against inhumane treatment," a department employee says. "That would come under some federal law, and it would be pretty complicated. We know it happened, but we don't have enough evidence to prosecute. It's very hard to get the information."

"It's a big, dirty business," Ron Catlin, a law enforcement specialist for the South Dakota Department of Game, Fish, and Parks, adds. "And when you're working with exotics or wild animals, many are either carnivores or something you don't want to pick up and put in your lap and say, 'Open your mouth and stick out your tongue.' Very few people want to walk into a cage with one of those critters and determine its origin. I've never had much success trying to interrogate one of those animals.

"A lot of states, including ours, have not allotted a terrible lot of time and manpower to this. We have other pressing issues that are scratching at our backs most of the time. And we just don't have the time or money."

Even if an undercover officer unearths evidence of wrongdoing, agencies must then deal with a judicial system that places wildlife crimes far down on its scale of priorities. Most judges neither understand wildlife crime nor take it seriously; penalties are usually misdemeanors that bring jail time only to the worst of the worst. What's more, state laws are so quirky that offenders repeatedly manage to escape prosecution. In Florida, for example, prosecutors sometimes cite primate smugglers for a minor infraction, such as not having wild-animal possession permits, rather than for the serious charge of illegal trafficking. As a result, offenders escape with a paltry fine instead of a criminal record.

Federal agencies such as the U.S. Fish and Wildlife Service are hamstrung by U.S. Attorneys who, by and large, are determined to focus their attention on anything but wildlife crimes. Jim Stinebaugh, a longtime Fish and Wildlife agent based in Texas, says that the trade in exotics there is largely unregulated: "We don't investigate people moving exotic animals. And with endangered species, for example, if someone's got barasingha deer out there that are captive-bred and have been for many generations, that doesn't get a U.S. Attorney excited. I've managed to prosecute people for killing the big cats, because you get no sympathy from anybody when you shoot a big cat in some type of enclosure. But the rest of it, there's very little regulation.

"Dope is one of my biggest problems," he adds. "To be a wildlife officer in Texas and to try to get someone prosecuted for violation of a permit when the U.S. Attorney's office is sitting there with a big stack of dope cases, well, it's hard to get in line."

Jim Harper was interested. He was the assistant U.S. Attorney, in Atlanta, who prosecuted the 1992 primate trafficking case against Antonio Alentado, Robert Troumbly, Tom Nichols, and others. Harper, who typically prosecuted cases involving drugs and violent crime, jumped on what he thought was a great case—a chance to shut down a trade that he believed had potentially deadly health consequences. The evidence had been amassed by a U.S. Fish and Wildlife agent, and because the case involved primates heading for the pet trade, the Centers for Disease Control and Prevention was also involved. Once Harper took on the case, he also got the U.S. Customs Service on board.

The case was largely based on violations of the Lacey Act, a century-old law that was enacted to protect wildlife from being sold illegally across state lines. Cases are rarely brought under the Lacey Act, and for good reason: Its provisions are so confusing that despite endless tutorials by the lead U.S. Fish and Wildlife agent, and despite the help of a Justice Department specialist, who had been dispatched from Washington, Harper was thoroughly befuddled. "I'd been on the case six months and I was saying, 'Tell me how this act works. What does it do?' What a stupid piece of legislation. It's impossible to understand."

Harper had other problems as well. The judge was so baffled by the case that he threatened to throw it out of court. The CDC, Harper says, rarely works with prosecutors and therefore was not helpful. What's more, neither the U.S. Department of Agriculture nor any other agency helped advance the investigation. As the case dragged on, Harper grew so frustrated that he tried to cut deals for plea bargains, a course of action he disliked because of the defendants' extensive involvement in the underground animal trade. But everyone else was happy, he says, most notably the judge.

"The judge called everyone back behind the bench—the private hallway leading to his chambers," Harper recalls. "We were all standing back there. This was off the record. He said, 'Tell me what you guys want me to do with this case. I'll do whatever you want.' He said, 'I don't understand it. If you guys understand it, just let me know and we'll make this case go away.'"

So they did. Nichols drew a one-year sentence on a misdemeanor charge (the judge wouldn't accept a felony plea), and Alentado, who pleaded guilty to one count of trafficking, received three months of home confinement. "It wasn't futile," Harper says. "We really did screw up their operations for about a year. Small victories."

-◄o►-

Others can also count small victories. In 1998, for example, a Montana deer-urine collector petitioned the state for permission to outdo Ray Hanson, his out-of-state rival: Instead of simply letting his decrepit deer die, the collector wanted to open his barn to paying "hunters." That way, he could squeeze every last drop of urine from them and, as gravy, also recoup his initial investment.

Like Hanson, this urine processor insisted that his proprietary collection process needed to remain secret, and he therefore declined to let state wildlife officials into his barn. The Montana Department of Fish, Wildlife, and Parks balked at the proposal, but the determined entrepreneur appealed the decision. The matter went to an administrative hearing officer, who, in siding with the bureaucrats, ruled that shooting the deer in such close quarters, with only a wooden wall to stop errant bullets, might endanger nearby humans. The deer would have to wait to die.

9

TIME BOMBS

Ringo is tethered to a sink pipe by a four-foot leash. The young pig-tailed macaque has been wiped down and toweled dry, his tail pulled through a disposable diaper that's fastened in the rear with three revolutions of duct tape. He's wearing a metal choker and a red-checked union suit that snaps up the front. Before him on the floor are a Teddy bear, a juice cup, and plastic toys, which occupy him intermittently. Ringo whimpers every minute, as if on cue. He grabs for the pant legs of passersby. He flings his toys across the room, then wails until they're returned. He grasps the sink from below and frenetically tries to hoist himself into the basin, feet first. But because the leash is too short, the two-year-old monkey is unable to complete his upside-down climb and he hurtles to the floor. He nonetheless keeps trying.

Ringo's home is a veterinary clinic in Cooper City, Florida, southwest of Fort Lauderdale. It was founded as a dog-and-cat hospital, but one long wing is now devoted to the care of native wildlife and exotic pets. This is Dr. Terri Parrott's domain. She treats animals that have been hit by cars or sprayed with BB-gun pellets. She sutures birds that have been at-tacked by foxes. Great blue herons, ill from eating mercury-laden fish, are brought to her for treatment and rehabilitation. One day a woman ar-rives carrying a Muscovy duck with a fish hook through its beak—a thick elbow of rusted metal whose barb can be severed only by the clinic's stoutest male wielding oversized shears. Muscovies are common through-out the South Florida suburbs, having been imported from Central and South America and then released by pet owners who grew tired of them. The black-and-white-plumed ducks, easily distinguished by red facial knobs, nest on balconies and invade swimming pools. They beg for food and, once fed, persistently demand more, refusing to look elsewhere for handouts. They transmit duck plague and avian tuberculosis to native birds. Large flocks descend on ponds and foul the water. Terri Parrott may care about the welfare of the Muscovies occasionally brought to her, but the birds are reviled by much of the public and, like raccoons and opossums, are considered a nuisance by Florida fish and game officers. They, in fact, would be happy to see the ducks disappear altogether, and some locals are helping in that effort: They trap the birds, transport them north, and sell them to New York-area restaurants, where they're appar-ently served to unsuspecting diners as Peking duck. At the same time, Florida's armadillos—a species that may carry human leprosy—are being poached for New York's Asian meat trade, and its river-turtle populations are being decimated for the same purpose. The state's birds are being slaughtered for a booming feather market. Coyote skulls, used for deco-rative purposes, are in demand. Floridians spray gasoline into burrows and ignite the fuel, then collect and sell the snakes and other animals that manage to make it out alive. A twenty-year veteran of the Florida Game and Fresh Water Fish Commission says that he's never seen such prolific dealing in wildlife.

The state's trade in exotic animals is also booming. Florida has ample space to accommodate its legions of breeders and dealers. It's estimated that Miami is the port of entry for three-quarters of the nation's legal wildlife imports and for most of the illegal shipments. The mild climate makes the state a wintertime dumping ground for northern petting zoos.

Theme parks, roadside menageries, and tourist traps lure customers with exotic species. An amalgam of immigrant cultures has fueled the demand for an unusually diverse array of pets and animals used for less noble purposes. In Miami's Little Havana, for instance, the Santeria priestesses send their clients to *botanicas* to obtain the sacrificial offerings integral to their religion: hummingbirds and woodpeckers (live or stuffed), vulture feathers and alligator teeth, turtle shells, deer hooves, goat organs, reptile eyes, and bats stuffed into bottles. A pair of Florida game officials once showed up at a Dade County house in time to rescue a mountain lion intended for sacrifice. As one officer recalls, another young cougar wasn't as lucky: They found it in the priestess's freezer. Wildlife officers have also stumbled on goats hanging from trees and monkeys burned alive as offerings to the gods.

Because Terri Parrott is one of the few Florida veterinarians who specialize in the treatment of exotic animals, pet owners eventually find their way to her. So do others. When the owner of a blind baboon died of AIDS, friends of the deceased arrived at Parrott's clinic with the animal and its high chair and said simply, "Here, take this monkey." She did. Not far from Parrott's office is the one-story, white-concrete home of Strictly Reptiles, the pet-trade wholesaler whose proprietors used to routinely throw injured snakes and other reptiles into their dumpster rather than provide them with medical care. It is Parrott who cared for the creatures that schoolchildren plucked from the trash bin.

Florida and federal wildlife authorities often deposit confiscated animals with Parrott. There has been a parade of lions. There was a tiger with cataracts—most likely the result of malnutrition, she says—that turned up at a gas station in Hialeah. There was a rare woolly monkey found in a car impounded after a police chase. In addition to Ringo, the current primate inventory includes a capuchin seized during a federal drug bust and a rare bonnet macaque—a young monkey so unmanageable that it is rarely removed from its small cage in the clinic's quarantine room. There's also a sleek, six-foot mountain lion once owned by Jose Canseco, the major league baseball star. The young puma's existence was revealed only when Canseco's garage door was inadvertently left ajar and the cat, which was being kept without the required permit, ran away and turned up at a neighborhood pool party.

Freed from its cage for exercise, the hundred-pound cougar swaggers across Parrott's examining room, then purrs like an appreciative house cat when scratched behind its ears. Because the animal has a kidney ailment, she says, placing it in a new home will likely be difficult. The tawny feline had been foisted off on a woman with two other big cats, but she paid little attention to the newcomer and it developed additional medical problems. So Terri Parrott reclaimed the illegally acquired pet and began the search for yet another home. Her best hope, she thinks, is the man caring for Babette the baboon. Arranging that adoption took three years, but it eventually worked out: Another veterinarian helped restore the monkey's eyesight, and the new owner built the animal a beautiful indoor cage. "It's like having a retarded child," Parrott says. "That was a hard one."

Finding Ringo a suitable home, she thinks, will probably be even more difficult. And it's not because of his unruliness, so evident on this winter day: The foot-and-a-half-tall monkey somehow manages to unsnap the leash from his metal collar and sprints across the veterinary examining room, swiping as he runs at jars, folders, and anything else not anchored. Parrott yells at Ringo and takes off in pursuit, but the monkey's quickness and low center of gravity give him what appears to be an insurmountable edge. She eventually corners the escape artist, however, and, with a rapid lunge, grabs hold and pins the monkey's arms behind his back, then ushers him to the sink. Ringo doesn't struggle but marches obediently across the room and allows Parrott to reattach the leash. This behavior, she says, is attributed to the hierarchy under which the young primate operates: He knows that she's dominant, and therefore he gives in to her commands.

But if that hierarchy is what allows Parrott to control Ringo, it also causes her unending concern; because of it, she says, anyone who owns a macaque as a pet faces a dire—albeit largely unknown or misunderstood—threat. "If I hit Ringo, he'll attack somebody else, because that's just their pecking order. My children, who are seven, five, and four, come in here, and if I yell at Ringo he tries to attack my kids. That's the way macaques are.

"What's going to happen," says Parrott, describing unsuspecting pet owners, "is that the parents are going to yell at the baby macaque, the macaque is going to bite the kid, and the kid is going to come down in eleven to twenty-one days with flu-like symptoms. Then they'll take him to the pediatrician, where he won't get treated correctly, and he'll die."

◄o►

Dr. Parrott says this almost matter-of-factly. She and a few colleagues have been saying it for years, although until recently few would listen. It wasn't that science didn't support their contentions: It has been known since the early 1930s that macaques carry *Herpesvirus simiae,* known as herpes B or B virus, which may cause a potentially fatal brain infection in humans. (Although *Herpesvirus simiae* is the widely accepted Latin form, the more accurate designation is *cercopithecine herpesvirus 1* [CHV-1]—nomenclature that recognizes that some three dozen other herpesviruses occur naturally in simian species.) The macaques typically carry B virus throughout their lives and shed it intermittently in saliva or genital secretions, particularly when they are under stress. Humans run the risk of infection only when the monkeys are shedding. But there are rarely any signs, symptoms, or other tip-offs to indicate when or if that's happening.

Because of this persistent threat—80 to 90 percent of adult macaques are believed to harbor the virus—those who work in close proximity to these primates are presumed to be in constant peril and are instructed to take so-called Biosafety Level 2 precautions, as prescribed by the National Institutes of Health: the use of lab coats, surgical masks, goggles, gloves, and other protective measures. As these workers know, such protocols have life-or-death implications. The virus has proved fatal in about 70 percent of known cases, and most survivors have suffered permanent neurological damage. In one late-1997 incident, for example, a young research assistant at Emory University's Yerkes Regional Primate Research Center died from B-virus complications after she was splashed in the eye with a body fluid when moving a rhesus macaque—the first time this route of transmission had ever been documented.

Contact with macaques was traditionally limited almost exclusively to zookeepers and biomedical researchers, who were aware of the herpes B threat and took appropriate precautions. ("B" represents the last name of the first documented fatality—an anonymous, twenty-nine-year-old physician who, while studying polio in 1932, was bitten on the hand by a rhesus macaque.) Documented B-virus infections have therefore been rare—the Centers for Disease Control and Prevention places the number in the United States at about forty—but a few years ago Parrott and other veterinarians began seeing a troubling trend that they feared would push the total higher: The monkeys were, increasingly, showing up in private hands. Macaques had entered the pet trade, constituting what a journal published by the CDC identified in early 1998 as a possible emerging infectious-disease threat.

Ringo was one of those pets. James Beekman kept the monkey illegally in his Palm Beach apartment, never securing the possession permit required by the state and ignoring the city's prohibition against owning primates. Authorities learned of Ringo after Beekman stopped on a Worth Avenue sidewalk—the chichi hub of Palm Beach—to let Debra Brewster and her four-year-old daughter, Catherine, play with the young macaque. Only later that Sunday did Brewster notice a bite mark on Catherine's shoulder, and a physician who treated the puncture wound recommended testing the monkey for disease. But because Beekman had no permit to keep Ringo, public-safety officials were unable to identify him and so were left to play a hunch: A year earlier, paramedics had responded to a "911" call from an apartment dweller whose pet spider monkey was having seizures. A fire-department rescue unit arrived to find the caller performing CPR on the tiny primate, but to no avail. From a photo, Debra Brewster identified that man as James Beekman.

Beekman denied owning Ringo, but he ultimately confessed after state wildlife investigators took affidavits, examined documents, and pieced together the truth: The thirty-one-year-old auto detailer had bought his pet macaque from James Anderson, the Fort Lauderdale dealer who ended up with most of the Harvard Medical School's cotton-top tamarins; Anderson, in turn, had purchased Ringo from Michael Powell, his South Florida colleague, who was the middleman for eighty-two animals that died in a six-month period. Seven days after the biting incident, Beekman finally turned Ringo over to the Florida Game and Fresh Water Fish Commission. Two and a half weeks later, Beekman was charged in county court with a five-count misdemeanor. Among the charges: secretly trying to resell the monkey to escape prosecution.

The seven-day lag left health officials guessing about the type of monkey that had bitten Catherine Brewster and about its disease status. As a result, the young girl was forced to undergo a series of medical tests and rabies shots, a regimen that Beekman dismissed in a newspaper interview as an overreaction. Not only had he diapered the macaque, slept in the same bed, and eaten off the same plate, but hundreds of people, he said, had held or kissed his pet with no apparent adverse consequences. Terri Parrott, however, was not quite as sanguine; after Ringo was deposited with her for safekeeping, she sent his blood off for testing. The results confirmed her worst suspicions: The macaque was herpes B-positive.

—<o>—

A couple of large cages sit behind Kevin Ivester's home in central Georgia, a hundred miles south of Atlanta. The impressive set-up gives his resident collection of capuchin monkeys shade, shelter, and room to move, along with a seasonal supply of pecans that fall from overhanging limbs. Capuchins have a life span of forty or more years, and so owning one of the cat-size monkeys can truly be a lifetime commitment. Sanctuaries are overflowing with monkeys abandoned by those unprepared for such responsibility, and interim caregivers such as Terri Parrott are continually asked to clean up the mess left behind by misguided primate enthusiasts like James Beekman. But it's unlikely that Ivester's group will ever be foisted off on others, because he is the model of responsible pet ownership: He has a strict regimen of daily care; he has a vast library of books, journals, and other research on the animals' needs; he even abbreviates vacations so that stand-ins aren't entrusted with his pets for more than three days. "My life," he says, "revolves around them."

Ivester bought his first monkey when he was a teenager, and he grew so attached to her that the two became college housemates: He lived in one room of a mobile home and P.J. in another. The amiable veterinary technician later decided that his capuchin would benefit from companionship, that a lifetime without another of her species was unfair, so in 1985 he went looking for a cage-mate. His search ended in a Tampa-area mobile-home park, where a marmoset breeder had caged on her porch a couple of "surplus" capuchins from the Dreher Park Zoo, an AZA facility in Palm Beach County. Ivester paid the breeder $400, and in return he got a two-year-old monkey and a receipt inscribed with a single line: "Guaranteed healthy & free of disease upon sale."

Ivester subsequently acquired two more capuchins (and another two were born at his facility) and at the same time became involved in campaigns to improve the welfare of captive primates. He is a director of the Simian Society of America, a small group of primate enthusiasts who work to discourage monkey ownership by those not up to the task. He is also a writer and coeditor of the society's *Primate Care Handbook*, a well-regarded volume whose pages about diet and psychological well-being are preceded by stern warnings: Monkeys are wild, unpredictable, and often vicious. Their bites can be life-threatening. Their food and veterinary care are expensive. They're destructive. They masturbate, copulate, and display their genitalia regardless of who's watching. They may harbor diseases. Their cages reek unless disinfected regularly. They sometimes require round-the-clock care.

"There are perhaps a limited number of individuals suited for the task of long-term primate caretaking," the book counsels. "Unfortunately, the story of 'see monkey–want monkey–buy monkey–tire of monkey' is all too familiar . . . and it is usually the monkey who ends up losing the most for our misjudgment in taking on such a responsibility."

The primate trade—much like the trade in exotic animals generally—is built on such impulsive errors of judgment. It's a business filled with cruelties, primatologists say, beginning with a newborn's removal from its mother. Adult males are forced into an adjoining cage, and the hysterical mother is so desperate to hold onto her offspring that she may have to be tranquilized. The traumatized, days-old monkey is packed into a crate and hauled off to an auction or shipped by air to someone who typically has no primate-care experience. The tiny monkeys are a child substitute for some buyers, who treat them accordingly: They're christened, outfitted in baby clothes, seated in high chairs, provided baby-sitters, and started on inevitably futile toilet-training regimens. For others, pet monkeys are status symbols, to be shown off in public, passed around among the curious, and subjected to endless stress and thoughtless abuse. Young monkeys are susceptible to measles, mumps, and other human diseases, and because adequate veterinary care is often difficult to find, many of them die.

Three- or four-year-old monkeys undergo dramatic personality changes, which usually carry unpleasant consequences for them and their owners: They become unruly and destructive, which confuses and upsets owners. The monkeys sometimes inflict life-threatening bites, so their teeth are extracted. They initiate troubling sexual displays, so the males are castrated and the females spayed. And many owners eventually stop having any physical contact with their monkeys, relegating them to basements or other out-of-the-way places where the social animals are left to spend the remainder of their lives entirely alone. Others are tagged for disposal. But hand-reared monkeys lack survival skills, and therefore can't be returned to the wild. Zoos don't want them. Animal shelters aren't equipped to keep them. Sanctuaries are overrun with others like them. In many instances, the only willing takers are the dealers who fuel the trade in infant monkeys. They reclaim the animals and sell them as year-olds to unsuspecting clients. Other sexually intact animals are designated as breeders, perpetuating the cycle, miserable as it is.

Public-health officials have other reasons to be concerned about primate ownership. Monkey bites can cause severe lacerations, wound infections, and potentially debilitating conditions such as osteomyelitis, an infection of the bone that may result in permanent deformity or, in chronic cases, require amputation. Although monkeys can infect humans with the Ebola virus, monkeypox, and other deadly exotic illnesses, it is much more likely that they will contract such human-origin diseases as tuberculosis, hepatitis A, shigellosis, and cholera, and either infect other monkeys or transmit the illnesses back to humans. Primates dumped into the pet trade after biomedical researchers are done with them may harbor a variety of infectious diseases that can be passed to humans, including hepatitis viruses and the HIV-like simian immunodeficiency virus. Because of such health threats, the National Association of State Public Health Veterinarians has recommended banning the private ownership of primates and outlawing further sale of them as pets.

Like the foxes and coyotes that pass along *Echinococcosis multilocularis* tapeworm eggs, which develop into cysts in the liver, lungs, and brain of humans, other animals can pose similarly grave threats. Rabies, which each year kills one or two Americans (but an estimated 40,000 to 100,000 people worldwide), may infect pets, livestock, and such wildlife as raccoons, foxes, and skunks—animals that are increasingly being moved across state lines by dealers and fox-pen suppliers.

Raccoon roundworm *(Baylisascaris procyonis)*, a parasite that lives in the intestines of raccoons, is passed on to animals and humans through the feces of the omnivorous mammal. The victims of raccoon roundworm are often small children with dirty hands, who unknowingly ingest the roundworm eggs through normal hand-to-mouth behavior. After the eggs hatch, the roundworm larvae can pass through the intestine and enter the bloodstream; once unleashed, they can migrate throughout the body, infecting the eyes, liver, and other organs, or they can tunnel through the brain. After a young Illinois boy died from chewing on wood chips contaminated with raccoon feces, an autopsy revealed more than three thousand migrating larvae in his brain.

Brucellosis, one of the most serious livestock diseases, also affects reindeer, giraffes, and other zoo stock, and can be passed to humans through contact with infected animals. There has been a recent resurgence in tuberculosis among captive deer and elk, threatening both livestock and humans. There have been several reported cases of Hansen's disease (also known as human leprosy) in patients who had contact with the nine-banded armadillo, which is sold at exotic-pet shows and auctions. Those who own macaws, cockatiels, and other parrots are at risk of being infected with the bacterium that causes the deadly avian chlamydiosis; in humans, so-called psittacosis, or parrot fever, produces dry, hacking coughs and, in severe cases, bloody sputum, but the disease can also result in hepatitis, encephalitis, and respiratory failure. Many reptiles—along with hedgehogs, sugar gliders, and other exotic pets—carry some strain of *Salmonella,* a bacterium that, when passed to humans, can cause cramps, diarrhea, fever, and, in rare instances, even death. "Little mice scare me as much as a tiger," says a Florida wildlife officer who has monitored the influx of threatening species.

Sometimes animals pass along mystery diseases. Not long ago, for example, jerboas imported from Egypt were shipped to Texas and were quickly unloaded in pet stores. Many who bought the long-tailed rodents, which are related to the kangaroo rats of western North America, were stricken with a rash. Other buyers suffered flu-like symptoms that lasted for weeks, withstood antibiotics, and, in the end, defied diagnosis.

Sometimes recasting wildlife as pets sets the stage for medical disaster. It happened in late 1995, when officials of the National Center for Infectious Diseases warned state veterinarians about the risk of plague posed by the interstate movement of prairie dogs. There was no evidence that the deadly disease had ever been transmitted to a pet owner from a wild-caught prairie dog, but two recent trends raised the specter of just such an occurrence: The furry rodents had suddenly become a big pet-trade commodity, and along with their popularity came a surge in reports of prairie-dog bites from hospital emergency rooms. "In a worst-case scenario, if animals are wild-trapped, transported within a couple of days, and placed in a pet store without any quarantine period, and without any dusting for fleas, then you could potentially have ill animals and infected fleas in the pet store," Dr. Kathy Orloski, a staff epidemiologist at the National Center for Infectious Diseases, says. "If you purchased that prairie dog and brought it home, you'd have a prairie dog that may be coming down with the symptoms of plague with infected fleas on it. You and anyone else in that household would potentially be exposed to those fleas."

The following year, five cases of plague among humans were reported in the United States, below the average of ten to fifteen. Two of those five died, and investigators attributed one of the deaths to a bite from an infected prairie-dog flea. In March 1997, another threat emerged: Prairie dogs that had been sent to a research laboratory in Texas the previous year were diagnosed with tularemia, a rare tick-borne disease, also known as rabbit fever or deer-fly fever, that in humans causes paralysis, coma, and sometimes death. Epidemiologists traced the infected rodent to Mark Schoebel, the Wisconsin animal dealer who, they learned, had previously sent another shipment of prairie dogs to the Boston University School of Medicine. An investigation revealed that some of those animals had also died of tularemia. (Schoebel assured Wisconsin health officials that he had not sent prairie dogs to other research facilities or retail outlets, and the investigation soon ended. In truth, however, Wisconsin records show that on July 10, 1996, one month after the prairie dogs reportedly arrived at his facility, Schoebel had sent a dozen prairie dogs to the Vanderbilt University Medical Center. What's more, that same month he also shipped another twelve of the rodents to an animal dealer in Chattanooga, Tennessee, and two hundred more to a Michigan dealer, who resold them through ads in *Animal Finders' Guide*.) With the threat of plague looming, and with the realization that humans inhaling bacteria from the lungs of infected prairie dogs also run the risk of contracting tularemia and pneumonia, health officials in Virginia and a few other states heeded the federal government's warnings and banned private ownership of the animals.

Health and safety concerns have led to similar bans in the United States and abroad. For example, some European nations have outlawed the private ownership of most monkeys and other wild animals. The governments of several Australian states have made it illegal to own pet monkeys. Since late 1972, the U.S. government has taken a variety of steps to restrict the importation and interstate movement of small turtles—measures designed to protect children from potentially deadly salmonellosis. In 1994, when the CDC learned that Egyptian fruit bats were being imported for the pet trade, it put a nine-month moratorium on further shipments. A review of the scientific literature showed that even American bat species may carry a variety of arboviruses (viruses also passed by flying insects and birds) and that African *Tadarida* species (distantly related to Mexican free-tailed bats) may be able to transmit the Ebola virus. As a result, the CDC announced that it would issue permits for importing or transferring bats only if they were destined for zoos or bona fide scientific researchers. That more or less shut down the retail trade in bats. The CDC's attention has since been redirected to imported rodents, which also carry a slew of diseases. These include viral hemorrhagic fevers, which begin with flu-like muscle aches and can progress to acute respiratory problems, severe bleeding, kidney failure, and sometimes death. Because the rodents act as hosts for such viruses, tests are needed to identify infected animals. But no such testing is performed at U.S. borders, nor does the federal government require quarantines or even visual inspections.

As a result, state and federal health officials fear that the importation of unfamiliar species without first establishing protocols may be courting disaster. "From a public-health point of view, there are a lot of things we don't know," Dr. Stephanie Ostrowski, a veterinary epidemiologist formerly in the CDC's Division of Quarantine, says. "If people want new creatures for the pet trade, there should be a plan and a way to do it safely. I wish some agency could test them, certify them as healthy, and microchip them before they go out to pet stores.

"If no one is performing up-front testing for zoonotic diseases," she adds, referring to diseases that can be passed from animals to humans, "then it's not a question of whether there's going to be a disastrous incident, but when."

◄о►

The federal agencies that regulate wildlife, including the USDA, the Fish and Wildlife Service, and the Public Health Service, have shown little interest in coming up with rules to head off such health-related disasters; these matters, officials of the three agencies say, are somebody else's responsibility. Instead, they all play a game of cross-your-fingers-and-hope-no-one-dies.

That indifference on the part of the federal government is just fine with the universities, drug companies, and other institutions that might be saddled with the long-term responsibility for potentially deadly animals, most notably the expensive-to-care-for primates. Even the nation's regional primate research centers, which, ironically, are funded by the National Institutes of Health, freely unload animals that may endanger the public.

New York University's Laboratory for Experimental Medicine and Surgery in Primates is a good example. LEMSIP was the biomedical research facility where unwanted zoo primates landed in the late 1970s, the lab that sequestered battalions of chimps for human AIDS- and hepatitis-vaccine research. It was here, for example, that Pet-a-Pet's young chimpanzee, Mario, was sent after Jack Crippen closed his Virginia petting zoo, thereby subjecting the animal to two decades of infectious-disease research.

In early 1995, New York University began planning to sell LEMSIP, setting off a scramble for its five hundred baboons, macaques, and other primates. From all indications, LEMSIP's chimpanzees were destined for the Coulston Foundation, the infamous research facility that had been cited by federal investigators a year earlier for failing to provide water to fourteen primates, killing four of them. Dr. James Mahoney, the assistant director of LEMSIP, didn't believe that some of the young chimps under his care could survive Coulston's brand of invasive medical research, and he quietly began seeking out alternatives. In fact, Mahoney was determined to spare chimps of all ages from the dreaded laboratory in Alamogordo, New Mexico, and he targeted sanctuaries as new homes. Despite his efforts, however, ownership of nearly one hundred of LEMSIP's chimpanzees was transferred to the Coulston Foundation.

The philosophical issues that guided Mahoney's quest are explored in his 1998 book, *Saving Molly: A Research Veterinarian's Hard Choices for the Love of Animals*. The Scottish-born NYU researcher, who took a keen personal interest in a number of the lab's chimpanzees (he talks with obvious familiarity, for instance, about Mario's mannerisms and personality), addresses a host of thorny issues in his writings: How can an animal lover like him subject chimps and monkeys to the pain of experimentation? Are all tests justifiable? And don't we owe a decent retirement to laboratory animals that have endured years of torturous experiments?

Mahoney believes that the former research subjects deserve everlasting peace. But in his rush to do right by his animals, Mahoney may have shown less concern for their new human guardians. For example, about fifty chimpanzees were sent to a huge California sanctuary whose work force is largely composed of volunteers with no background in caring for primates that may pose a human-health risk. Another fifteen chimps were relocated to a sanctuary just south of Montreal (Canada's first for surplus laboratory primates). Quebec health authorities were troubled by the relocation: Animals that may have become chronically infected with human hepatitis or HIV, and that were previously housed in a laboratory that maintained Biosafety Level 2 standards, were now roaming an indoor/outdoor facility with few safety protocols. Care of the chimps was largely entrusted to community volunteers with no related experience or biosafety training. What's more, Quebec had no formal policies to ensure the protection of sanctuary visitors.

It's possible that the chimps posed no medical threat to their new guardians, but no one could say for certain. Quebec health officials spent several futile months requesting copies of the animals' complete medical histories. Without full disclosure, devising a safe environment for workers is reduced to a guessing game. Guess wrong, and people may die.

In mid-1997, the Yerkes Regional Primate Research Center sought to dispose of forty sooty mangabeys infected with simian immunodeficiency virus. A strain of SIV isolated from sootys (SIV_{sm}) is a close relative of human immunodeficiency virus type 2 (HIV-2), which can cause AIDS in humans. In fact, SIV_{sm} has been shown to be directly transmissible to other species, and there is widespread speculation that this simian virus evolved into HIV-2 after jumping the "species barrier" and infecting humans. This cross-transmission happened, it is believed, when people in West African nations—the natural range of mangabeys—butchered infected monkeys.

In 1992, the CDC reported that two laboratory workers—including one who had handled blood specimens without gloves—had developed antibodies to SIV. Six years later, CDC researchers confirmed that four animal handlers exposed to baboons and green monkeys were infected with another monkey retrovirus.

So far, the humans infected with SIV_{sm} (at least five have now been identified) and simian foamy virus have suffered no adverse health consequences, nor have their sexual partners been infected. But these monkey viruses are not thoroughly understood, and there is some concern that they may mutate and, like HIV-1 (which is responsible for the global AIDS epidemic), spread between people. Therefore, relocating a troupe of SIV-positive mangabeys obviously requires careful deliberation.

The Yerkes staff members charged with finding a new home for their infected mangabeys were repeatedly frustrated. For example, two Texas primate facilities rejected their overtures after expressing worries about the animals' health status and the possibility of monkey-to-human transmission of SIV. Finally, in late 1998, Yerkes worked out an agreement with Wild Animal Orphanage, a sanctuary in San Antonio, Texas.

The Yerkes Regional Primate Research Center was unusually secretive throughout the entire search process, refusing to answer public inquiries about its plans for the infected mangabeys. In fact, officials of the Texas Department of Health learned of the finalized arrangement with Wild Animal Orphanage only after receiving an anonymous tip.

Texas health officials were immediately concerned about the transfer. Because the sanctuary is open to the public, they worried that visitors might be put in jeopardy. A veterinary inspector with USDA's Animal and Plant Health Inspection Service worried about the sheer number of primates at the sanctuary, which had already contracted with a facility in Wisconsin to provide permanent housing for some of its research primates, including ninety-four stump-tailed macaques (some herpes B-positive).

Carol Asvestas, who with her husband, Ron, operates the sanctuary, tried to quell the fears by spelling out the specifics of the deal: Yerkes had agreed to finance the construction of a building to house the mangabeys. The building would be on land outside the city limits that the sanctuary had purchased to house retired research primates. And Yerkes had agreed to train the sanctuary's two permanent employees in Biosafety Level 2 protocols.

"Since Ms. Asvestas indicates that every effort is being made to protect her and her employees, and there will not be public access of any kind to the animals in her new facility, the shipment of these animals into the state does not seem to pose a significant threat to the public health of the state, and action by this department to block this shipment is not warranted at this time," Jim Schuermann, an epidemiologist in the Texas Department of Health, wrote in his recommendation to his superiors, including the chief of the Communicable Disease Control Bureau.

Notwithstanding Schuermann's guarded endorsement, the transfer raised troubling questions, including the most obvious: Is a private sanctuary the appropriate home for monkeys infected with a virus whose effects on humans are still uncertain? Even though the sanctuary's two permanent employees have been schooled in Biosafety Level 2 standards, which is recommended for exposure to SIV-infected monkeys, will they appreciate the need for such precautions and faithfully heed the guidelines?

Although primate centers provide their workers with ongoing safety training, sanctuaries are unlikely to do so. Wild Animal Orphanage employs two full-time keepers—the only ones trained by Yerkes—and relies heavily on a "volunteer" maintenance staff composed in part of individuals performing court-ordered community service. Although scientific primate centers have rigid security systems, Asvestas's sanctuary has been vulnerable and its new facility may be as well. In April 1997, for instance, an intruder had a hand mangled by a tiger when he and a buddy broke in to the sanctuary, possibly to steal a cougar. A month earlier, a tiger escaped from its cage, apparently after someone tampered with the door. In late 1997, a capuchin monkey escaped from its cage. The USDA was concerned enough about Wild Animal Orphanage that, in March 1999, the agency charged the Asvestases with violations of the Animal Welfare Act and proposed a ninety-day license suspension. Among the alleged violations detailed by APHIS inspectors: The sanctuary operators failed to "maintain structurally sound housing facilities for nonhuman primates in good repair so as to protect the animals from injury, to contain the animals securely, and to restrict the entrance of other animals."

Primate centers undergo continual scrutiny for their adherence to standards of humane care and occupational guidelines. As a USDA-licensed exhibitor that offers tours to paying customers (the mangabey building, however, will not be open to the public), the sanctuary is inspected regularly by a veterinarian chiefly for the purpose of evaluating its compliance with Animal Welfare Act standards—the primates' diet, the size of their cages, and the like. Primate centers rely on the federal government for their budgets; Wild Animal Orphanage is a not-for-profit organization that solicits donations. What happens if, in five, ten, or fifteen years, the sanctuary can't raise enough money to stay in operation? And who will take responsibility for the infected mangabeys if they outlive the sanctuary operators or if the place is closed for reasons of health, finances, or natural disaster? A case in point: Thousands of animals escaped their cages when Hurricane Andrew devastated parts of South Florida in August 1992. A month after the storm, fifty macaques and twenty baboons that had been housed at a research center south of Miami were still at large. Some of the facility's thousand-plus primates were shot by National Guard troops, while feral dogs later invaded the compound and ripped the arms and legs off of thirty free-roaming monkeys. "We predict a large number of these new exotics will adapt and establish breeding populations," an inspector with the Florida Game and Fresh Water Fish Commission wrote in a memo. "This includes a new population of primates, because they are too elusive for complete recapture."

Finally, there are more personal issues. Since the long-term consequences of exposure to simian immunodeficiency virus are still unknown, why expose the general public to the virus? Even if a sanctuary worker or volunteer infected with SIV suffers no health-related problems, testing positive for the virus during HIV screening will still have serious repercussions. Their health-insurance premiums are likely to be higher. Their employment in the health-care field may be problematic. And they are certain to experience immeasurable psychological stresses. Sanctuary personnel have been exposed to these risks and other potential consequences only because the Yerkes Regional Primate Research Center and New York University's LEMSIP didn't want to take responsibility for their own actions. Their disease-carrying primates are now someone else's problem.

◄o►

Presumably, those seeking to relocate unwanted macaques would not be as undiscriminating. After all, the risks of SIV may be uncertain, but there's incontrovertible evidence that herpes B kills humans. It has done so more than twenty times, according to medical literature. And in all likelihood, additional deaths from this monkey virus have gone undetected.

More than sixty years after Albert Sabin, the oral-polio-vaccine pioneer, implicated *Herpesvirus simiae* as the agent that killed the eponymous Dr. B., little is known about the macaque-borne virus. What's certain, however, is that rhesus, Japanese, pig-tailed, and virtually every other macaque species (more than a dozen) carry herpes B, and that up to 90 percent of adult macaques are infected. Like herpes simplex in humans, monkey B virus is characterized by a lifelong infection that resides in the nervous system and generally remains latent. Studies of both wild-caught and captive macaques show that, with age, the proportion of B-virus-positive individuals increases dramatically. At any given moment, research shows, about 2 percent of infected macaques shed the virus via saliva, urine, feces, and fluid from their eyes. This typically happens when a monkey is under stress or ill, or during breeding season. A human bitten, scratched, sneezed on, or spit at in the midst of this shedding runs the risk of infection.

Why only a small number of bite and scratch victims are infected with the virus is among the mysteries that have confounded researchers. There was speculation that some strains of herpes B are more virulent than others, but that doesn't appear to be so. Another theory—also now discounted—was that those infected with human herpes carry antibodies that protect them from the simian variety. Also unexplained is why some victims live and others don't. "Eighty percent of them go on to die," a physician who has studied the virus says. "And those who don't die wish they had."

That's because the disease is catastrophic. What begins with fatigue and flu-like symptoms progresses to headache, vomiting, double vision, difficulty swallowing, sensory loss, convulsions, and other manifestations of encephalitis, an inflammation of the brain. Death usually takes about four weeks, but survivors suffer pain, paralysis, neurological damage, and, this same doctor says, disabilities so severe that it's hard to think the quality of life justifies survival. Some infected individuals are permanently institutionalized.

There are other troubling aspects about the disease. Doctors know little about it, and a definitive diagnosis requires a test that only a few laboratories can perform. What's more, monkey owners often don't report bites or scratches out of fear that their pets might be confiscated, so some of the numerous deaths caused by influenza-like or viral encephalitis symptoms, but never diagnosed to conclusion, may in fact be attributable to herpes B. Finally, there is the possibility that infected individuals may initially suffer only mild symptoms, and the latent virus emerges later. When that happens—far removed in time from any exposure event—who would ever suspect a monkey-borne disease?

Given such threats, it's reasonable to expect that zoos, biomedical researchers, and others that house and display macaques would take uncompromising precautions to ensure that these animals never leave institutional control. In fact, however, many seem to take no precautions at all.

Throughout the 1990s, even though zoos and biomedical researchers well understood the threat of herpes B, they nonetheless unloaded macaques by the dozens on the same breeders and dealers given their other surplus exotics. This was particularly evident in the earlier part of the decade, when zoos concerned about the liabilities associated with harboring B-virus-infected macaques rushed en masse to get rid of the animals. The official species studbooks maintained by curators at AZA-accredited zoos show that all the usual suspects shared in the potentially deadly largesse. From the Columbus Zoo: Japanese macaques to Jim Fouts, nine months after the Kansas dealer was caught by *60 Minutes* selling zoo surplus at auction. From the Kansas City Zoo: Japanese macaques to Little Ponderosa Livestock Company, the Illinois dealer and auctioneer. From the Buffalo Zoo: Japanese macaques to New York dealer Edward Novack. From the Cincinnati Zoo and the Cleveland Metroparks Zoo: Japanese macaques to Northland Wildlife, whose owner pleaded guilty in 1993 to a federal charge of illegally selling monkeys. From Burnet Park Zoo, in Syracuse, New York: Japanese macaques to Lamkin Wildlife Company, a Texas pet-trade supplier. From Ross Park Zoo, in Binghamton, New York: Japanese macaques to both Lamkin Wildlife and Novack. From Henry Doorly Zoo, in Omaha: Japanese macaques to Northland Wildlife a year after the dealer's indictment on multiple counts of illegally importing, transporting, and selling primates. From the Los Angeles Zoo: Celebes macaques to Texas dealer Buddy Jordan. From Bucknell University: seven Japanese macaques to Animal Kingdom Zoo, in New Jersey, Burton Sipp's primate-dealing stronghold. And remarkably, from the California Regional Primate Research Center, in Davis, one of the NIH-funded research centers: nine Japanese macaques to Tom Nichols, of Georgia, the primate trafficker whose operation was finally busted by the U.S. Fish and Wildlife Service and a federal prosecutor in Atlanta.

In 1993 and 1994, zoos in Milwaukee, Pittsburgh, and Syracuse dumped more than twenty Japanese macaques on Ashby Acres, Robert Crowe's animal-dealing operation in New Smyrna, Florida. Pittsburgh "donated" nine, including at least five herpes-B-positive animals that had been kept in a quarantine area in the zoo's basement, away from public view. Lee Nesler, general curator of the zoo, told a reporter for the *Pittsburgh Post-Gazette* that Crowe's park has separate colonies of infected and uninfected macaques, and that the public would see only the latter. The relocation, added zoo spokeswoman Kerry Ford, was prompted, in part, by concern for worker safety.

But there was obviously no concern for Crowe's clientele—whether the auction-goers or the retail buyers—who apparently ended up with the potentially lethal animals. Crowe had four Japanese macaques before receiving the zoo castaways, and in the years that followed, his reports to the state game commission still showed just four. An official of the Florida Game and Fresh Water Fish Commission, who has inspected Crowe's operation, says the public is rarely allowed on the grounds, there is no separate colony of infected macaques, and he can't remember ever seeing more than the four Japanese macaques that Crowe owned before Pittsburgh and the other zoos sent him theirs. So where are the others, including those infected with the virus? Crowe will only say that he gave away the Pittsburgh Zoo's macaques before ever even bringing them on his property. End of conversation.

The dumping of zoo macaques has been so rampant that when Dr. Stephanie Ostrowski of the CDC reviewed primate transfer patterns from AZA institutions, she documented about two hundred Japanese macaques "lost to follow-up," along with another two hundred celebes macaques. Add to this the lion-tailed macaques and those species for which there are no official studbooks (the databases Ostrowski relied on for her calculations, according to her 1997 presentation at a meeting of zoo veterinarians).

The fallout is a pet trade teeming with macaques. They're for sale at Woods & Waters, Lolli Brothers, and other exotic-animal auctions. Macaques are flowing from roadside menageries to dealers, and from there to private homes. Macaques are being cross-bred with other species, creating hybrids whose capacity for B-virus and SIV infections is unknown. Five advertisers offered macaques in a recent issue of *Animal Finders' Guide,* including a South Florida broker selling rhesus monkeys, at one time the favored species of biomedical research. Their ranks also included an Idaho man with no USDA license; a Wisconsin primate dealer with pregnant snow macaques; and Bellona Arsenal Farm, in Midlothian, Virginia, whose inventory included three adult macaques, exact ages unknown.

Macaques, like other pet monkeys past infancy, bite and scratch. Many attacks are unprovoked; and children are often the targets. Testing of the animals, which can grow to forty pounds and become frighteningly aggressive, frequently reveals a herpes-B infection. But many macaque owners are either ignorant of the monkey-virus threat, uncon-cerned about it, willing to accept dealers' assurances that it's a nonissue, or are willing to ignore it, even if lives may be in jeopardy.

In a recent nine-month period, for example, twelve macaque bites were reported to the Arizona Department of Health Services. One in-volved a woman who took her pet into hiding after it bit a five-year-old child. (This ploy was intended to spare the monkey the fate suffered by its mother and sibling, who were euthanized after testing positive for herpes B.) Another case involved a four-year-old who was severely bitten by a macaque at an unlicensed day-care center in Phoenix. The facility's operator immediately transferred ownership of her macaque—one of her eight pet monkeys—to a local animal dealer, putting it out of the reach of health officials. Because the monkey could not be tested for herpes B, the young victim had to be hospitalized for four days and then needed prolonged outpatient care.

There was also the case of an infant macaque that tested positive for herpes B after a veterinarian treated it for vomiting and dehydration. At least five individuals—including three family members—had extensive exposure to the monkey through changing diapers, kissing it on the lips, preparing and washing baby bottles, sharing food, and swapping chewed bubble gum. Even after the veterinarian explained to them the risks of herpes B, the owner refused to leave her pet monkey at home and even brought it with her to a doctor's office for her own B-virus blood-test appointment. Three weeks later, she left the B-virus-positive macaque with one of her employees for the weekend. The employee took the monkey to a bar, where it bit another patron on the face.

◄○►

Nineteen months after his pet macaque bit four-year-old Catherine Brewster, James Beekman finally had his day in court. The state had of-fered Beekman a series of plea bargains, but each time he refused. The sticking point was always the same: He wanted the right to own mon-keys again. In fact, he wanted Ringo back. But the state deemed Beek-man unfit. Wildlife officers vowed to prohibit him from owning dangerous animals. And so the lawyers talked, deals were explored, and the case dragged on.

Throughout those long months, Ringo was confined to Terri Parrott's clinic. After the monkey twice tested negative for herpes B, the veterinarian decided to "give him a life." That's when she freed Ringo from quarantine, outfitted him in the union suit, and attached his leash to the sink pipe, where he could watch an ongoing procession of animals and humans. The former generally eyed him with indifference; the latter called him by name, asked how he was doing, stopped to hand him a toy or flip him a treat. Ringo became a popular resident of the veterinary clinic's exotic-animal wing, and the fear he would have otherwise engendered dissipated somewhat after doctors declared young Catherine Brewster free of the dreaded herpes B virus.

Over those same nineteen months, Terri Parrott also watched the threat from macaques escalate. She says that the monkeys became especially popular with Latino families in the Miami area, who often keep them without the required permits. "Nobody would even know they had a monkey until it got loose," she says. "They're the ones I'm worried about, because, like many other pet owners, they have no education about what they've got." Parrott also worries about the danger to the Florida wildlife officers she works with, who must snag macaques found roaming neighborhoods or encroaching on unfamiliar houses. She also recalls the girls from New York who showed up at her clinic in search of treatment for their pet spider monkey. The animal, it turned out, was a macaque.

Although state public-health veterinarians have proposed shutting down the primate trade, Parrott doesn't totally oppose the idea of monkey ownership. In fact, although some lawmakers and wildlife agencies would like to outlaw the private ownership of carnivores and other dangerous animals, Parrott believes that many exotic species are by and large appropriate companion animals. On the whole, she says, cougars make good pets. Parrott's longtime assistant breeds and sells marmosets (squirrel-size monkeys), which she endorses. She happily entrusts rare animals confiscated by wildlife officials to private citizens. She acknowledges that there's an ugly side to the ownership of exotic animals—the confiscated pets heaped on her are a constant and troubling reminder—but an outright ban, she thinks, is unwarranted. "'Exotic' people are very unusual," she says. "I wouldn't be in business if they weren't dedicated to their pets. They're more dedicated than a lot of dog and cat owners."

But if Terri Parrott condones the ownership of capuchins, squirrel monkeys, and spider monkeys, she draws the line at macaques. Time bombs, she calls them.

Ringo, for example, is still a baby, but in two more years, she says, he's going to be a full-grown male with big teeth and a surly attitude. Many macaques in private hands are about that same age, as the species has come into widespread popularity only recently. And age brings not only aggressiveness but also the onset of sexual activity—triggers, it is believed, for the shedding of herpes B. The convergence of all these factors—more aggressive, infected macaques exposed to greater numbers of unsuspecting humans—is what particularly troubles Parrott and like-minded colleagues, including Stephanie Ostrowski. The result, they predict, will be more cases of herpes B.

The Centers for Disease Control and Prevention could presumably put an end to the private trade in macaques by enforcing the foreign quarantine regulations of the Public Health Service Act, which decree that since October 10, 1975, imported primates and their progeny may not be redistributed to the pet trade. Public-health officials believe that the CDC will finally stop looking the other way when pet owners or their neighbors die—a certain outcome, they predict. "I was told that they need to see a body count before they'll take a really strong look," Parrott says. "We're still waiting."

Some contend that fatalities have already occurred, but that the deaths have gone unreported because B virus is difficult to identify. "It's very probable there have been a number of people who died from B virus and haven't been diagnosed," says David Davenport, an infectious-disease specialist at Michigan State University in Kalamazoo who has studied the disease. It's only conjecture, Davenport says, but he believes that as the number of macaques in the population increases, the probability of such deaths likewise grows.

None of this, however, seemed to concern James Beekman. He wanted his pet macaque returned, and so on May 5, 1998, nineteen months after Ringo was confiscated, he headed for the huge judicial complex in downtown Palm Beach. Then the unexpected happened: Beekman learned that Court TV was preparing to broadcast the trial, and his resolve to reclaim his monkey dissolved. He decided to forgo the limelight for a plea bargain.

The negotiations dragged on for four hours, but a deal was finally struck: Beekman agreed to plead guilty on three charges, including one count of failure to protect the public. Adjudication was withheld on another count, and the state dropped the last count—failure to have documentation showing the source of his wildlife. Beekman also agreed to forfeit his monkey and to pay more than $3,100 in court fees and restitution, including $500 for Catherine Brewster's medical bills. In addition, he was placed on probation for two years.

Not long after the court action, Ringo got a reprieve. Terri Parrott's only placement option was biomedical research, which for her was unthinkable. So she and some coworkers decided to adopt the young macaque and share the responsibility for his care. Parrott thinks it's a good arrangement, since everyone at the clinic had become so attached to the monkey. Ringo, she says, will be treated well.

Surprisingly, Beekman earned his own form of absolution: a Florida fish and game officer recanted his pledge and agreed not to oppose Beekman's new wildlife-possession application. If after three years Beekman has met the terms of the plea arrangement, the primate enthusiast will again be free to sleep with a monkey, eat off the same plate, and—barring intervention from the CDC—expose both himself and others to the threats of a killer virus.

10

GOING, GOING, GONE

Thomas Solin arrived in the vicinity of Buckhorn Flats Game Farm, in Almond, Wisconsin, early on a Saturday morning in September 1997. Solin, a conservation warden, had driven the hundred miles from his home near Madison to examine the acquisition and disposition records of Stanley Hall, the game farm's owner, and also to deliver an order of quarantine issued by the Wisconsin Department of Agriculture, Trade and Consumer Protection. It was routine work for Solin, whose responsibilities include monitoring the state's game farms for compliance with regulations of the Department of Natural Resources. But for the veteran warden, the routine was broken by something entirely unexpected: the pointblank shooting of a penned trophy animal, exactly the sort of infamous "canned hunt" that's often whispered about but rarely seen.

The quarantine order that Solin carried had been imposed because Stan Hall had recently acquired a couple of nonnative mule deer but couldn't produce the required documents to show their place of origin. Wisconsin has strict regulations governing the importation of mule deer and other cervidae, and health officials in the state were on high alert because Hall's trading partners included a Michigan game farmer suspected of shipping deer without first performing health tests. There had been an outbreak of bovine tuberculosis in Michigan deer, and the importation of infected animals could pose a grave threat to wildlife, as well as to the state's lucrative livestock industry. What's more, humans could be at risk from exposure to infected animals or from consuming dairy products made with unpasteurized milk.

The Michigan outbreak was being closely watched by state agriculture and wildlife agencies, but Wisconsin's had the most pressing concerns. More than two dozen TB-infected deer had been identified in Michigan in 1995, and another twenty-plus the following year—a startling number, inasmuch as only eight cases of the highly communicable disease had previously been documented in wild deer across the United States. A single TB-infected cow found in northeastern Wisconsin had spooked state agriculture officials, who feared that the incident might somehow be linked to the Michigan outbreak. Their worries were compounded by an unalterable geographical reality: Wisconsin shares two hundred miles of border with Michigan's Upper Peninsula. The TB outbreak had so far been confined to a five-county region in Michigan's lower reaches, but wildlife officials in the state wouldn't rule out the possibility that whitetails in the Upper Peninsula could be similarly infected. Wisconsin officials grew so concerned that there was half-joking talk of erecting a deer-proof fence along the entire Michigan border.

The possibility of animal-health problems at Stan Hall's place was unrelated to the confirmed bovine tuberculosis cases, but troublesome nonetheless. Michigan wildlife officers had recently seized records from game-farm owners suspected of moving elk and deer in and out of the state without the required paperwork and without first having them tested for disease. Indictments were expected, but Michigan investigators were stymied by the intricacies of the paper trail. One subject of their investigation, for example, was the owner of, or a partner in, four different game farms, and animals were moved among them until it was nearly impossible to determine their true origins. Auditors faced a task not unlike one undertaken by a New York state investigator who, a few years earlier, had tried to chronicle the movement of bears to and from such facilities as Catskill Game Farm. He gave up after a few days, explaining that deciphering the business records of organized-crime families—which he had once been called on to do—was much easier.

The presence of diseased animals—even if confined to game farms—terrifies wildlife officials, because there are no assurances that native herds won't be infected. In South Dakota, for instance, the owners of Bear Country U.S.A., a drive-through park, have, on their nearby ranches, domestically raised elk that are infected with chronic wasting disease, an infection related to mad-cow disease that causes the animals' slow, horrific, and certain death. One of the three pastures on which the infected elk live is next to Wind Cave National Park, which abuts Custer State Park—home to most of the state's wild elk. If a ranch gate opens or an infected pen-raised elk comes in nose-to-nose contact through a fence with its wild cousin, animals throughout the Black Hills could be in jeopardy.

Tom Solin's inspection of Hall's records was being conducted in the throes of peak game-farm activity. Most game-farm deer are moved in September or October—before the bucks' inevitable mating-season fights begin, and in advance of the canned-hunt patrons who typically come out in the fall. In addition, does have usually weaned their fawns by then, so the females can be relocated in time for November breeding. Solin had been in contact with Michigan wildlife investigators, who speculated that the game farmers under investigation may have illegally shipped deer to Wisconsin in the previous three weeks. A thorough examination of Hall's records, Solin figured, might reveal whether the undocumented mule deer, which are native to the western United States, had come by way of these Michigan operators.

Although Hall is one of more than four hundred deer farmers in Wisconsin, Solin was particularly familiar with his business dealings. Hall had recently received some unwelcome notoriety after a magazine alleged that one of his clients had been part of a hunting hoax. A year earlier, Steven Futch, a U.S. Marine Corps major from Pasadena, California, had sold an article to *Buckmasters Whitetail Magazine* and several other North American publications chronicling his deer-hunting exploits. In the story, titled "Carrot Patch Buck," Futch graphically described a two-day Wisconsin excursion that had netted him a once-in-a-lifetime trophy buck: "As I settled the cross-hairs on his shoulder, I heard the farmer announce, 'That's the big one.' Those whispered words played over and over again in my mind as the evening silence was shattered by the crack and boom of my rifle. The buck wheeled and lurched forward to his final resting place in the oak leaves on the floor of the forest which had borne him." The article was accompanied by a photograph of a beaming Futch, rifle at his side, next to his fourteen-point monster.

But there was one problem, according to the *Wisconsin Outdoor Journal*: The carrot-patch buck, the magazine claimed, had actually been shot on the grounds of Hall's game farm in November 1994, blown away inside a fence that precluded anything even remotely resembling a fair chase. According to the magazine's account, Futch was found out when taxidermist Klaus Lebrecht, who had been brought the deer's antlers for replication, and who had positively identified the "rack" as belonging to a pen-raised animal, later stumbled on Futch's article. Labrecht knew those antlers, and he knew something was amiss.

At the time, Dick Dickinson, a special agent with the U.S. Fish and Wildlife Service, was investigating the shooting of a huge buck under suspicious circumstances, and the paper trail led him to Lebrecht. *Wisconsin Outdoor Journal* got wind of the investigation—which concluded that no law had been broken—and assigned Richard Wulterkens, a freelance writer, to look into it. By the time Wulterkens finished his reporting, Futch's story appeared to have unraveled: For starters, Futch was photographed beside his trophy kill wearing nothing but camouflage, in violation of Wisconsin's laws, which decree that hunters wear blaze-orange clothing. His account told of a hunting partner killing his deer with a bow and arrow, which is illegal during Wisconsin's gun season. What's more, Wulterkens reported that the carrot-patch buck had been bottle-fed and hand-raised by Kevin Kimball, another Wisconsin deer farmer with whom Hall often conducted business. Kimball, who had raised "Little Lyle" as breeding stock and sold him to Hall, told Wulterkens that the deer was so tame it was "little more than a cow."

Futch stood by his narrative and sued *Wisconsin Outdoor Journal* for damaging his reputation. The magazine countered by producing Hall's 1994 annual report to the Wisconsin Department of Natural Resources, which listed one Steven Futch as having taken one adult white-tailed deer at Buckhorn Flats on November 10. But Futch claimed—as he still does today—that the carrot-patch kill was the real deal, and he pressed ahead with the case. The two sides finally reached a confidential out-of-court settlement, but no retraction was ever printed.

―◦―

Buckhorn Flats Game Farm sits on two forty-acre tracts, split down the center by a road. One of the parcels is nothing but open field, with a scraggly corn crop that provides the resident deer with food and some cover. About fifteen acres of the other tract is given over to a pole barn, a four-to-five-acre pen, and various facilities for Stan Hall's deer-farming business, while the remaining twenty-five or so acres is covered with jack pine and scrub trees. Circling the property on foot takes all of about twenty minutes.

There are two wooden towers on the property, one overlooking the cornfield and the other back in the trees. With binoculars, it's possible to see both towers from the roads on either side of the fenced-in acreage. Deer ambling along the property or lying in the timothy grass are also usually visible through the fence. Some scarcely move when you appear, so acclimated are they to humans.

There are typically thirty to forty, sometimes as many as fifty, of these white-tailed deer out in the rear part of the compound. Some are born and raised on the property, whereas others come by way of dealers like Mark Schoebel, Reston Animal Park's bear-cub supplier. From the road it's a pastoral setting, but this is actually the Buckhorn Flats shooter pen, where rifle-toting customers climb a ladder and wait in the tower for one of the deer to wander by. It's never much of a wait.

Buckhorn Flats is a so-called canned hunt—a privately operated shooting ground whose customers are assured that they won't leave empty-handed. There are many incarnations of canned hunts. An animal is shot point-blank in its cage. Or a big cat is trucked to a prearranged spot and shot by a waiting client when the cage door is opened. Or a game-farm elk walking to its afternoon feeding—lured by the bell to which it has grown accustomed—is shot in its tracks from beside the trail it always follows. Or an animal is drugged and released into the woods, where it is too disoriented even to run. Or an animal raised at a petting zoo, accustomed to the outstretched hand of humans holding food, is set free inside the fences, its instinct to approach someone with a rifle, not to flee from him. Or dogs tree a cougar, and a hunting guide uses his cellular phone to round up someone who'll pay to kill it; when a price is agreed on, the location is revealed. Out-of-town patrons sometimes choose the deer they'll kill from photos sent them. Some canned-hunt operators show would-be clients pictures of the antlers that a buck shed the previous year. Because a deer's antlers grow to more or less the same dimensions year after year, the canned-hunt operator can calculate "rack" size using standard trophy-scoring systems, such as that of the Boone and Crockett Club. If you're willing to pay the right price, the deer and its antlers are yours. And if you can somehow convince the antler-size scorers that the deer was killed on a real hunting trip, rather than at an open-air trophy shop, you'll qualify for the record books.

What exactly constitutes a canned hunt is the subject of ongoing debate. When the U.S. House of Representatives considered the Captive Exotic Animal Protection Act of 1995, the ill-fated legislation sought to ban the trophy hunting of nonnative species within enclosures of less than one thousand square acres. Some hunters say that, depending on the terrain and the kind of animal being stalked, it's possible to simulate actual hunting conditions on even a hundred acres. Others, including many avid hunters, take a harder line: that because a fence makes escape impossible, such hunting—whether on ten acres or ten thousand—should be outlawed.

Whatever their yardstick, sportspersons who decry canned hunts agree with David Croonquist, Assistant Chief, Law Enforcement, of the Colorado Division of Wildlife: "I don't consider those hunts. The hunting community believes in the elements of fair chase. The shooting of an animal raised inside a fenced enclosure of any size is not a hunt. There is a difference between shooting and hunting."

In mainstream hunting magazines, those who patronize the worst of these operations have been likened to assassins. The National Rifle Association has denounced "canned shoots," proclaiming them the antithesis of fair chase. The NRA opposed the canned-hunt legislation, however, branding it yet another attempt to erode the nation's hunting heritage. So did Safari Club International, an association of big-game hunters based in Tucson, Arizona, even though its code of ethics calls for both fair chase and the humane harvesting of wildlife—provisions that are presumably intended to distinguish this self-proclaimed conservation group from the "slob hunters," as they're often referred to, that patronize canned hunts.

By any standard, Buckhorn Flats is one of those widely denounced canned hunts. There is no fair chase inside its fences; in fact, there is no chase at all: You can peer into the cornfields from one tower, and from the other tower you can simply wait for the passing parade, shoot one deer as it plods by, or else hold out for another or another or another, which will inevitably follow. Buckhorn Flats is nothing but target practice, a no-muss-no-fuss way of obtaining a rec-room conversation piece without having to spend hundreds of hours traipsing through Wisconsin forest. You can be in and out of Buckhorn Flats in a day, on your way home with your kill at the taxidermy shop and, if you've got the imagination of a fiction writer, an incredible story to tell.

The criticism heaped on canned hunts like Buckhorn Flats has prompted a few states to enact legislation banning these shooting grounds (though sometimes grandfathering in existing operations). In other states, however, the ranks of canned-hunt operators are not only growing, but entrepreneurs also are devising clever new twists. In Montana, for example, one would-be operator sought permission from the state to combine his canned hunt with an exotic-meat business; after all, he figured, the shooter usually only wants a trophy, so why let the meat go to waste? The state agriculture department took the position that the idea, which would have relegated the animals to open fields for killing, violated Montana's slaughter laws. Much to the relief of the state fish and game department, which considered the proposal an ethical travesty, a court turned down the businessman's appeal.

Wildlife and agriculture departments also fear, with justification, that irresponsible canned-hunt operators both foster the spread of disease and upset the natural order by introducing new species. In a number of states, for example, swine imported for hunting have taken up permanent residence, displacing native species and bringing with them the threat of pseudorabies and brucellosis. In Indiana, a veterinarian with the state agriculture department says, feral pigs released for hunting have proven to be a particular menace. "We originally thought there were about fifty, but later learned there were a whole bunch more," she says. "The Department of Natural Resources put out a notice to deer hunters that said: If you see these things, shoot them. Along with your deer license you can shoot all the wild boars and feral pigs you can find, because they're not supposed to be here anyway." But open season on the pigs hasn't eliminated them. "They're still out there," the veterinarian says.

Despite the recurring bad publicity about canned hunts, Stan Hall hasn't been hurting for customers. His annual roster typically includes a dozen or so shooters, although in one recent year he got twice that. Most come from towns south and east of Almond, though some travel great distances to get to Buckhorn Flats: Citronelle, Alabama; Groverton, Georgia; Gillhead, North Carolina; Long Island City, New York. The client list has included an obstetrician/gynecologist from the far-west reaches of Virginia and a dentist from Bennington, Vermont. Because patrons of canned hunts aren't bound by the take limits imposed on real hunters by state fish and game laws (they're restricted only by the size of their bankroll), a Houston man paid Hall to kill five animals on a single day in November 1996.

But not all of Hall's clients come away happy. One man, after paying to shoot a deer advertised to be worthy of inclusion on the Boone and Crockett Club's list of notable trophies, complained to the state Department of Natural Resources that the animal's antlers fell short of the mark. (Hall responded by offering him a cut-rate deal on a buck the following season.)

Others, though, return to Buckhorn Flats year after year. Their ranks include E. Wayne Pocius, a Pennsylvanian who on some days has left Hall's property with three "trophies," including a reindeer. Pocius (pronounced "pokus") is an official scorer for Safari Club International, whose code of ethics demands fair chase. In that capacity, Pocius is called on to judge whether animals killed by members of the organization meet the requirements for record-book entry. His own achievements include the Safari Club's record for a whitetail taken with a bow and arrow—a feat made all the more incredible by his ability to have it captured on videotape.

Pocius is featured in a series of videos, demonstrating for novices and experts alike the fine art of stalking and hunting deer. The series also features such luminaries of the hunting establishment as Thompson Temple, of Ingram, Texas, an outfitter whose company owns two game preserves in Hill County (an area north of San Antonio that's overrun with hunting ranches) and who in 1976 established a record book for exotic trophies taken in the United States. For Jim Stinebaugh, a veteran agent of the U.S. Fish and Wildlife Service, Temple's renown has its roots elsewhere. "He had a deer he bought from Michigan that was going to upgrade the gene pool on a big ranch called Anacacho Ranch in southwest Texas," Stinebaugh recalls. "I think he paid $5,000 for this big, old deer with monster horns that was on its last legs. He brought it down here and it was almost dead when it got here. The veterinarian worked on it and couldn't do any good for it. They took it down and put it on the Anacacho Ranch. The deer was fading fast; he couldn't get on his feet, so Thompson shows pictures to some hunters in the area and gets an attorney out of Florida who pays him $10,000 to shoot this big deer. Well, Thompson takes him and rides him around and around the Anacacho Ranch for fifteen or twenty miles in a big circle and whispers, 'Wow, there he is; he's right under the tree.' Well, the deer is lying there; he can't get up. He turns his head and looks at Temple, and the attorney lets the air out of him with his .270 and goes home with a big trophy. Thompson, being the entrepreneur he is, had already set up a deer contest, and they rushed off and won."

—◦—

Tom Solin parked on the north side of Buckhorn Flats to prepare paperwork for his Saturday meeting with Stan Hall. A nearby rifle shot got Solin from his car, and with the help of binoculars he saw three men beside a truck in the corral behind Hall's pole barn. Three bighorn sheep were at the far end of the five-acre pen, and before long one of the men headed toward the animals, in the hope, it seemed, of moving them to a different location.

As Solin watched from afar a second member of the group grabbed a rifle, leaned over the hood of the truck, and took aim. He heard a single shot and watched one of the bighorns fall to the ground. The three men then got into the truck and drove the hundred feet to the carcass. It was September 27, 1997. Solin noted the time as 7:35 a.m., then headed for the entrance to the ranch.

As Solin reached the foot of the driveway, a red pickup came around the pole barn and stopped near his car. Stan Hall and two men got out of the truck: a taxidermist from a nearby Wisconsin town, Solin later found out, and the shooter, a principal in an accounting firm in Logan, Utah, who reportedly had paid Hall $5,000 for the kill. There was a freshly gutted bighorn sheep in the bed, its great horns curled in near-360 degree arcs. The animal's left-rear leg hung over the edge of the truck, and trails of blood stained the license plate and rear bumper.

Solin identified himself, showed a badge, and grilled Hall about an uncased rifle in the truck, which is illegal in Wisconsin. He also advised Hall that shooting the bighorn sheep was against the law, that only deer could be shot on game farms, and that he would refer the matter—as mandated by state law—to the local sheriff. Hall disputed both charges (six months later, when the *Milwaukee Journal Sentinel* learned of the incident, Hall also disputed Solin's contention that the sheep was killed in the small pen). While Hall and Solin argued, the taxidermist drove the carcass to the nearby woods so that the shooter could pose with his trophy. Kneeling before the trees with the sheep, the accountant wouldn't have to explain away the fences, animal trailer, or Stan Hall's house in the background of his "hunting-expedition" photos.

Hall produced for Solin two health certificates that showed the origin of his bighorn sheep, which had been shipped in a week and a half earlier. A Michigan certificate revealed that three four-year-old males—named Spanky, Rocky, and Bombay—had come from a Michigan dealer who supplies deer, elk, and other animals to operators of canned hunts. Solin says it's his experience that names usually indicate that the animals are zoo castoffs, but in this instance he had no way of proving that. Another four-year-old male had been sent to Hall by Roger Karber, a South Dakota game farmer whose elk have come from the Bramble Park Zoo, an AZA member in Watertown, South Dakota, and whose bighorn sheep have come from the Buffalo Zoo via dealer Ed Novack.

Following the picture-taking session, the taxidermist skinned the bighorn carcass. Hall used a small chain saw to cut off the sheep's feet and remove the horns from its skull. The Utah "hunter" watched as the taxidermist laid the horns out on a wagon, measured them, and prepared them for mounting.

Solin pored over Hall's records, searching for clues about the unaccounted-for mule deer that he had come to investigate. A week later, in his Madison office, he discovered a number of discrepancies and inconsistencies in the documents: Hall reported buying five deer from another dealer, but the dealer didn't report selling him any. A Michigan deer farmer claimed that he had bought twenty-one deer from Hall, but Hall's records contained no trace of the transaction. Three to six mule deer had been shot on Hall's property, but his records reflected the acquisition of only one of these animals. Hall's records also indicated that, in nearly every instance, white-tailed deer were killed on his ranch, but records of the taxidermist who handled many of the mounts there showed that other species were in fact killed. And there was one last matter to puzzle through: A reindeer had been shot at Hall's ranch in October 1996, but where it came from was a total mystery.

◄○►

There are dozens of exotic-animal and "alternative-livestock" auctions across the country, but none compare with Woods & Waters, in Delphos, Ohio, and Lolli Brothers Alternative Livestock & Bird Sale, in Macon, Missouri. These two auctions—the largest east and west of the Mississippi River—are the linchpins of the exotic-animal industry. Animals move between these hubs and the nation's smaller sales, then to mom-and-pop breeders, penny-ante dealers, and individual pet owners, a true wholesale-retail chain of distribution. Animals from these auctions also move directly to canned hunts. In fact, Solin's missing reindeer passed through the Lolli Brothers auction on its way to Stan Hall's place, although it would take the game warden an entire year to learn that.

Without huge regional auctions like Woods & Waters and Lolli Brothers, the exotic-animal industry would be turned upside-down, possibly even crippled. Breeding stock would be harder to come by. Middlemen would lose ready access to their predictable supply of babies, which are the foundation of the pet trade. Roadside zoos would lose a prime source for their seasonal attractions and would in turn have a difficult time unloading their unwanted fall inventory. Hunting-ranch operators would be denied one-stop shopping for their trophy stock, requiring them to spend considerably more on travel and transportation to acquire deer, elk, bison, addax, and the like. More important, though, the demise of the Delphos and Macon auctions would force big-time and jerkwater dealers to deal with one another more openly, to exchange business cards and telephone calls, to buy and sell merchandise without the welcome cover of anonymity and with at least the semblance of a paper trail. In fact, the ability to conduct business incognito, to profit from such often-detestable commerce without any acknowledged responsibility, without any notion of who is buying animals, or why, is what makes these auctions so appealing in the first place.

"It was a whole other culture," says a onetime regular at Delphos and Macon, who, of course, asks not to be named. "Nobody would ask you who you were. It was really hard to find out who people were, what their names were. Most of them didn't even put their last names on their business cards. There was this one sleazebag girl from Michigan who used to bring these baby monkeys, just loads of them. She was personally really dirty, and not a nice person. Everyone would talk about how disgusting her place was. But she had what people wanted. She had the monkeys.

"You would never really know who these people were. If they had a place, then maybe. You would see their truck, and the truck would say the name. But you had to be very careful not to be too curious about who they were and where they got their animals from. That was never asked. They would talk about others sometimes, but not really about themselves."

Although selling at auction may cut into your profit margin (commissions are typically 10 percent for sales over $50, twice that for cheaper winning bids), it eliminates after-market hassles. "If you sell directly to the end user," this former auction patron adds, "then you've got that burden of them calling you back and saying, 'The monkey is biting.'"

Because auction houses like Woods & Waters and Lolli Brothers are regulated by USDA, monitored by state wildlife agencies, and open to the public, sellers have the it's-perfectly-legal pretense to justify their nameless horse trading. But a closer look at the buyers shows what the action is really about.

Lolli Brothers, April 1995: The proprietor of Dixie Wildlife Safaris, a hunting ranch in Frostproof, Florida, goes home with eight sika deer hauled in from Illinois and Minnesota. Steven Forest, the owner of Adventure Safaris, a hunting ranch in Bandera, Texas, buys Père David's deer and a fallow deer. Theodore Fitzgerald, a Michigan game farmer, buys two dozen Russian hogs. Ten months later, Fitzgerald is indicted on thirty-one counts of violating state game laws. Among the allegations:

that he brought Russian boars into the state that hadn't been tested for disease; he's also charged with dumping animal carcasses and parts in a river not far from Hunter's Quest, his shooting preserve, and later plea-bargains his way out of a felony charge by agreeing to close the canned hunt and dispose of his animals.

The 1996 lineup at Woods & Waters is more of the same: Operators of canned hunts in Cheboygan, Michigan; Homer, New York; and Tioga, Pennsylvania, leave with trophy stock. An adult rhesus macaque—a potential carrier of the herpes B virus—is sold to the operator of a pet store in northern Indiana whose sideline is peddling a bizarre collection of bib overalls, boxer shorts, parachute pants, and other custom-tailored monkey fashions. Animals from Indiana and New York are sold at the auction and transported by the new owners directly to Mid-America Animal Auction, in Cape Girardeau, Missouri, to be sold again. A male-female pair of thirteen-week-old pet lions is sold to a man from Alabama. A two-week-old pet cougar is sold to a man from Pennsylvania. A newborn bobcat is sold to an exotic-animal dealer from Shelbyville, Indiana, who, just five days later, unloads it at an auction in New Castle, seventy miles away.

Another buyer at the 1996 auction is Ronald Morrow, who is the high bidder on seven Russian hogs that have been trucked in from Iowa and Michigan. Two years earlier, Morrow had been found guilty of civil violations of the federal Animal Welfare Act and, as punishment, was fined $50,000 and barred from being licensed under the act for ten years. The penalties leveled against Morrow stemmed from numerous charges brought by USDA, including dealing without a license, refusing to allow inspections, and multiple counts of animal neglect; concurrently, local prosecutors filed eight animal-cruelty charges against him in an Ohio municipal court (a city prosecutor agreed to dismiss the charges after Morrow upgraded his facilities). At the time, a veterinarian touring Morrow's compound with a USDA inspector reported that a cougar and other animals were so sick or emaciated that euthanasia was the only viable treatment alternative. The veterinarian described a three-and-a-half-foot tall pile of animal carcasses and bones in various stages of decomposition. He described animals with hacking coughs, lameness, pink-eye, parasitic infections, and patches of missing hair. And he witnessed wild pigs—like the ones Morrow bought at Woods & Waters— including a group of eight housed in the stall of a barn that was two feet deep in manure. "One small pig was seen running around the premises with a broken leg," he wrote about another section of the compound. "One dead pig was present in a mud wallow in one pig enclosure and a skull of a larger pig was present next to it." But when you raise your number at Woods & Waters, no one asks your name, background, or credentials. You just go to the office and pay for your purchases.

Some of the animals consigned to these auctions are stuck in an endless loop of misery. In late 1995, for instance, a Michigan sanctuary operator named Shannon "rescued" an adult male serval and a pair of two-week-old lions that were offered for sale at Woods & Waters. Shannon fought back tears as she recounted the convoluted tale of how she was forced to give up these lions and some of her other big cats, how both a serious illness and "habitat reconstruction" at her preserve required that the animals be temporarily transferred elsewhere.

Unable to find them suitable homes, she turned to a friend—an Ohio "exhibitor" whose *Animal Finders' Guide* ads read like this: "Siberian Tiger Cubs born 2-2-95. Big beautiful fluffy babies. Nicest you will ever see. $1000." Or this, from two springs later: "Liger female, 12 weeks old. Very beautiful and friendly. Mother is a Siberian tiger, father is an African lion. $1500." He put Shannon in touch with a California dealer who for three decades has been dumping exotic cats into the pet trade and who counts the Cincinnati Zoo among her suppliers. She knew just the right person to take Shannon's animals: the owner of a top-flight sanctuary in Missouri. Conversations ensued. Shannon inspected the sanctuary. Everything checked out. And weeks later the sanctuary owner came to haul away two tigers and a lion, including one of the Woods & Waters pair.

Shannon at first was troubled by some aspects of the transfer, including the type of truck and cages used for the long trip back to Missouri. But a month later, she made a surprise visit to the facility and found her three big cats in good health. Buoyed by the visit, she subsequently sent another four lions—including the second Woods & Waters cub—to the Missouri sanctuary.

There was soon trouble, however. The owner of the sanctuary refused Shannon's request for a visit, saying that the animals had been moved to a satellite facility. There were more requests, and more refusals. Then Shannon spotted an advertisement in *Animal Finders' Guide* asking for donations of unwanted big cats. The phone number listed was that of the Missouri sanctuary.

Shannon became nervous and started asking questions about the sanctuary. She talked to state and federal investigators, game wardens, and anyone else who might have information. And as her inquiries continued, she became increasingly suspicious. Finally, she was told by someone she won't name that some of this sanctuary's cats had been shipped to canned hunts; other were killed on site, their meat packaged and their hides hauled off to a local taxidermist. What's more, she was told, the remains of two lion carcasses were apparently found in a burn heap.

Shannon tried to find an attorney. She called law-enforcement agencies in Missouri. She called animal-welfare groups. She called the USDA and the U.S. Fish and Wildlife Service. She vowed to get justice, if her cats had in fact been turned into dog food or collectibles. And she would return to the auctions, if necessary, to save more cats from the horrendous fates to which they had been subjected.

As she continued telling her story, Shannon's voice wavered. There was a long pause, and finally she managed to speak a single sentence. "You have to understand," she said, no longer able to fight back tears, "these cats were my *babies*."

◄○►

Despite the fates suffered by animals sold at auction, the breeders, dealers, ranchers, and petting zoos keep shipping them there for sale. Both Lolli Brothers and Woods & Waters are favorite dumping grounds for seasonal menageries like Reston Animal Park: In 1996 alone, it consigned to the Lolli Brothers auction ring a coatimundi, four female elk, four miniature horses, four llamas, six angora goats, a nilgai antelope, and a sheep. The following year it sent two llamas, one water buffalo, four nilgai antelopes, two baby blackbuck antelopes, two elk, one miniature horse, and six one-month-old fallow deer.

Naturally, exotic-animal dealers flock to the auctions. Their ranks include William Fitzhugh, M.D., whose operation in Midlothian, Virginia, was shut down in November 1995 after the federal government alleged that he failed to maintain complete records and violated numerous animal-care standards of the Animal Welfare Act—charges that Fitzhugh denied. The suspension was lifted on September 26, 1997, just in time for homecomings at both Lolli Brothers and Woods & Waters: Fitzhugh shipped to the auctions three Dexter cattle, along with eight donkeys, a two-month-old zebra, two young camels, a nine-week-old Asian water buffalo, five Bennett's wallabies, two white-throated capuchins, a pair of months-old vervet monkeys, a Siberian lynx, two binturongs, two Arctic fox, and a three-day-old dama gazelle named Bones.

Henry Hampton, the North Carolina animal dealer who disposes of many of Six Flags Wild Safari's animals, trucks dozens of them directly to auctions, including Woods & Waters and Lolli Brothers. Eric Mogensen, who runs Zoological Animal Exchange, the AZA-accredited animal supplier, did not put Woods & Waters on one of his health certificates, but instead listed Dick Osting, the auction's proprietor, as the recipient of the scimitar-horned oryx and other species sent to him by AZA zoos. Choctaw Preserve, a Texas hunting ranch whose suppliers include dealer Jim Fouts, disposes of its unwanted elk at the Missouri auction. Private zoos from Reno, Nevada, to Hazlehurst, Wisconsin, to New Castle, Pennsylvania, unload their animals at the Lolli Brothers auction. So does Curtis Krebs, who for years has been handed exotic Asian and South American bears by AZA zoos in Baton Rouge, Louisiana; Cincinnati; Cleveland; Houston; Little Rock, Arkansas; Miami; Oklahoma City; San Diego; and Tampa, Florida, but whose Smoky Mountain Zoological Park, in Pigeon Forge, Tennessee, has never been open to the public.

—◆—

Tracking an individual animal to and from auction, and perhaps back again, is usually impossible, which is of course the point of these sales. Occasionally, however, it's possible to follow how one animal has been shunted from place to place.

In 1994, for example, a three-year-old male reindeer named Honker was walked through the Lolli Brothers auction ring. Honker was born at Northern Splendor Reindeer Farm, in the Yukon town of Whitehorse. The Canadian game farm, which has been in operation for more than a decade, sells pedigreed animals that are acclimated to human contact: They are used to being hand-fed, for instance, and they don't shy away from people walking in their midst.

An Iowa couple bought Honker and a three-year-old female—another animal consigned by Northern Splendor Reindeer Farm—at the Lolli Brothers auction, and from that pair they built a small herd. Equipped with a game-farm license, the couple also raised zebras and elk—a pastime they relished. "We truly enjoyed and learned much from our birds and animals through the years," the wife says.

But when her husband died, the elderly widow found it too difficult and too expensive to care for the animals. Friends in her northern Iowa community volunteered to represent her at the Lolli Brothers auction, and it offered to send a truck for the animals. On September 20, 1996, a veterinarian signed a health certificate testifying that Honker and his five companions—the youngest of them five months old—were free of brucellosis, tuberculosis, and other diseases, and could therefore be moved across state lines. The following week, the entire herd was hauled two hundred forty miles to Macon, Missouri. Days later, Honker was again sold to the highest bidder. Selling the reindeer bull was "a painful experience," his owner says, but an unavoidable one.

If you want to sell a reindeer, there's really no better place to go than Lolli Brothers. Woods & Waters by and large attracts the underclass of the exotics trade, while Lolli Brothers hosts the dealers with the biggest trucks, the most expensive trailers, and in some cases, the ability to obtain surplus animals from AZA zoos—an asset that earns them reverential whispers throughout the auction-house risers. What's more, the

Reindeer Owners & Breeders Association holds its annual meeting during the Lolli Brothers four-day September sale—an event that Honker's owner recalls nostalgically.

The spring and fall sales at Lolli Brothers follow the same basic schedule, although the April event typically goes on an extra day. The pre-auction festivities begin with a swap meet: pheasants, guinea pigs, porcupines, bear and lion cubs, and other miscellaneous species are set out in a yard, flea-market style. Beside this area is the bird barn, inside of which are some three hundred fifty cages. The building echoes with a cacophonous mix of roosters crowing, geese shrieking, and everything from tom turkeys and trumpeter swans to cameo peahens and pheasant pigeons sounding off in discordant unison. On some days, the temperature in the barn feels even colder than the subfreezing temperatures outside. A Spaulding peacock (price tag, $110) stands in a cage barely longer than its body; with its tail feathers sticking through the wire mesh, the great-plumed bird cannot turn or otherwise move, so it is forced to remain in this one position for the entire day, and maybe a second or third day. The auction begins Tuesday with the sale of reptiles. There are six baby iguanas in a bag, all guaranteed by the seller to have tails, the $10 asked-for opening bid a mere one-fifth, it's claimed, of the going pet-store price. There is a Colombian red-tail boa, average of thirty-one babies per clutch. There are Bangkok tree dragons (six per bag), a commodity no one else is importing into the United States. There are very friendly, very rare, giant Asian pond turtles. A twelve-foot reticulated python is brought before the crowd—a snake so friendly, the seller says, that he'd trust his four-year-old with it.

The pet-shop animals follow: prairie dogs, sugar gliders, albino pygmy hedgehogs, chinchillas, short-tailed opossums, flying squirrels, and a bucketful of white and chocolate-colored descented, neutered ferrets. The cages brought into the sale ring get bigger and bigger, and the bidding escalates in tandem: ringtail cat ($140), genet ($150), North American porcupine ($200), bottle-raised female Patagonian cavy ($400), North American river otter ($300 for the male, $800 for the female). The top bid for a trio of young, hand-tamed fennec foxes is $350 each, which doesn't meet the seller's reserve, so the animals are withdrawn. Many are similarly "no-saled," reclaimed by their owners and held for auctions elsewhere.

It goes on like this all day, a nonstop procession of small animals in cages, boxes, and Tupperware containers, the bigger animals walked in by men holding their leads. The primates, bear cubs, and big cats will follow. Then the kangaroos and other marsupials, along with muntjac deer and a variety of hogs. Tuesday will end with the sale of ostriches, emus, and the other ratites. And the auction will wrap up Friday with the sale of alpacas and llamas, or perhaps miniature horses and donkeys.

Behind the sale barn is a warm room, where the babies are kept until it's their turn in the ring. The corrals are back here as well, with pen after pen of elk, donkeys, deer, and bison. The enclosures are outfitted with tags to identify the consignor. A few owners are on hand, laying out for passersby the merits of a breed or individual animal—the great disposition of the zebu cows, the investment potential of the llama. There is a Kansas dealer with her six-month-old, declawed cougar, which is available for trade (litter box included). There is a baby serval for sale and a terrified-looking week-old camel, whose spindly legs seem barely sturdy enough to support its weight. A South Florida dealer with a baby capuchin cuts a deal to bypass the auction ring, and the young monkey is put in its carrier and walked to the buyer's car. A Michigan dealer has brought a half-dozen eleven-week-old bear cubs, which are kept in a trailer outfitted with heat lamps. Crowds encircle him at the advertised feeding times and watch with rapt attention as the young bears struggle with one another to reach the nipple of the formula-filled bottle. The dealer outfits himself in a hooded sweatshirt for protection against claws as the Teddy-bear-sized animals crawl over him, hang from his shoulder, cling to his back, wrestle in his lap. These acrobatics bring an appreciative buzz from onlookers, many of whom discuss the merits of bear ownership.

Day two at Lolli Brothers is reserved for sheep, goats, hogs, buffalo, yaks, and exotic cattle, such as Watusis. The International Miniature Zebu Association has its membership meeting in April, while the Missouri Buffalo Association has staged special fall sales. Wednesday is also reserved for the taxidermy auction, where you can bid on anything from a bear head or zebra-skin rug to more elaborate mounts: a fisher attacking a porcupine or a stuffed chipmunk holding a miniature golf club with a ball teed up before it.

On Thursday, the lineup includes deer, elk, and such rare hoofed stock as gazelles, impalas, and Père David's deer, followed by zebras, camels, and such genetic anomalies as zebra-donkey crosses. Reindeer are also sold on this third day of the auction. September is when reindeer typically sell, in some cases snatched up by those hoping to lease them for Christmas displays.

On September 26, 1996, Honker was walked before the crowd. When the gavel finally came down, the winner proved to be Stan Hall. Honker, it turned out, was the reindeer whose origins had eluded conservation warden Thomas Solin.

The Lolli Brothers veterinarian signed a new health certificate, copying the disease-test results from the Iowa certificate. Dr. G. W. Spencer indicated on the paperwork that the reindeer would be shipped by truck and that Hall would be acting as transporter. He noted where and when the disease test had been performed, and he listed the purpose of the move as "breeding." In nearly every instance, the health certificates for animals bought at the Lolli Brothers auction list nothing else. But when this one reached the Missouri Department of Agriculture, along with the rest of the auction health certificates, a state worker examining it added this notation: "Animal is for slaughter."

Two weeks later, on October 10, the caribou was in fact killed at Hall's Buckhorn Flats Game Farm. The shooter was William Backman, Jr., of Aurora, Indiana, the chairman of Aurora Casket Company, not far from Cincinnati. Backman is an appointed member and former officer of the Indiana Natural Resources Foundation, a not-for-profit organization founded in 1990 by the General Assembly to further the state's conservation goals. Backman, like Wayne Pocius, is an official scorer for Safari Club International. And, like Pocius, Backman is one of Hall's repeat customers: On the same day a year earlier, he had paid to kill a white-tailed deer and another reindeer.

On this Thursday in 1996, Backman killed three animals on his "hunting" expedition. He then brought the carcasses to Spring Creek Taxidermy, twelve miles away in Amherst, Wisconsin. Hall's game-farm records noted that his client had taken three white-tailed deer, but taxidermy records show that to be a lie: Backman actually killed one white-tail, one mule deer, and five-year-old Honker.

11

END OF THE LINE

The Primate Rescue Center is hidden in an out-of-the-way Kentucky valley, its almond-shaped acreage bounded on one side by a meandrous stream and on the other by a quarter-mile slope that connects it with neighboring tobacco and dairy farms. Halfway down that single-lane incline—the only way in or out of the privately operated sanctuary—you get your first look at a string of eighteen-foot-high poles. From this vantage point, the silver-colored shafts appear to be the result of some sort of freakish impulse—a half-dozen behemoth spikes out of place on this remote swatch of tree-lined earth. From ground level, however, the poles make perfect sense: They form a thirty-by-sixty-foot rectangle that hugs the side of a hill. Woven stainless-steel mesh is wrapped around the perimeter of the structure and across its top. The enclosure has three padlocked entryways, one of which leads to a new redwood-shingled building that's outfitted with facing rows of "night" cages. It's a hundred thousand dollars' worth of corral, and from all appearances, the seven young chimpanzees inside the structure seem happy to be there.

Certainly, this open-air enclosure, with its grassy yard and collection of toys, is an improvement over the great apes' former homes: small, indoor cages suspended off the ground at New York University's Laboratory for Experimental Medicine and Surgery in Primates. When the university began planning to sell the laboratory in 1995, its assistant director, James Mahoney, who deposited chimps that were infected with hepatitis and HIV with sanctuaries in Quebec and elsewhere, also courted April Truitt, the operator of the Primate Rescue Center.

Truitt initially resisted Mahoney's overtures, insisting that she was even ill-equipped to care for the "naïve" apes offered her—that is, chimps that hadn't been used in biomedical research. "I told him we don't even have cages, we don't know what chimps need," she says. "I knew that chimps were big, that their care required another level. And I knew enough to know that feeding five chimps would cost as much as feeding fifty monkeys and take as much manpower. I didn't want that responsibility, and viewed it as being as serious as a heart attack."

At the time, Truitt had about three dozen monkeys, nearly all of which are still at the sanctuary. There is a pair of endangered siamangs (tree-dwelling apes native to the forests of Sumatra and Malaya) that had gone from the Greater Baton Rouge Zoo in Louisiana to animal trafficker Thomas Nichols, then to a Missouri couple who tired of the apes' deafening calls and passed the animals on to Truitt. There is a baboon that had been used as a research blood donor at the New York University lab. There is a snow macaque from the Cincinnati Zoo that was chased off its exhibit by dominant males. There is a cynomolgus ("Java") macaque that was slated to be killed for rabies testing after it severely bit one owner and then another; the monkey was spirited from Maryland the night before its scheduled execution and deposited with an Ohio dealer, who in turn unloaded it on Truitt. There is a rare mona monkey that landed in an Arizona dog pound after it bit someone. There is a five-year-old Japanese snow monkey that had gone from a zoo to a pet shop to a basement cage; when the owner's wife became pregnant, the five-year-old macaque was deemed a health threat and disposed of. There is a guenon named Baby that a Long Island woman had bought from a neighborhood pet store. The once-sweet monkey, who was accustomed to being handled, savagely attacked the woman and for three weeks scared off any humans who tried to enter the loft the woman had built to house her pair of pet primates. Truitt cut a hole in a wall and, with food as bait, lured Baby into a carrier and relocated her to Kentucky.

There is also a bizarre-looking capuchin named Sweetie Pie. The elderly monkey appears from a distance to be hump-backed, but she's actually frozen in a permanent sitting position by a severely twisted spine. Sweetie Pie's owner had a provision in her will directing that, upon her death, her beloved pet of three decades be euthanized and the two buried together. But the family veterinarian refused to put Sweetie Pie to sleep, and the deceased's sister kept the monkey for six months before handing her over to an Ohio dog pound. Truitt was given an ultimatum: Take the deformed primate or it would have to be euthanized.

Truitt's sanctuary is also home to former research subjects, including a macaque named Dusty who was housed at a Midwestern university. A laboratory worker sought out Truitt and vigorously lobbied her to take the monkey. The animal, she explained, had only one more available vein, and when a catheter could no longer be inserted, the macaque would be destroyed.

"I kept saying, 'No, I really can't take another single animal,'" Truitt recalls. "I already had the revelation that these lab animals were somebody else's responsibility. But she kept at it. She said she convinced her bosses to let Dusty be relocated. 'He is very special to me,' she said. 'Will you take him?' I said, 'No, but I will help you find another place for him. We'll see what his herpes B virus status is. I will really work with you.'

"But of course I knew what the monkey's prospects were, and how many places I would refer her to—none, basically. Who the hell wants an old, singly caged male macaque that has been used for God knows what kind of research? But she kept telling me how sweet he was, how she goes in the cage with him. She was so persistent I finally said, 'Okay, I'll take him.'

"So I went to pick him up. I had seen pictures of tethered laboratory monkeys, but I had never seen single macaques spinning around in their cages, attached to a drug delivery system. I assumed there was some kind of pharmaceutical research being done there. Dusty was almost completely bald, and was the saddest-looking thing.

"When he got to my place, he would throw himself down the minute he would see you, to be petted and given attention. He was a little aggressive, though, and also had some behavioral problems; we were trying to get him to pay attention, but he was really not responsive.

"Then the lab worker came to visit him, and I was talking to her about operant conditioning as a training method. She had alluded to getting the monkeys in her lab to push levers, so I asked her how they did it. What was the reward system? How did she train them? And she said, 'Well, first we make it so they have to hit the lever thirty times.' And I said, 'How can you work up to thirty?' And she said, 'Well, if they don't do it, they won't feel good.' And I said, 'What do you mean?' And she said, 'If they don't do it, they don't get the cocaine.'"

Looking after a few dozen abandoned pets, unwanted zoo animals, and whacked-out, drug-addicted research subjects was really not so hard, Truitt says. Once the cages were built, the day-to-day care and feeding became almost second nature. But she knew that looking after chimpanzees—no matter what Jim Mahoney of LEMSIP told her— would require an enormous commitment. Truitt resisted for about six months but finally agreed to take four chimps. Shortly thereafter, she consented to take three more—a decision that saddled her with a prodigious financial burden: "One day it was three thousand dollars," she says of her sanctuary expenditures. "The next day it was three hundred thousand. I don't know how it happened."

It happened like this: In addition to the hundred-thousand-dollar outdoor cage, Truitt and her husband, Clay Miller, spent another $250,000 of their own funds on the adjoining building, which is outfitted with a kitchen, heated concrete floors, and a chimp playroom complete with skylights. There is excavating equipment. There are increased veterinary bills. There are large produce bills. And there are salaries for two full-time keepers, who do most of the day-to-day work: Rachel Weiss, a former employee of the Yerkes Regional Primate Research Center, in Atlanta, where she cared for a chimpanzee named Jerom, the first of his species to die of AIDS after being experimentally infected with the human immunodeficiency virus; and Becky Wagner, a former volunteer at the Cincinnati Zoo and the Duke University Primate Center, in Durham, North Carolina, who first worked at the sanctuary as a summer volunteer. (Wagner won the job over Elizabeth Griffin, the young Yerkes research assistant who, in late 1997, died from herpes B-virus complications after being splashed in the eye with a body fluid when moving a rhesus macaque.)

Even with many of the capital improvements complete, running the facility costs about $125,000 a year. It appears to be money well spent, because the Primate Rescue Center is an impressive, well-maintained operation that provides its residents space, attention, and a genuinely safe haven: They are not rented out for commercials or dragged around to shopping malls for photo-taking sessions. They are not sent off to auctions. There are no babies for sale, and loans are made only in rare cases and only after Truitt has visited a recipient's facility and thoroughly checked it out. Instead, the animals are simply afforded a decent environment in which to live out their lives—something no one else was willing to give them.

It is, in short, a model sanctuary. For her part, though, Truitt would like to close the place down, because she thinks that sanctuaries are nothing but a temporary—and ultimately futile—fix for a problem that needs a far better solution.

—◦—

For Truitt, the route to sanctuary operator began in the fall of 1987 with a classified ad in *USA Today:* Monkeys for sale. Her husband saw the notice and, following a telephone inquiry, made arrangements to visit Monkeys Unlimited, which, he would later discover, was a notorious primate mail-order operation run out of a filthy Cincinnati warehouse. (The owner of Monkeys Unlimited, Randy Davies, who dumped huge numbers of baby monkeys into the pet trade, shut down the business a few years later but has since resurfaced in the Phoenix area, where, to the dismay of Arizona health officials, he sells baby macaques via newspaper ads.) Clay put down a deposit on a twelve-week-old, $1,800 "Java" macaque named Gizmo, then waited for the right moment to break the news to his wife. "We were watching TV," Truitt recalls, "and he said, 'Gee, honey, wouldn't it be nice if we had a monkey?' At the time we had an African gray parrot and a couple of cockatiels. We had a big house with plenty of space, and he just thought, wouldn't this be a nice thing? I did not think this would be a nice thing, and I said so. But unbeknownst to me, his deposit had been taken. He went to Cincinnati and brought him back."

Truitt assumed that Gizmo would be both the beginning and end of their collection, that she could learn to live with a lone monkey. But then she ordered and read a book about primate care that detailed the latest research on the need for social enrichment, including companions—a theory that ran counter to the conventional wisdom in the pet magazines.

"I began thinking about where I could get another one without us having to go back to that awful place, Monkeys Unlimited," she says. "I started looking around and wondering, 'Do others have monkeys?' And then one day I was in the drive-in window of the bank and somebody pulled up in the next car. I had Gizmo on my shoulder—he went around with me for the first year of his life—and the guy said, 'My friend has a monkey he's got to get rid of and is trying to find a home for.' He told me that his friend worked at a factory up the street, so I called there and finally found him. I drove out to his house, which was a dump. He had JoJo in an outdoor cage. It was Thanksgiving, it was getting cold, and he was going to stick JoJo in another awful cage and put him inside the house. But there clearly wasn't enough room, so he really wanted to get rid of the monkey. We made a deal to trade a gun and $200 cash for JoJo. That was number two. And it just went on from there.

"We went looking for buddies for Gizmo and JoJo. We started frequenting auctions and talking to other people, because they seemed to be the experts and surely we could learn from them. We were traveling a lot—just visiting places to see what people were doing out there. We bought some animals at auctions, and we even traded with a few dealers and roadside zoos. We knew that Monkeys Unlimited was doing a great business. They were selling the hell out of these primates, but they were doing a crappy job providing information about follow-up care. So on some level, as businesspeople, we thought maybe we could do that. But we will do it better. We will be the ethical ones. We will instruct people. We'll find out about better care, and we will tell people what that entails.

"But that was before our monkeys started biting, and before they became aggressive, and before we realized that the secret of the whole monkey trade is that there are no adult pets. Then we started finding these animals in basements; after they had bitten someone, people would just chain them up and stick them in a birdcage or something. There were nothing but unhappy endings.

"Then I visited Primarily Primates [a large sanctuary in Texas] and started to understand that there was something else going on, that the dealers weren't taking all of these animals, that there was no use for a lot of them. And I got to understand that there were animals that needed to go someplace, but people didn't know where. And then I either got hooked up with a humane society or someone referred someone else to me, and suddenly there was a monkey that needed a place to go, right now. Do you say yes or no?

"And that was the beginning of it. Once you start looking and a couple of people get your number, the animals are everywhere. They are just literally everywhere."

◄○►

They are indeed. Renters vacate apartments and leave their exotic pets behind. Birds and reptiles are seized from people trying to smuggle them into the United States in their suitcases, coat pockets, and beehive hairdos. Trailers full of big cats are abandoned at highway rest stops. Animal-control officers pick up lions and leopards that are spotted roaming around residential neighborhoods. Monkey owners attacked by their pets leave the animals at shelters. Courts rule that exotic-animal collections violate zoning or health laws and decree that the animals be sent elsewhere. Wild animals are taken from people who don't have the permits that are required to keep them. Collectors die and leave behind menageries that their heirs are unwilling to care for. Court-appointed receivers are handed control of animals that are assets in bankruptcy or divorce proceedings. Monkeys spill, hundreds at a time, out of universities and biomedical research labs. Pet owners lose interest in their animals, tire of the responsibility, or can no longer afford the care: In a single year, for example, one AZA zoo logged more than three thousand phone calls from individuals seeking to donate their unwanted exotic pets.

There is, of course, a well-established system to deal with discarded dogs and cats: Bring them to the pound and after a week or so they'll be ushered into the carbon-monoxide chamber or administered a lethal injection—procedures that are carried out millions of times annually in the United States (estimates range from four million to four times that). But exotics are generally spared the IV barbiturate, and so game officers and humane societies looking to find them homes must instead try to scare up a rehabilitator, sanctuary, or licensed exhibitor. It's a process that invariably takes weeks, even months, and typically involves a nationwide search that depends almost exclusively on luck. And it's a process that, despite the best intentions, often has an unhappy ending, much like the rescue effort that sent Jake the cougar from Virginia to a fictitious wildlife refuge in Connecticut: A state biologist drove the ten-month-old cat from an SPCA to an arranged meeting place in a Philadelphia parking lot, where he was transferred to a man who claimed to be building a private zoo. Apparently, no such zoo exists.

Cindy Carroccio, who with her husband, Jim, owns Austin Zoo, in Texas, is forever being sweet-talked, badgered, and pleaded with by those hoping to unload an animal. Not long ago, a Vermont man offered her a crippled, twenty-year-old elephant that he had rescued from a circus; shortly thereafter, a man from Texas tried to give her a pair of unwanted reticulated giraffes that had somehow ended up on his property. A woman from an animal shelter in Houston had a confiscated black panther to donate. An anonymous caller offered her his timber wolf.

"I'm offered tigers by the truckload," says Carroccio, whose small, privately operated zoo is relatively unknown outside the Texas capital. "I could build an enclosure a day and fill it." Some pet owners don't bother to call but simply deposit their animals at the gate in the middle of the night. Someone once managed to sneak guinea fowl into the zoo—she suspects in an ice chest—and dropped them over the fence into the chicken yard.

Austin Zoo's collection includes one of Baylor University's retired black-bear mascots. In the past, the university entrusted its bears not to a zoologist but to an undergraduate member of a campus fraternity, who'd get a crash course in animal-care techniques from his predecessor. The bear that Carroccio agreed to take had been given a diet rich in Dr Pepper and Oreos and wore down its canines on the fence in which it was contained. The university agreed to contribute $9,000 of the $50,000 that was needed to build an enclosure for its once-adored, no-longer-wanted mascot, and after much haranguing by Carroccio—who threatened to take her case to the news media—Baylor finally reimbursed Austin Zoo $1,400 for two junk-food-related root canals and the removal of a damaged tooth. Because it has become increasingly difficult to place unwanted mascots, in 1998 Baylor University decided to phase out its tradition of live bears.

During a recent summer, Austin Zoo agreed to take a black bear cub, bought at auction, that had been kept illegally by a couple in Buffalo, New York. That same summer, a Louisiana veterinarian passed along to Carroccio another auctioned animal: a baboon that had escaped from its owner's horse trailer and was pestering residents of a mobile-home park. The vet rescued the monkey as trailer-park vigilantes were preparing to kill it, then spent a year trying to find the animal a home before Carroccio volunteered. Also that summer, Austin Zoo took in a pair of tiger cubs—their claws intact—that a sheriff had found in a trailer alongside a four-year-old child. The tigers later escaped, showed up on a neighbor's doorstep, and were hauled off to the local animal shelter. The owner tried to reclaim her pets but was threatened with a child-endangerment charge. With her husband in jail and her days given over to a drug-rehabilitation program, she finally agreed to relinquish custody of the big cats. No one but Carroccio would take them.

No one ever wants them. In fact, finding a home for dispossessed exotics is such a formidable job that wildlife agencies often end up depositing them with the very dealers and roadside menageries that are responsible for creating the glut of unwanted animals in the first place. A state biologist tells of a division chief who wanted to bust a horrendous menagerie for animal-welfare violations but was ordered by his boss not to. In years past, the division chief was told, the zoo's operator had agreed to take the exotics found wandering the streets. His facility may have been squalid, and the animals may have been in jeopardy, but he had provided the state fish and game agency with an enormously valuable service, and as payback he was therefore to be left alone.

Former assistant U.S. Attorney Jim Harper, who in 1992 prosecuted Tom Nichols, says that he wanted to bring in zookeepers and seize the Georgia dealer's animals, but the U.S. Fish and Wildlife Service refused. "I kept saying, 'Let's take the animals,'" Harper recalls, "and they said, 'We don't have any place to keep them; it costs so much to feed them.' I said, 'I thought the whole thing was about cruelty to animals and disease, and now you guys are telling me we're going to leave the animals with Nichols and let him dispose of them any way he wants?' 'Yes,' they said.

"At one point I was so exasperated by the U.S. Fish and Wildlife bureaucrats' unwillingness to take the animals, I said, 'If you get the cages and someone to feed them, they could put the animals in the woods by my parents' home.' I was just trying to find some solution, but they still wouldn't seize the animals.

"The bottom line is that they don't take the process seriously. Because if you took it seriously, you'd do what you've got to do. If the animals are held illegally, you seize the animals."

—◦—

In the winter of 1997, the Animal Protection Society of Orange County, in Chapel Hill, North Carolina, opened a 2,900-square-foot wildlife shelter to handle ever-increasing numbers of injured native species. It is a spectacular facility, complete with operating and recovery rooms, quarantine areas, and a diagnostic laboratory. Not far from the new building, on the society's thirty-seven-acre rural campus, are a three-acre fenced-in dog park, a two-stall horse barn, and a pair of raptor cages—one of them a hundred feet long—for the rehabilitation of birds of prey. Peek through the slats and a great-winged bird, just regaining its ability to fly, peers back warily from within its cavernous temporary quarters.

The nonprofit humane society was incorporated in 1962 and for its first seventeen years was essentially a foster-care network: Injured and wayward animals were kept at the homes of volunteer members until they were adopted or nursed back to health. That system was shelved in 1979, when the county built a shelter and contracted with the Animal Protection Society to operate it. Then, about ten years ago, the society hatched a plan to build a sanctuary that would double as its own permanent headquarters. The new wildlife shelter is one more piece of that ambitious blueprint.

Although most of the animals that pass through the shelter are domestic pets or native wildlife, there has also been a trickle of unfamiliar species, including an emu, an armadillo, prairie dogs, chinchillas, iguanas, and a sika deer. Staff members realize that these *nouveau* animals probably foretell a trend, but they haven't yet formulated any policies to deal with exotics. They know they'll soon have to, however, because the organization's overarching principle is that no animal—be it a wood duck, dachshund, or Barbary ape—is ever turned away.

Some shelters have a hard-and-fast rule about the fate of their charges: If an animal isn't adopted after four or five days, or if it can't be rehabilitated and returned to the wild, it's euthanized. There are no exceptions. "At our shelter, we take into account a lot of factors, such as sociability—how socialized it is and how healthy it is," says Amanda Graham, former associate director of the Animal Protection Society. "And some animals are given longer than others." It's a policy, she adds, that would probably be applied to exotics as well: If the shelter received a monkey, for example, its health and ability to survive adoption would be evaluated, and an effort would be made to find it a suitable home. A decision would then be made whether to place the monkey in one of those homes or instead to euthanize it.

For many, killing a monkey or a kangaroo is a far more disturbing prospect than putting down an orphaned coonhound or alley cat. And willfully killing a healthy giraffe or an African lion is unthinkable. But for shelter officials, who one day may face such decisions, life or death ultimately could hinge on bottom-line considerations. "If we got ten monkeys tomorrow, we would be struggling with how to facilitate them," says Graham, who has been a consultant to the Animal Protection Society since leaving her full-time position there. "I think we are proactive in many areas, but there is a limit on how proactive you can be. We may know that we have to have housing if we were to get ten monkeys, but we also know that those resources may need to be used for a spay-neuter clinic or something else. To tie up those resources may not be the best thing. Besides, for me—having seen the suffering and abuse many animals endure—there are a lot worse things than a humane death."

Just considering these issues puts the North Carolina shelter well ahead of its counterparts, most of which barely have the wherewithal to deal with companion animals, and which therefore happily cede exotics to privately run sanctuaries. Wildlife agencies generally consider sanctuaries the best alternative for displaced animals, while the news media typically laud these operations for their selfless work on behalf of the dispossessed. For their part, local governments have refused to clean up what zoos, dealers, and irresponsible pet owners leave behind. With sanctuaries providing that service, tax dollars need not be spent.

But placing unwanted animals at a sanctuary may be only a Pyrrhic victory. Sanctuaries are usually not licensed, regulated, or inspected by any state or federal agency, so their animals may be underfed, in need of medical attention, or caged with incompatible or menacing species. Because the operators of sanctuaries need no experience or credentials, they frequently employ a learn-as-you-go approach to caring for animals. Responsible sanctuaries either render their animals reproductively inactive or keep breeding-age males and females separate—an obvious strategy to ensure that the cycle is finally broken. But there's no requirement to do either, and it's not unusual for sanctuary operators to breed animals for auction or sale to the pet trade—a way of generating funds, they argue, to pay for the other animals' care. There's also nothing to prohibit sanctuaries from dealing their animals to exotic-meat vendors or pelting out animals—that is, killing them and selling them as taxidermy mounts. A sanctuary may even sell its rescued animals to operators of canned hunts.

Although the public and news media generally regard privately operated sanctuaries as being well run, these refuges collectively resemble a dysfunctional foster-care system. Many of them are nothing but animal-dealing fronts that intensify the very problem they purport to be fixing. Others are overseen by those whose good intentions blind them to the wretched, even inhumane, conditions to which they subject the animals in their charge. Yet others have evolved into little more than pyramid schemes: They continually seek out and stockpile more animals, because each wave of new arrivals offers a fresh fund-raising opportunity.

"Most of the sanctuaries don't deserve the name," says a veterinarian who has monitored these sanctuaries for a federal agency. "The more I think about it, the more I realize it's an impossible situation they put themselves in. They probably all start out saying, 'Look at that animal: It's not being taken care of well. I can do it, and that will be fun.' And they start with one animal. Then they get another, then several, and maybe some have babies. All of a sudden the feed bills are huge and they don't have an independent source of income. So what do they do? They sell off one animal now and then to help pay for feed for the rest of them. Then maybe they get into breeding because they need a continuing source of income, and they haul off to auctions the ones that aren't working out.

"And then there are the sanctuaries that instead do fundraising. Some of them do a pretty good job and are working toward doing it better. They have a goal of getting up to being a really nice facility that's like an AZA-accredited zoo. But think about it: What is the financial foundation of this place? It's based on the incredible efforts of one or two people. If they get hit by a car tomorrow, their heirs are going to sell every damn animal as fast as they can, or give them away. It's just setting up for disaster."

The Missouri Primate Foundation, thirty-five miles south of St. Louis, in Festus, is billed as a sanctuary for chimpanzees and monkeys that have been rescued from medical research and other inhumane settings. In April 1998, Mike and Connie Casey, the founders of the operation, admitted to a reporter for the *Jefferson County Leader*, the local newspaper, that their rescue work was sometimes financed by the animals themselves: A seven-year-old chimpanzee had recently been used in a national TV commercial for Old Navy clothes; a service called "Chimparty" let those attending company picnics and other social events interact with a young ape. But missing from the page-one feature story, which detailed the Caseys' commitment to the animals' well-being, were details of their not-so-altruistic activities: rare baby chimpanzees advertised for sale ($30,000) in *Animal Finders' Guide,* along with pig-tailed macaques ($3,500), weeper capuchins ($3,000), spot-nosed guenons ($1,000), and other monkeys. "Expecting moms," their ad trumpets. "Babies available SOON!"

I. B. (Trey) and Bethan Chapman ran Alamo Tiger Ranch, a Colorado sanctuary, until the USDA put them out of business forever in early 1998. The couple publicly claimed to have rescued abused and neglected animals, then to have rehabilitated them by offering "a great home with lots of love." In truth, the USDA charged them with physically abusing big cats. They sold animals. They rented animals for commercials. They charged for photo sessions and tours of the so-called sanctuary. And despite the news media's faithful recitation of their rescue claims, the truth was otherwise: A leopard and other endangered big cats were "donated" by California firms that provide animals for Hollywood productions. Three tigers were purchased for movie appearances from a Missouri dealer. And Alamo Tiger Ranch bought a pair of adult cougars from Black Pine "Animal Park," in Albion, Indiana, yet another dealer/sanctuary that's home to rescued, rehabilitated, and retired animals (including some from the Ringling Brothers and Barnum & Bailey Circus, which in turn is treated to tiger cubs bred for sale at the refuge). Black Pine's owners sometimes try to pre-sell a litter of tiger cubs months before the birth. Their clients include a man in Boise, Idaho, who bought a female mail-order mountain lion cub as a way to get started in the cougar-breeding business. But the moneymaking scheme was abandoned when the would-be entrepreneur didn't buy a companion, and the cougar was sold. A year later, the animal escaped its cage and mauled a seven-year-old boy.

—◄o►—

From the far end of the great outdoor cage at April Truitt's Kentucky sanctuary, there is a clear line of sight to a nearby garage. But because the garage door is beneath a darkened carport, and because the entryway is fifty or sixty yards away, seeing what's inside the garage, even when the door is open, is nearly impossible.

Even with a dead-on view from just beyond the portico, it's hard to get a true read. It's clear that there's a seven-foot-high cage in there, and behind that cage there are one or more aluminum cages just like it. But peering through the bright sunlight into a room lit with fluorescent bulbs, you can see only two pairs of eyes and the indistinguishable outlines of animals.

Move under the carport, just steps from the entryway, and the forms begin to take shape. But something looks decidedly wrong, and only by going inside, where five cages are arranged in an L-shape, can you really appreciate what you've been trying to make sense of.

There are five more chimps in these cages. The enclosures are clean and well maintained, but the animals are old and hideous looking: Their faces are bruised, scarred, and splotched with white patches, as if they had been smeared with typewriter correction fluid. Their hair—what's left of it—has no sheen. Their ears jut out like bowl-shaped antennae. Some have crooked teeth. Their eyes are sunken. Their foreheads overhang their brows. They look almost like humans in misshapen chimp costumes. And they are frightening: When they shriek and rattle the cages, which some of them do unexpectedly and with great ferocity, it's hard to not flee for the yard. In fact, these chimps—unlike the cute five-year-olds playing in their enclosure—are like a ghastly circus sideshow that you can bear to look at only once. Leave the garage and you never want to return.

These are the so-called Dahlonega Five, named for a northern Georgia town not far from the chimps' former home. For twenty-plus years the animals lived in a concrete bunker, never seeing daylight. They received little veterinary care. There was rarely fresh water. They were emaciated. The doors on their cages—in truth, old jail cells—were rusted shut. The drains didn't work and the walls leaked, so storms sometimes flooded the floors of the cages with a half-foot of rainwater. The chimps had nothing to sit on, nothing to occupy them but mounds of garbage. Years' worth of crumpled newspapers, shoved into the cages as bedding, was never cleaned out. The walls were encrusted with feces. The building reeked. The kerosene heaters often didn't work. It was a hellish environment, although, like many of the other delusional good Samaritans involved in their missions of mercy, the keeper of these great apes considered her operation a bona fide sanctuary.

Because the chimps had in fact been rescued from awful fates, the claim of sanctuary is technically defensible: One of the Dahlonega Five came from a carnival, another from a pathetic roadside attraction in Florida. There is a circus castoff with a vitamin B deficiency; without injections she had seizures that crippled her hands and feet, as if paralyzed. The group also includes a former pet that's missing half of a finger. At one time there were other chimps at the Georgia sanctuary, including two who died of unknown causes.

Like the stories of most rescues, this one is convoluted: One day a woman called Truitt to ask for her help. She had been in a car wreck, she had a heart condition, her health was failing, and for various legal reasons her five chimps appeared destined for a nearby wildlife preserve that, to her mind, couldn't provide them adequate care. She wanted Truitt to come to Georgia and help her find the chimps a more suitable home.

Truitt receives phone calls and e-mails like this one almost daily. It's a never-ending list of crises, and Truitt, a fortyish transplant from New Jersey who can still call upon that overbearing Northeastern attitude, feels personally responsible for the fates of all the primates involved. The rescue and reconnaissance missions are rarely simple, but the Dahlonega Five undertaking was complicated by a fast-moving series of unexpected events, including a hospital-bed plea from the chimps' owner that Truitt should inherit her pets. "Suddenly," she says, "I was the proud owner of five chimps that I didn't even know."

Truitt needed temporary housing for the chimps, and she enlisted the aid of Dr. Sally Boysen, the director of the Comparative Cognition Project at The Ohio State University Chimpanzee Center, who is a veteran of many other chimpanzee adoptions and rescues. Boysen contacted the Yerkes Regional Primate Research Center, which agreed to house the chimps for six months, provided that Truitt could transport them to the center's field station in suburban Atlanta. That meant tranquilizing the animals, but no one who was qualified to perform the procedure would help: The Knoxville Zoo refused. The head veterinarian at Zoo Atlanta, an AZA member that proudly heralds its rescue of Ivan the gorilla from a Tacoma, Washington, strip mall, where the great ape had been caged most of its life, would not dispatch a veterinarian on her staff seventy miles to save the lives of the five chimps. Only Chicago's Brookfield Zoo was willing: George Rabb, its director, listened to Truitt's telephone plea and then instructed his veterinarians to provide her all the necessary assistance. A team equipped with medical gear arrived by air the following day.

With the Dahlonega Five safe at Yerkes, Truitt began the search for a permanent home. Her first choice was Austin Zoo, and Cindy Carroccio consented. "And then she came to Atlanta to meet them," Truitt recalls. "She needed to fall in love, but she didn't. Instead, she saw Hazel eating shit off the wall, spreading it around, finger-painting with it. That is the reality of those animals. I don't know if it's like that with all big chimps, but that is what those guys were doing, and that is what they do for entertainment. She thought about what that was going to look like to the public and came back a couple of days later and said, 'I just don't think I can do it.'"

Carroccio, whose private zoo has for the past few years been run like a bona fide sanctuary (no animal sales or purchases, and no breeding), says there were other reasons as well: She had no experience with chimps and worried that she might do the animals more harm than good. Furthermore, the high cost of keeping the chimps might have siphoned funds that are needed to adequately care for the zoo's other animals. "It's a juggling act," she says. "You have to decide what you can do legitimately. I can't save them all."

Truitt had few other immediate options, primarily because of her refusal to compromise on any animal's well-being. For her, decisions about placement are clear-cut and nonnegotiable: If a sanctuary sells animals, if it uses its animals in such moneymaking endeavors as road shows or photo shoots, or if its facilities aren't well maintained, she doesn't deal with it.

Others willingly overlook such shortcomings if the animals are facing euthanasia or are being rescued from horrific conditions. Judging by its 1998 list of big-cat rescues, Turpentine Creek Wildlife Refuge, in Eureka Springs, Arkansas, must certainly be doing the Lord's work: A year-old male bobcat was brought there because it was too rough to stay in its owner's house. A two-and-a-half-year-old female bobcat was brought from Oklahoma, where its elderly owner was unhappy because the animal could not be litter-box trained. A male cougar that had been confiscated from its nonpermitted owner arrived from Kansas. There is a female cougar, its legs half the normal length, that had bitten the owner's son and was facing euthanasia. A six-month-old cougar was rescued from an oil-soaked garage. A woman feared that her ex-husband might seek revenge for their divorce by harming their pet cougar, so she brought it to Eureka Springs. A ferocious eight-year-old Bengal tiger arrived from a roadside zoo, where it had been cared for temporarily after the owner died. A three-year-old Bengal tiger, malnourished from a diet of dog food, came from a Dallas-area humane society. And four tigers, including a crippled male Bengal, were retrieved from a paraplegic Texas man who reconsidered the idea of keeping large cats after a cougar injured his son.

Turpentine Creek Wildlife Refuge, however, is hardly the model sanctuary. "I had seven tigers neutered because our breeding was getting out of hand," cofounder Hilda Jackson admitted in an interview. A year and a half later, the refuge's newsletter proclaimed: "Our breeding is finally under control. We do not intend to have any more than one or two litters of cubs each year. We are trying to schedule them for when the most people can enjoy them."

Turpentine Creek charges visitors admission fees, just like a private zoo. It charges for photo shoots. It sells memberships. In early 1998 it began a partnership with a local illusionist, whose nightly show includes such acts as turning a girl into a sixteen-month-old tiger. Turpentine Creek's Web site and promotional materials are filled with photos of staff members posing gleefully with the tame and magnificent tigers, thereby encouraging even more private ownership of these animals. And the deaths that some of the animals have suffered there are troubling: A Bengal tiger found its way into the cougar cage, where it killed one animal and tore into the leg of another. Jackson wrote in a newsletter about a capuchin with frostbite found chewing on its tail, its feet and hands bleeding. An illness had kept her away from the compound for days, so neither she nor apparently anyone else knew about the monkey's condition. The capuchin's health deteriorated over the ensuing weekend, and on Monday morning it was finally brought to the veterinarian. "He checked her out and said that he would have to amputate one hand, one arm to the elbow, both legs to the knees and her tail," Jackson wrote. "He was not sure that he would not have to amputate more later. We made a decision that this was no way for a little monkey to live so we had her put to sleep."

◄○►

Truitt's list of acceptable facilities is, not surprisingly, woefully short, and six months after the Dahlonega Five had been pulled from their filthy concrete bunker, Yerkes wanted the aging chimps out. And so Truitt borrowed a truck and brought the group to Kentucky. "We don't have a proper place for those animals," she says. "That is something that I criticize others for, and here I was doing it. So what do I do? I asked myself. Do I euthanize them and take whatever comes down the pike, let people massacre me for doing that? I almost did."

She would have been legally entitled, because chimpanzees born in captivity—unlike their wild-born cousins—do not receive the full protection of the Endangered Species Act, and may therefore be euthanized without government permission. Of course, where these animals were born is impossible to determine: The Florida roadside attraction is long gone, and there is only a last name and no known address for the circus employee who bequeathed the chimp with seizures. The *North American Regional Studbook for Chimpanzees* offers possible explanations about the chimps' lineage: The manual lists numerous young chimps that were born at zoos in Los Angeles; Philadelphia; Pittsburgh; Portland, Oregon; and other cities that were "lost to follow-up" in the late 1960s and early 1970s, fates unknown. It's possible, for example, that the Dahlonega Five's ranks include one of the two young chimps sold by the Detroit Zoo to International Animal Exchange in 1969. Or maybe the two-year-old chimp sent by the Baltimore Zoo to an undisclosed location in 1968 is the one called Zulu. It's impossible to say.

Truitt would like to find out, but she has more immediate concerns: She has started to retool the caging in the redwood-shingled building, changes that will allow the two groups of chimps to shift in and out of the yard, letting them each have a half-day's use of the outdoor enclosure. (It is hoped, however, that the two groups will eventually be introduced, giving them all greater access to the yard.) While she continues the search for a permanent home, she can get the five aging chimps out of their small temporary cages and allow them to move freely across turf after two decades of inhumane confinement.

Whether she'll actually find them a new home is doubtful. In October 1998, U.S. Representative James Greenwood, a Republican from Pennsylvania, and then-Speaker of the House Newt Gingrich introduced legislation that would establish sanctuaries for chimpanzees used in research by federal agencies. The Dahlonega Five wouldn't qualify, but the bill included a provision that permitted other chimps to be admitted for this lifelong care. It may be moot, however, because the legislation was not reintroduced when a new Congress convened in 1999, and when a coalition of animal-welfare groups championing the measure unraveled, the creation of such sanctuaries became an even greater long shot.

As a result, Truitt seems resigned to caring for a dozen chimps, four dozen monkeys, and, despite her insistence that the inn is full, whatever else may be dropped off at the top of her road. She has decidedly mixed feelings about that role: The animals deserve proper care, she says, but mom-and-pop sanctuaries like hers clearly aren't the answer. Instead, research should take care of its own surplus. Let the breeders, dealers, and auction houses that profit off the animals bear financial responsibility for the mess they've created. If zoos aren't willing to provide cradle-to-grave care, then they should at least fund a network of regional retirement homes; proclaiming animals lost to follow-up—as if they had somehow vanished—hardly absolves them of responsibility. And the misguided pet owners should be required to contribute to the animals' ongoing care. In only a handful of instances, Truitt says, have former monkey owners offered to help pay for their food, shelter, or medical care. Most assume that it's now her problem, her duty.

For the moment, however, she and others so inclined will have to assume responsibility for the growing number of unwanted exotics. From beside the huge outdoor chimp enclosure, that doesn't seem like an altogether terrible thing: On this sunny fall day, the seven young primates are swinging across the mesh, playing tug-of-war, or lounging inside sections of huge concrete pipe. The two-foot-tall chimps, which earnestly thrust their hands through the fence in hopes of getting a treat, are so much fun to watch that caring for them seems like it would be almost a welcome task. But Truitt sees it otherwise: The young chimps may be cute, but one day their hair will thin, their faces will have white splotches, their foreheads will overhang their brows. "One day," she says, "these guys will look just like them." She is pointing toward the garage, but the bright afternoon light makes it impossible to see more than vague shadows hunched over in the tall metal cages.

12

THE CAPTIVE KINGDOM

I once saw a gorilla blush.

Her name is Mandara. She was born at the Milwaukee Zoo in April 1982 and three years later was sent to the National Zoo, where she lives today. Gorillas are among the elite group of "charismatic megafauna" that zoo directors rely on to bring patrons through the gates. But Mandara has a special place even within this special hierarchy: She not only is a clear favorite of visitors to the National Zoo's ape house, but she also has a loyal following among the bands of gorilla enthusiasts who travel from zoo to zoo in hopes of being acknowledged with eye contact, a nod, or some other telling gesture. Members of Mandara's fan club—a symbol of adoration that none of the National Zoo's other gorillas can claim—even wear buttons imprinted with her picture as a display of their allegiance and affection.

It's not hard to understand this fascination with Mandara. Her features are more human-like than those of the zoo's other gorillas, some of whom have long, sloping foreheads or faces that seem too large even for their massive frames. She is relatively small, not particularly imposing, and often so serene that the idea of entering her cage seems almost risk-free (it's not). Unlike some of the other gorillas, who show little interest in humans, Mandara occasionally sits tranquilly beside the thick floor-to-ceiling wall of shatterproof glass, letting visitors get literally within inches of her. In the outdoor yard, she sometimes makes eye contact with a visitor and, with an "ET"-like gesture, points a wavering index finger in his or her direction. And Mandara is a caregiver of much renown, the much-heralded "supermom" of North American gorillas: She not only gave birth to three offspring during the 1990s, deftly nurturing and disciplining her babies before adoring crowds, but in 1992 she also stole away the newborn Baraka from his mother, Haloko, and raised the precocious ape as if he were her own. Mandara's motives are uncertain, but one popular theory holds that she sensed Haloko's maternal ineptitude and wanted to ensure able care for the group's newest member. Twenty-five-year-old Haloko, who had shown no interest in raising her previous babies, didn't protest the kidnapping but simply gave in to her younger cage-mate.

Mandara was the first gorilla I was introduced to on arriving to begin my year-and-a-half-long volunteer stint at the zoo. The keeper-aide program I was recruited for required a full day's work each week, and the first morning's orientation included nothing that required a zoology or biology degree: This is a mop, this is a pail, and this cage—an off-exhibit horseshoe where Mandara's group is fed—is where the disinfecting routine will begin. There was one inviolable precaution: Mandara, who was watching the briefing through a metal grid in the sliding security door, would, I was advised, probably try to entice me with twigs or hay, and I should stay away. The reason: If I took her gift, she would seize my finger and not let go. We would be joined through that mesh, I was warned, and if no keepers were nearby to pry me free, I would remain hopelessly pinned there.

Sure enough, once the hosing and swabbing began, Mandara tried to coax me her way. She stared at me from behind the steel door and pressed foliage through the grating. When I ignored the offer, she stuck a longer piece through the opening and waved it. When I still declined the come-on, Mandara dropped strands of hay onto the floor I had just hosed, then she lured me her way with eye contact. I moved to within a few feet of the door—steadfastly refusing to take the bait—and marveled at the sight of her, the smell of her, and the sound of her smacking her lips together. She sat hunched beside the door, her head angled at a sort of seductive tilt and her mouth upturned in what looked like a smile, poking the bouquet of hay stalks at me.

I dropped the hose and the squeegee and debated whether to ignore all the warnings and take the offering. Being so close to such an impressive animal was unlike any experience I'd ever had, and for minutes I stood there utterly transfixed. But without warning, Gus, the huge male silverback who presided over the zoo's largest gorilla family, sprinted around a blind corner, charged our way, and smashed the security door with such force that I thought it would break off its hinges. Mandara, the mother of Gus's first-born son, squealed and took off down a passageway. I bolted for the cage door, certain that the giant gorilla had busted through the hatch and was in hot pursuit. Thus began an hour-long initiation rite that nearly convinced me to quit on the spot: Every time I entered the cage to clean, Gus appeared and slammed his enormous palm against the grating. And with each deafening reverberation I dropped the shovel or hose and ran for the exit, sure that even the thick metal couldn't withstand his crushing blows. The battle for dominance was clearly a mismatch, and it finally ended when Gus saw his pathetic human counterpart cowering by the cage door, too nervous to enter and finish swabbing the concrete floor. After that, he eased up on me.

By mid-afternoon, in fact, Gus was downright civil: He bluffed a few charges in my direction, but otherwise let me be. And when I served up popcorn for an afternoon snack, he let me watch the feast from a few yards away. The rest of the group gave me the once-over, but none showed much interest. Mandara, meanwhile, continued her offerings, at one point shoving a large branch through the cage with such force that it nearly impaled me.

By day's end my terror had been replaced by the excitement of being so close to the gorillas, Mandara in particular. The only remaining task was to bring the trash barrels outside, and I was warned that we would be passing a male named Mopie who didn't always take a liking to new-comers. "It's nothing to worry about," the volunteer coordinator assured me. "It will just be some cage-rattling."

So we wheeled the hay-filled barrels down a walkway behind Mopie's cage, and as I passed the huge male he looked up at me but didn't budge. On the return trip, however, as I talked enthusiastically about my new volunteer position, Mopie had a change of heart: From the corner of my eye I saw the four-hundred-fifty-pound behemoth rise off his knuckles and sprint directly at me. As he approached, he reached down with his right hand and, while still charging full speed, scooped up a softball-size pile of poop and flung it through the cage bars. The huge turd struck me in the chest, but, too shocked and terrified to even react, I kept walking down the corridor until we were out of the gorilla's view. Then my knees buckled and I slumped against the concrete wall. I surveyed the results of the assault: Gorilla feces dripped off my coveralls, and the splattering mess also left foul stalactites hanging from my beard.

I felt sick, almost too weak to move, and my interest in spending an-other Saturday in the ape house immediately vanished. But volunteer co-ordinator Rob Shumaker, who had seen other newcomers subjected to the same indignity, had a different take on the pummeling: "Hey," he said, "I think Mopie really likes you."

"Why would you think *that*?" I asked.

"Because Mopie has really good aim. If he didn't like you, he would have caught you right between the eyes."

But if Mopie liked me, he never let on. Keepers speculated that he was troubled by my beard—that he confused me with a handler at another zoo who had apparently used a hose with a high-powered nozzle to move the gorillas from cage to cage. Whatever the reason, the massive ape tried his best to terrify and annoy me during my entire volunteer tenure, and he found great success.

The other gorillas accepted me, or at least didn't seem to object to my presence. Even Gus ambled in from the yard one afternoon and sat in an overhead tunnel—his broad mouth fixed in what looked like a grin—

and placidly watched me clean his quarters. We were at times separated by just a few feet, and after that we had a pretty good understanding: I would treat him with courtesy and respect (no eye contact, stand back from the cage when he led his group in from the outdoors), and he'd forgo the intimidation.

Mandara, on the other hand, did more than just tolerate me: She sought me out, sat beside me, and continued her offerings. In return I would talk to her, bring friends and family to meet her, and sometimes slip an extra banana into her lunch bucket. And one afternoon, as my favorite gorilla held out an orange rind to me, a keeper who was scratching her back through the wire mesh good-naturedly accused the teenager of flirting. Mandara's head rolled from side to side, as if she were embarrassed, then she looked skittishly over her shoulder at me and, for one brief moment, I saw her blush.

◄○►

Although I resigned my volunteer position a half decade ago, Mandara still ambles over to the glass to sit beside me. One dreary Sunday in the spring of 1997, when the ape house was virtually deserted, she scampered by to show me her newborn son, K'tembe, who looked like a tiny backpack on his mother's shoulders. It felt like old times.

My nostalgia soon disappeared, however, because the place had changed dramatically: Gus and his first son, Kejana, had been relocated to a bachelor troupe at Disney World's Wild Animal Kingdom, in Orlando, Florida, breaking up a family that had been intact throughout most of the 1990s. Kuja, who grew up with Mandara in Milwaukee and then Washington, was designated as Gus's replacement, but he's an inept leader who gets bossed around by the females and hassled by the youngsters. He's also been a sexual dud, and if he doesn't eventually figure out the mating routine he'll in turn be replaced by Mopie or an interloper from another zoo.

If that happens, Kuja may also be headed for Orlando. Or perhaps for Gorilla Haven, a private sanctuary in north Georgia that's planning to begin housing "excess" male apes in 2000. Yet again, the zoo establishment

has embraced the notion of entrusting its genetically useless or socially inept animals to private hands—this time, to a couple of well-to-do Chicago
transplants who had their own versions of the sanctuary epiphany: Steuart
Dewar wanted to earmark proceeds from the sale of his computer business to help the world; on meeting Koko the signing gorilla, Jane Dewar's
greeting of "I love gorillas" brought an enthusiastic reply of "love gorillas
you!" The idea for the sanctuary came a few years later.

But if the fates of Kuja and Mopie are uncertain, Mandara's future
seems clear. In all likelihood, she'll be afforded every opportunity to continue breeding. After all, the public loves babies, particularly gorillas.
They flocked in great numbers to see Kejana, K'tembe, and the others.
And then they enthusiastically went off to see the baby rhinos, the baby
elephant, and as always, the baby giraffes.

Zoo officials insist that such births are part of carefully scripted
species-conservation plans, and sometimes they are. But often those pronouncements are just public-relations blather, because giraffes and other
nonnative species are in fact merely living museum pieces. They or their
offspring will never be repatriated to the wild; their survival is in no way
tied to the fate of their wild cousins; and there is no blueprint for succeeding generations. Births just happen.

And when they do, the expendable two-year-olds—along with the
aged, out-of-vogue, and reproductively spent—become sacrificial lambs
that are cast off, resold, and laundered on paper until they become officially "lost to follow-up." Animals that are supposedly part of grand conservation schemes are recast as just more fodder for the dealers, brokers,
auction houses, and sanctuaries that exploit them for profit, subject them
to abuse, relegate them to unsuitable environments, or even worse, use
them to breed new generations of product for their mercenary commerce.

How is it that trusted public institutions proclaiming themselves to be
ardent conservationists, committed defenders of wildlife, and teachers of
the interrelationships among all living things can so cavalierly dispose of
rare animals? Why is it that zoos can devote resources to the preservation of habitat in distant corners of the globe but can't provide cradle-to-
grave care to captive members of the very species they purport to be

saving? Are zoo animals nothing but crowd-luring props, to be blindly disposed of when they're no longer useful? Society castigates those who treat their mutts in such fashion.

The people who are responsible for ensuring the well-being of exotic animals, monitoring the spread of zoonotic diseases, and enforcing wildlife laws have among them a long list of strategies for cleaning up the mess created by zoos and others involved in the exotic-animal trade: Overhaul USDA's Animal and Plant Health Inspection Service. Impose a tax on the sale of exotics, and earmark the proceeds for state-funded sanctuaries. Set up statewide wildlife courts. Mandate the sterilization of big cats and other exotic pets. Require the licensing and inspection of sanctuaries. Close loopholes in the Endangered Species Act. Shut down exotic-animal auctions. Prosecute veterinarians who are caught selling blank health certificates or falsifying these documents. Consolidate responsibility for the oversight of exotics within a single state agency. Ban the private ownership of macaques and other disease-carrying primates. Rewrite the Animal Welfare Act to guarantee nonnative species more-humane treatment. Coordinate town-by-town campaigns to outlaw the ownership of wild and dangerous animals.

These are practical and potentially effective strategies, but their adoption would require calculated blueprints, adroit lobbying, legislative muscle, wide grassroots support, and well-funded campaigns. Rewriting state laws would pit advocates of change against politicians who kow-tow to the exotic-animal merchants. Overhauling the policies of federal agencies would require the cooperation of bureaucrats who are determined to maintain the status quo. Enlisting the assistance of a justice system overwhelmed with murder and mayhem would be a hard sell. And members of the American Zoo and Aquarium Association prefer to circle the wagons rather than to admit publicly that their policies are flawed or that their peers are engaged in questionable activities.

Ironically, AZA institutions may provide the greatest resistance to meaningful change. The association's one hundred eighty-three members like to paint all critics as animal-rights extremists bent on shutting their gates—a knee-jerk strategy designed to engender wide public support and squelch dialogue about their misdeeds or shortcomings. AZA zoos are in collective denial about facilitating the private trade in exotics, insisting that their unfortunate—often inadvertent—role in such smarmy business ended years ago. Instead of acknowledging that animals may in fact be ending up in unsatisfactory places, the AZA damns its critics with all-out public-relations warfare.

It happened in early 1999, when a California newspaper prepared to publish a multi-part series that promised to document shortcomings with the zoos' disposal procedures. A month before the series was published, Jane Ballentine, the AZA's communications director, circulated a question-and-answer sheet to members debunking the reporter's anticipated findings. Ballentine promised that the association's headquarters would read each installment as it appeared on the newspaper's Web site and quickly prepare canned responses for public-affairs directors to recite for local reporters. "We hope that you will continue to not comment to the media about other members' policies and practices," Ballentine said in a fax. "We need to present a unified front."

To keep the front united, Ballentine and Sydney Butler, the AZA's executive director, schooled zoo directors in how to answer thorny questions. For example, AZA zoos challenged the series' conclusions because the reporter was not professionally trained to interpret data she collected. "We have no way of knowing how she decided to input her information, therefore the validity of her analyses is suspect to us," PR directors were instructed to answer. *Why do animals go to private hands?* Tell reporters this: "Many private individuals and organizations have contributed greatly to Species Survival Plans for a wide variety of animals including rhinos, Arabian oryx, cheetah, lemurs, Mexican grey wolves, California condors, black-footed ferrets . . . the list goes on." *If you say wild animals do not make good pets, why are they going to the public?* In studbooks, the term "public" is used to designate a variety of recipients. "These can include state licensed wildlife rehabilitators and facilities, farms or ranches or qualified individuals that are employees or docents with a zoo." Of course, "public" can also mean pet-shop owners, backyard breeders, and those whose profits are generated by auction sales.

The sorry truth is that zoo directors are almost never willing to criticize one of their own for violating the public trust. What's more, zoo directors prefer to conduct even routine business with the secrecy of freemasons. When I asked about one hundred sixty or so of them for consecutive-year reports showing nothing but numerical changes in mammal collections, like frightened children they enlisted Sydney Butler to contact me about my motives and my organization. In the end, fewer than two dozen zoos provided me with reports that even remotely matched my benign request, even though the numbers I sought were readily available in their annual reports. Most ignored me, while others might as well have. The Louisville Zoo, for example, sent two packets, each containing a peacock feather, a pair of complimentary passes, and a brochure detailing the zoo's admirable conservation goals. That certainly beats releasing data that might shed some light on the zoo's disposal practices: Two year-old dromedary camels sold to an Indiana dealer whose zeedonks and other animals end up at an auction in Wapakoneta, Ohio. An aging Hartmann's zebra sold to Larry Johnson, the California dealer who used a bogus Louisiana post-office box as the destination for his alleged giraffe shipment. A pair of two-year-old Masai giraffes sold to International Animal Exchange, which a few months later shipped a group of giraffes to Keihin Choju Trading Company, a Japanese animal dealer. And greater kudu, put through the mark-down routine in the AZA *Animal Exchange* newsletter: $1,000, then $750, and finally $500. When the listings brought no takers, four of the large-horned antelopes were sold to Ed Novack, the New York pet-trade supplier whose much-publicized role in facilitating the sale of a wild boar from the San Diego Zoo to a Canadian canned hunt supposedly made him a pariah.

—◦—

But dramatic change, fortunately, does not require the blessings of the AZA. Many member institutions are owned by cities or counties, in some cases by states, and their animal-disbursement records are therefore available under the applicable open-records or freedom-of-information laws. Zoo directors have tried to exempt their parks from these statutes, but when threatened with legal action by newspapers, for example, they have reluctantly handed over copies of transaction reports, invoices, correspondence, and other documents that expose their institutions' inner workings.

Members of zoo-support organizations—aided, if necessary, by lawyers who have litigated Freedom of Information Act disputes—need only demand ongoing access to disposition records, which can then be abstracted and reproduced in newsletters and on Web sites. Similarly, a lone volunteer in each state capital can sort through health certificates and exotic-animal import permits—a means of both checking the veracity of zoo documents and monitoring the activities of dealers, roadside zoos, universities, and others that move exotics.

Add to the mix the annual reports to the U.S. Fish and Wildlife Service, and it's also possible to follow the movement of endangered species within states. A listserv or e-mail network would permit the fast and easy exchange of information on local zoos. A small battalion of volunteers could methodically scrutinize and verify virtually all of the legally executed exotic-animal transactions in the United States, then release its findings accordingly. For example, if Six Flags Wild Safari sends more hoofed stock to canned-hunt supplier Henry Hampton, would-be patrons who are offended by such practices could find that out. If the National Zoo sends more animals to Burton Sipp, the New Jersey pet-trade supplier and roadside-zoo operator, members of the congressional committees with oversight of the Smithsonian Institution would know. If it's revealed that a petting zoo like Reston Animal Park continues to dump its animals at auctions or with dealers such as Mark Schoebel, those concerned about the welfare of animals might know enough to take their children elsewhere. And although Tulane and Harvard—like other private universities—are not required to disclose their contracts with vendors, their affiliated primate centers would not be able to keep hiding all the pipelines into the pet trade. Alumni, donors, and others who find such practices repugnant would have the facts available to them.

◄○►

Disclosure, however, is not a cure; it's only a window on hypocrisy and potentially unethical behavior. Actually changing the way that zoos conduct business would require difficult decisions, because the alternatives are themselves controversial. As a result, they're choices best left to the taxpayers—the animals' rightful owners—rather than the public servants entrusted with their care.

In some ways, the zoos' misguided animal-disposal practices are only the result of public demand and shortsightedness: Everyone wants to see babies, so the zoos comply. No one asks about the dispossessed animals, so the zoos don't tell. That, in fact, may be how communities would like their zoos to be run: Let animals not controlled by the AZA's Species Survival Plans breed indiscriminately. Let nature take its course, so that each year there will be a flood of new babies on exhibit. Then send the unwanted adolescents and the older, nonbreeding "surplus" to International Animal Exchange for overseas disposal, to Bob Crowe for resale at auction, or to Craig Wagner, the fugitive sanctuary operator. In short, maintain the status quo.

A second option is to let the breeding continue but to euthanize humanely all unwanted animals. This would reduce the dealers' inventories and in turn cut off a major source of product for the pet trade, auction houses, bogus sanctuaries, canned hunts, and so on. The lost revenues would probably not be significant, since zoos more or less give away many of these animals. But some could be recouped by using the euthanized animals as feed for the zoos' lions and other carnivores. Higher-priced animals, such as giraffes, moose, and even monkeys, could be sold to exotic-meat vendors. (Monkey is a prized delicacy among some African expatriates, who have so far been unable to find a legal source in this country.) This practice would be repugnant to many, but is it any worse than an animal landing in a deplorable roadside zoo, or even in the jail cells that for two decades were home to the Dahlonega Five?

A third option is to demand that the breeding be selective, that contraceptive measures be employed across the board so that a giraffe may be born every four or six years instead of every two. That would require a dramatic shift in both the public's attitude about zoo animals and the zoos' educational and promotional plans: Zoo officials would have to tone down the baby-mania and teach their patrons also to appreciate the adolescents, the elderly, and the nonphotogenic has-beens. And zoo visitors would have to understand that further breeding might doom that once-cherished two-year-old to the auction ring or even the slaughterhouse.

And there is a final option: Let the breeding continue unchecked, but instead of euthanizing animals, keeping the elderly on exhibit, or sending the surplus to dealers, provide them all with a retirement facility. Give the animals cradle-to-grave care; in return for their years of public service, let them simply live out their lives in peace.

Zoo directors would rightly maintain that the funding for such facilities simply isn't available. Therefore, taxpayers can decide whether they want to provide their animals that kind of haven, or whether it's too great a price. Each community could fund its own retirement home; alternatively, there could be statewide or even regional facilities. Ideally, these old-age homes would be operated by keepers from AZA zoos—the most qualified and, unlike management, the ones with the greatest interest in the animals' day-to-day well-being. As publicly funded facilities, these sanctuaries would be inspected and audited. And they could double as interim shelters for exotics with nowhere else to go—the lions seized in drug raids, the monkeys rescued from basement birdcages. Depending on budget, charter, and so on, these nonzoo animals could be either provided with permanent homes or euthanized, thereby removing them from the endless loop of exotic-animal horror stories. Local, state, and federal wildlife officers would never again have to let tigers remain with their abusers simply because there was no available cage space.

Whatever the choice, the decision should be the public's. After all, animals are legally deemed property, and these assets belong to citizens, not to zoo directors who have in many instances proven themselves unworthy of guardianship. But pending any decision, communities should at least demand that their zoos sterilize every animal that's sent to an unaccredited institution. If these animals are no longer necessary to the goals of a Species Survival Plan, then permitting them to further fuel the underground trade in exotics is the height of negligence. What's more, every zoo animal should have implanted in it a microchip that will identify its origin. The convenient "lost to follow-up" designation is not acceptable, and this low-cost technology could help make zoos accountable for their indifference.

◄o►

If history is any guide, zoos will fight all attempts to make their affairs public and to change the way in which they do business. They will instead crank up the public-relations machine and regurgitate the undeniable proof of their value: More than 120 million people visit AZA member institutions each year. Zoos encourage visitors to assist in conservation projects locally and internationally. Educators use zoos as parts of their classroom curriculums. Outreach programs take animals to hospitals, nursing homes, and inner-city camps. Zoos helped save some animals from extinction, including the California condor, American bison, black-footed ferret, and red wolf. Zoos are saving endangered species and staving off global threats to wildlife. And perhaps most important, zoos afford the public a connection with wildlife that is not otherwise available—an up-close, in-person experience that instills in many the desire to do more to help protect those and all other species.

If that's true, then perhaps this stewardship should be extended to all captive animals. Because in twenty or thirty years, for example, when Mandara's baby-making years have passed, her fan club will no doubt have found itself a different idol. The gorilla once so adored will be just another aging, listless member of the troupe, the forty-plus matriarch whose celebrity status will have all but disappeared. Of course, I'll still go to see her. I'll sit beside her at the glass, just like old times, even if she doesn't have a baby to show me.

Geraldine Rockefeller Dodge died in the summer of 1973, and a foundation bearing her name was created the following year. Although the foundation's directors were left to establish the areas for grant-making, they followed three of the suggestions outlined in Mrs. Dodge's will: encouragement of the arts; projects local to Morris County, New Jersey, site of the deceased millionaire's estate; and prevention of cruelty to animals.

Over the following quarter-century, the Geraldine R. Dodge Foundation became a well-known benefactor of projects in all three program areas. The philanthropy is probably best recognized for its ongoing support of National Public Radio, but its beneficence is much more far-reaching. It funds North America's largest poetry festival, underwrites the Presidential Scholars program, and awards grants to outstanding new teachers. It supports a New Jersey crafts center that offers an artist-in-residence program as well as the Web site of the *New Jersey Reporter*, a bimonthly magazine that analyzes an array of critical issues facing the Garden State. In the animal-welfare arena, the foundation has funded everything from local spay-neuter clinics to projects with much wider significance: a global question-answering service for children and teachers interested in species and habitat preservation; the Center for Wildlife Law, which analyzes state, national, and international wildlife policy issues; and *Birds of North America*, a highly regarded reference work. In addition, it offered grant money for "Virtual Dog," a three-dimensional, computer-based animation system that provides veterinary students an alternative to using live animals in their medical educations.

These last grants are a natural for a foundation bearing Geraldine Dodge's name, because the reclusive niece of John D. Rockefeller was certainly an animal lover. Her thirty-five-room New York City mansion was filled with animal paintings. Known as "the first lady of dogdom," she and her husband, Marcellus Hartley Dodge, the chairman of Remington Arms Company, founded New Jersey's Morris and Essex Kennel Club. The couple's 380-acre estate, Giralda Farms, was the site of many high-profile dog shows, and in recognition of her work, Mrs. Dodge was inducted into the American Pointer Club Hall of Fame the year after her death. She was also permitted to keep native white-tailed deer on her New Jersey estate and made provisions in her will for their humane care.

Although the Geraldine R. Dodge Foundation does not ordinarily support book projects, it made an exception for this work. And it did so at a critical moment: The Center for Public Integrity, which for a decade has investigated government-accountability and ethics-related issues, has traditionally relied on foundation support for its projects, but no grantmaker was willing to lend its support for this one. After a year and a half of research, the project was in jeopardy. The Dodge Foundation rescued the book, and a year later it reaffirmed its commitment with a second grant.

In retrospect, the reluctance of other foundations to fund this project is not entirely surprising, because issues related to animals are hot buttons: Zoos are either conservation strongholds or cruel, unnatural anachronisms. Hunting is rich tradition or barbaric sport. Animals feel joy, anger, love, and sorrow, or nothing more than cold, hunger, and physical pain. Animals are merely property, to be owned and sold as one sees fit, or they're valued natural resources that should be left to live as nature intended. Human economic interest either should or should not take precedence over saving a species on the verge of extinction. For some, animals may be subjected to any abuse in the interest of finding human-disease cures; for others, the lives of animals are as important as those of their human counterparts.

These are contentious issues, and the debate has increasingly been framed in such a way that there's no middle ground: Criticize zoos, for example, and you're somehow aligned with animal-rights activists who liberate primates from university laboratories or parade naked in front of fur stores.

Ironically, even Geraldine R. Dodge, whose posthumous bequest enabled the project to go forward, couldn't escape the chicanery and controversy that so often accompany animal-related undertakings. In her case, the issue was the humane relocation of the deer that roamed her New Jersey estate. Although she had originally been licensed by the state to maintain a herd of ten, their number grew to a hundred by the time she died. The executor of her estate, Fidelity Union Trust Company, took great pains to place the deer in accordance with its client's wishes—that is, somewhere they would be well cared for.

Finding such a wildlife preserve is no easy task. Although the deer were bequeathed to St. Hubert's Giralda, an animal shelter founded years earlier by Mrs. Dodge, the facility was ill-equipped to keep them. Herbert W. Ball, a vice president of Fidelity Union Trust Company, contacted those permitted in New Jersey to keep deer, with no success. He called wildlife commissions and permit holders in other states but still came up empty. Releasing the deer into the wild was not feasible, because their captive breeding had left them unable to avoid hunters and predators.

Ball was himself an animal enthusiast, and his commitment to finding the deer a good home was serious. With the estate's natural browse having been entirely eaten by the large herd, and the trees stripped bare of leaves that the deer could reach, Ball's bank provided commercial corn and oats. Neighbors gathered apples from their trees, which Ball collected for the Giralda Farms orphans.

At the end of 1976, after a year of futile placement attempts and even more births among the deer, Ball took the suggestion of New Jersey game officials and contacted Stanley LeVan, the owner of a Pennsylvania game preserve. After touring the grounds with Ball, LeVan agreed to rescue the animals. Ball and everyone else connected with the operation was pleased, because LeVan would be relocating the deer to a preserve set aside for the protection of wildlife.

New Jersey fish and game officers provided trap boxes, and LeVan began removing the deer the following spring. By the time the operation concluded, more than a hundred deer had been humanely removed from the Dodge estate. "Neighbors in Madison will surely miss their longtime friends," a local newspaper observed, "but a good home for them has been found." Accompanying the article was a picture of Ball saying goodbye to the friendly deer.

Unfortunately, there was something that Ball didn't know: LeVan was the proprietor of Hemlock Acres Hunting Club. Despite everyone's best intentions, about three dozen of Geraldine Dodge's deer ended up in a Pennsylvania canned hunt. "We guarantee our guides will show you game in one day," the club's brochure boasted. "We had a 98% kill on one-day hunts last year. You pay only for animals you kill."

But it could have been worse for the executors of the Dodge estate. Before LeVan removed thirty-four deer from Giralda Farms, another eighty were relocated within New Jersey, thereby saving the animals from such an unhappy fate. Those deer, it turns out, were sent to Great Adventure amusement park and wildlife refuge, in Jackson Township. The drive-through attraction was later renamed Six Flags Wild Safari.

SOURCE NOTES

AND ACKNOWLEDGMENTS

The primary sources of information for this book were interviews and public records. The records that formed the foundation of the reporting are certificates of veterinary inspection, known familiarly as health certificates. These documents, which chronicle the movement of animals across state lines, have traditionally been overlooked sources of evidence about the trade in exotic species. In fact, the keepers of the records in a number of states said that no one had ever before asked to see them.

The author, either alone or with an assistant, personally visited twenty-seven state departments of agriculture and reviewed an estimated two million health certificates (primarily, those chronicling the movement of cattle, swine, and horses) in search of those that might best document the trade in rare species. Assistant Patricia Jamison individually collected copies of health certificates from three states, including two with unusually voluminous records (Oklahoma and Texas). Friends and hired assistants collected records in Arizona, Colorado, Maine, Oregon, South Dakota, and Washington. The records of Minnesota, Nevada,

New Hampshire, and North Dakota, came via Freedom of Information Act requests. A decision was made early on not to seek records from Alaska and Hawaii, primarily because of the relatively small number of animals moving from these states to the contiguous forty-eight states. For a variety of reasons, the capitals of the remaining eight states were bypassed. Tennessee officials, for example, claimed that health certificates were exempt from release under the state's Freedom of Information Act; a Utah official promised for nine months to send the requested documents but ultimately refused. Some rural states, including New Mexico and Vermont, have few federally licensed dealers and exhibitors, and veterinary officials reported that their files contained only a handful of certificates for exotic species. California does not routinely keep copies of health certificates for exotics leaving its borders. As a result, documents from these eight states were gathered from the "incoming" files in Kansas, Missouri, Ohio, and other major exotic-animal crossroads.

Ultimately, I collected about three thousand health certificates. Some certificates document the interstate movement of one or two animals; others detail the movement of dozens, including, in some cases, multiple species. Information from more than twenty-two hundred of these certificates—including such unique identifiers as tattoos and health-test result numbers—was added to a database created for this project. This offered the ability to document the trading partners of those involved in the exotic-animal business. In some cases, the database entries showed the movement of individual animals from state to state to state.

I placed a high level of confidence in the accuracy of health certificates, since they are completed by an accredited veterinarian and, in some states, must be signed by an animal's owner. For example, in New Jersey, North Carolina, Texas, and other states, the owner/agent statement reads: "The animals in this shipment are as certified to and listed on this certificate." Virginia health certificates also carry a warning: "It is a felony to forge a public record, certificate, or attestation; or to utter a forged public record, certificate, or attestation."

Because these records are completed with an owner's knowledge and input, and because these particular records were gathered directly from state files, they were believed to be accurate. It is possible, however, that some transactions listed on the health certificates never actually happened. For example, someone may have made a last-minute decision not to ship an animal. Or an animal may have died between the time the certificate was mailed to the state department of agriculture and the animal was to be shipped. Attempts were made to verify the accuracy of these transactions, but it was not possible to verify all of them.

Information from the health certificates was augmented with a wide variety of other data, most of which I computerized in like fashion. I examined abstracts of every case involving an alleged violation of the Animal Welfare Act and recorded details of more than four hundred of them in a separate database. Another database was created to record the animals listed in the American Zoo and Aquarium Association's *Animal Exchange* newsletter. Information from more than sixty-eight hundred notices throughout 1995 and 1996 was computerized, providing the wherewithal to track the number of animals offered by individual zoos, the asking price, and other pertinent facts. Yet another database included information from two years' worth of advertisements in *Animal Finders' Guide* magazine. The identities of advertisers were determined using CD-ROM versions of reverse phone directories and such Web sites as InfoSpace.com. Information from approximately one thousand of these ads was computerized. In addition, I computerized more than one thousand records gathered from promotional brochures, Web sites, and such secondary sources as newspapers and magazines. Still another database cataloged hundreds of transactions taken from the annual reports of a few dozen individuals and organizations granted federal permits to trade in endangered species. Like health certificates, these records are completed by the permit holders and therefore offered assurances that the listed information was accurate. Finally, these databases were supplemented with thousands of records from species studbooks maintained by personnel at zoos accredited by the American Zoo and Aquarium Association, along with hundreds more transactions culled from three reports published by the AZA Contraception Advisory Group.

I relied on many other sources of information to help piece together the identities of those trading in exotic species. These included court records, taxidermy records, and Internal Revenue Forms 990, which detail the fiscal activities of certain not-for-profit organizations. In addition, I relied on such industry publications as the *Directory of Alternative Livestock & Bird Owners*, the *Breeder Directory of the Exotic Wildlife Association*, and *Who's Who in International Live Animal Trade & Transport*. Also valuable were computerized records made available by state departments of fish and game; for example, the Florida Game and Fresh Water Fish Commission provided a printout with the names of nearly five thousand individuals and organizations with permits to display wildlife or keep exotic animals as pets. These helped identify recipients named—but not otherwise identified—on captive-bred wildlife registration reports to the U.S. Fish and Wildlife Service. The U.S. Department of Agriculture's Animal and Plant Health Inspection Service provided a host of indispensable materials, including annual listings of licensed dealers and exhibitors and facility inspection reports. The U.S. Fish and Wildlife Service also provided printouts from its Law Enforcement Management Information System (LEMIS) database, which tracks the flow of species to and from the United States. Many valuable materials, including species studbooks and copies of the *AZA Animal Exchange*, were available from the library at the National Zoological Park, in Washington, D.C., which is operated by the Smithsonian Institution.

Also of great use was the *Directory of Zoological Parks and Aquariums*, published annually by the American Zoo and Aquarium Association. In addition to background information about the association and its members, the directory also includes the AZA's bylaws and Code of Professional Ethics. I used one provision of the code, which is included in part II (Mandatory Standards), as an ethical benchmark throughout the research process. Section 2(e) reads: "A member will make every effort to assure that all animals in his/her collection and under his/her care are disposed of in a manner which meets the current disposition standards of the Association and do not find their way into the hands of those not qualified to care for them properly."

◄◦►

More than three hundred fifty people were interviewed for this book. Many requested anonymity, thus the unattributed quotations throughout. Their assistance, as they know, was greatly appreciated.

Happily, some of those who helped can be named. The list starts with Charles Lewis, the founder and executive director of the Center for Public Integrity, who gave the project the sort of ongoing, unqualified support that would make any writer envious. Without the endless backing of the organization, this book would never have been published.

I am similarly indebted to Bill Hogan, the Director of Investigative Projects at the Center for Public Integrity. I was lucky to have had such a talented editor working with me, and even luckier to have such a good friend.

A host of other people at the Center for Public Integrity were also instrumental in helping the project get going and get to the end. They include Barbara Schecter, the Director of Development; Bill O'Sullivan, whose editing was invaluable; and researchers Eric Wilson, Dan Steinberg, Melanie Strong, Joshua Dine, and Patricia Jamison. Special thanks to Erin Gallavan for months of exhaustive research. Special thanks also to Peter Newbatt Smith for his extraordinary efforts helping to ensure the accuracy of the text.

I am grateful to Joel Fishman, of the Bedford Book Works, for doggedly working on my behalf, and I'm similarly grateful to Peter Osnos and Geoff Shandler, of PublicAffairs, for this opportunity.

A number of people were kind enough to volunteer their time, including Abby Green, Sandra Bemis, and Christina Zuccaro. I am particularly grateful to Nivia Quintela and Kelly Gordon, whose painstaking volunteer efforts were at times the equivalent of full-time employment.

I had the good fortune of dealing with especially helpful federal government employees, most notably Circee Pieters, at the U.S. Fish and Wildlife Service. I am similarly grateful to Mary Maruca and Kim Deskins Logan, also of the U.S. Fish and Wildlife Service, as well as

Tanya Fisher of the U.S. Department of Agriculture. Dozens of state-government employees also went out of their way to help me retrieve documents. In particular, I'd like to thank Jean Roush, of the Missouri Department of Agriculture, and Dee Rhodd, of the Kansas Animal Health Department.

Finally, thanks to the Geraldine R. Dodge Foundation for its generous support.

About The Center
for Public Integrity

The Center for Public Integrity began operation in May 1990. It is a nonprofit, nonpartisan, tax-exempt educational organization founded so that important national issues can be investigated and analyzed without the normal time or space limitations. Described as a "watchdog in the corridors of power" by *National Journal*, the Center has investigated and disseminated a wide variety of information in more than thirty-five published Center reports since its inception. More than 3,000 news media stories have referenced the Center's findings or perspectives about public service and ethics-related issues. The Center's books and studies are resources for reporters, academics, and the general public, with databases, backup files of government documents, and other information available as well.

As with its previous reports, the views expressed herein do not necessarily reflect the views of individual members of The Center for Public Integrity's Board of Directors or Advisory Board.

If you would like access to the most recent findings of the Center, including additional information not contained in this book, you can visit the Center's Web site at www.publicintegrity.org, or subscribe to *The Public i*, the Center's award-winning newsletter.

For more information or to become a member, contact the Center for Public Integrity:

The Center for Public Integrity
910 Seventeenth Street N.W.
Seventh Floor
Washington, D.C. 20006
E-mail: contact@publicintegrity.org
Internet: www.publicintegrity.org
Telephone: (202) 466-1300
Facsimile: (202) 466-1101

PUBLICAFFAIRS is a new nonfiction publishing house and a tribute to the standards, values, and flair of three persons who have served as mentors to countless reporters, writers, editors, and book people of all kinds, including me.

I.F. STONE, proprietor of *I. F. Stone's Weekly*, combined a commitment to the First Amendment with entrepreneurial zeal and reporting skill and became one of the great independent journalists in American history. At the age of eighty, Izzy published *The Trial of Socrates*, which was a national bestseller. He wrote the book after he taught himself ancient Greek.

BENJAMIN C. BRADLEE was for nearly thirty years the charismatic editorial leader of *The Washington Post*. It was Ben who gave the *Post* the range and courage to pursue such historic issues as Watergate. He supported his reporters with a tenacity that made them fearless, and it is no accident that so many became authors of influential, best-selling books.

ROBERT L. BERNSTEIN, the chief executive of Random House for more than a quarter century, guided one of the nation's premier publishing houses. Bob was personally responsible for many books of political dissent and argument that challenged tyranny around the globe. He is also the founder and was the longtime chair of Human Rights Watch, one of the most respected human rights organizations in the world.

.   .   .

For fifty years, the banner of Public Affairs Press was carried by its owner Morris B. Schnapper, who published Gandhi, Nasser, Toynbee, Truman, and about 1,500 other authors. In 1983 Schnapper was described by *The Washington Post* as "a redoubtable gadfly." His legacy will endure in the books to come.

Peter Osnos, *Publisher*